The Senate Munitions
Inquiry of the 1930s

Recent Titles in
Contributions in American History

The Senate Munitions Inquiry of the 1930s

Beyond the Merchants of Death

Matthew Ware Coulter

Contributions in American History, Number 177

Greenwood Press
Westport, Connecticut • London

Library of Congress Cataloging-in-Publication Data

Coulter, Matthew Ware, 1956–
    The Senate munitions inquiry of the 1930s : beyond the merchants
of death / Matthew Ware Coulter.
        p.   cm. — (Contributions in American history, ISSN 0084–9219
; no. 177)
    Includes bibliographical references and index.
    ISBN 0–313–30394–0 (alk. paper)
    1. United States. Congress. Senate. Special Committee to
Investigate the Munitions Industry—History.   2. Military-industrial
complex—United States—History.   3. Defense industries—Government
policy—United States—History.   4. United States—Military policy.
5. Military readiness—United States—History.   I. Title.
II. Series.
    HD9743.U6C68   1997
    338.4′76234′0973—dc21   97–1692

British Library Cataloguing in Publication Data is available.

Library of Congress Catalog Card Number: 97–1692
ISBN: 0–313–30394–0
ISSN: 0084–9219

First published in 1997

Greenwood Press, 88 Post Road West, Westport, CT 06881
An imprint of Greenwood Publishing Group, Inc.

Printed in the United States of America

The paper used in this book complies with the
Permanent Paper Standard issued by the National
Information Standards Organization (Z39.48–1984).

10 9 8 7 6 5 4 3 2 1

To my parents

Contents

Preface

The Senate Munitions Inquiry, often called the Nye committee after its chairman, Senator Gerald P. Nye, first interested me during my undergraduate years in the middle 1970s. With the Vietnam War coming to an end, questions about American foreign policy and military action formed an important part of the campus environment. I do not remember when I initially learned of the munitions inquiry, but it may have been in a course on the politics of national defense in which Adam Yarmolinsky's *The Military Establishment* was required reading. At any rate, I first wrote about the inquiry in a graduate history seminar in 1980 and quickly learned that it might be difficult to expand upon the prevailing interpretation. After presenting my research, the professor forcefully asked me, "What was Nye really up to?" Then he provided the answer, explaining the committee's isolationist motives.

The Nye committee as a group of wrong-minded isolationist cranks, busying themselves with a simplistic search for evil arms makers, is a view presented in many American history survey textbooks. For a topic so often mentioned in textbooks, little research and writing has been published. Only one book on the committee exists, *In Search of Peace* by John E. Wiltz, a study that left me believing that there were questions still to be explored.

This book takes the committee's work seriously and presents the major figures of the inquiry as serious people. To what extent they were wrong-minded is a question I have tried to leave for the reader to answer. The court of history is entitled to render judgment only after all the arguments have been heard. This study is intended to supplement existing arguments in the case of the munitions inquiry of the 1930s by attempting to add to prior studies and build from them. I am indebted to those scholars who have labored in the vineyard of American history between the World Wars.

I am grateful to Dr. Robert A. Divine, Dr. Frank Freidel, Dr. Chris Grooms, Dr. William Kamman, Dr. David M. Kennedy, Dr. Ronald Marcello, Dr. Lin Moore, Dr. Donald K. Pickens, Dr. Gustav Seligmann, and Dr. David L. Wilson for their critical readings of all or parts of the manuscript. I have tried to incorporate their perceptive comments into the final version. I am responsible, of course, for any and all errors as well as for the interpretation.

My home institution, Collin County Community College, assisted in many ways. Teaching, researching, and writing in such a supportive environment made it much easier to complete the study. My colleagues in the History Department were especially helpful.

Wendy Chmielewski, curator of the Swarthmore College Peace Collection, Dwight Miller, senior archivist of the Herbert Hoover Library, and Raymond Teichman, supervisory archivist of the Franklin D. Roosevelt Library, were very helpful. The Franklin and Eleanor Roosevelt Institute provided support for my research at the Franklin D. Roosevelt Library. Lynn Zelem, production editor at Greenwood Press, always provided rapid answers when problems arose.

Finally, I thank my daughter, Monica. She was five years old when I started this book and ten years old when I finished it. At times when I could not see the end of the tunnel, she provided the light I needed. Her cooperation and encouragement made it possible for me to complete the project.

The Senate Munitions
Inquiry of the 1930s

Chapter 1

Perspectives on the Munitions Inquiry and the Interwar Years

During the years 1934 through 1936, many Americans pondered the state of the armaments industry and its leaders, the so-called merchants of death. The U.S. Senate's Special Committee for the Investigation of the Munitions Industry, often called the Nye committee for its chairperson, Gerald P. Nye of North Dakota, led the effort. Historian John E. Wiltz authored the only book-length study of the committee, *In Search of Peace*, published in 1963. Wiltz concluded that the committee's main achievement was to debunk the merchants of death thesis, defined as the assertion that "people who profited from war . . . bore responsibility for war." As a result, by the end of the 1930s "hardly anybody bothered with merchants of death."[1]

In the last third of the twentieth century, events have allowed for a new study to supplement *In Search of Peace*. In the 1960s and 1970s, the Vietnam experience led to the questioning of earlier assessments about isolationism and foreign policy. Writing in 1972, historian Richard D. Burns noted that "in the debates of the 1950s over the validity of American foreign policy in the 1930s many seemingly 'deadend' issues, such as the arms traffic, were spurned by diplomatic historians—an attitude which was unfortunate and shortsighted." In the 1980s, the Iran-Contra affair, with its allegations of secret deals to trade missiles for hostages, of illegal weapons shipments to rebels in Latin America, and of shadowy intermediaries such as Adnan Khashoggi, raised issues reminiscent of the munitions committee hearings. By the 1990s, the collapse of the Soviet Union and the end of the cold war served to further open historical debate over twentieth-century foreign policy issues.[2]

Contrary to Wiltz's conclusion, Americans continued to be bothered by the activities of arms merchants. Even before the publication of *In Search of Peace*, President Dwight D. Eisenhower drew on the work of the Nye committee while drafting his "farewell address" in 1961. In early January, Eisenhower discussed the upcoming speech with businessman and friend Ellis D. Slater. "The boss

commented that Du Pont years ago was always accused of fomenting wars,"
Slater recorded, and "now that point of view has subsided with respect to that
particular company, but he is disturbed because of the interrelation of our
economy with real disarmament. . . . The more successful we are in effecting
disarmament, the more disastrous the effect will be in many directions from the
standpoint of the economy." Ten days later, Eisenhower spoke to the nation
about a "conjunction of an immense military establishment and a large arms
industry" and warned Americans to "guard against the acquisition of unwarranted
influence, whether sought or unsought, by the military industrial complex." A
generation later, Eisenhower's speech showed up in the popular film *JFK*, in
which director Oliver Stone suggested that leaders of the military-industrial
complex conspired to murder President John F. Kennedy. From the perspective
of 1990s popular culture, the munitions makers were capable of nefarious
actions.[3]

"What? Our Technology Worked Perfectly . . ."
Source: Jeff Danziger, *The Christian Science Monitor*, 31 December 1993, 20. Copyright
  1993, The Christian Science Publishing Society.

Other observers in the 1990s also focused attention on the arms makers. In a
1993 editorial cartoon, *The Christian Science Monitor* depicted a mother and
child, both missing a leg, and identified them as "Third World Victims." An
overweight manager, sitting behind his desk, was labeled as one of the "land
mine manufacturers in industrial nations." The same paper asked readers to
"ponder the industry" in a 1994 editorial on the barbarity of land mines.
Estimating that perhaps 100 million mines had been planted in over sixty
countries, the *Monitor* noted that the devices were "almost impossible to

detect—except perhaps by unsuspecting children. What were these men thinking?" Companies in perhaps fifty countries produced an average of ten million mines every year. The *Monitor* did not limit criticism to the mine producers and noted that many of the companies were state-owned. Still, the paper made clear that those who built and distributed the deadly weapons bore some blame for the "unconscionable irresponsibility of randomly scattering antipersonnel devices." In 1996, the *Monitor* published an essay which stated that "we must destroy the economic viability of land mines and eliminate their 'profitability' as weapons." By that time, enough interest had been generated to produce an international conference on land mines.[4]

Contrary to the thrust of Wiltz's *In Search of Peace*, the munitions investigation went well beyond a chase of phantom death merchants. The Nye committee's chief accomplishment comes not from disproving a merchants of death "thesis," but rather from providing a wealth of information about the extensive modern military sector of American society. The main body of the munitions committee's history lies in its ninety-three days of hearings, during which committee members questioned over 200 witnesses. The committee's subpoena power provided access to private files, and they reviewed thousands of letters, reports, and memoranda. The committee's investigators devoted hundreds of hours to combing through records of armament companies and banking institutions. The resulting collection of over 4,900 exhibits provides the best available view of the arms industry of the early twentieth century, a time when most of the important communications were in writing. The extensive phone and electronic communications of the late twentieth century make activities within organizations harder to document, so the hearings and exhibits of the committee offer probably the best look historians will ever get of the modern armaments industry.

Historical assessments of the munitions investigation fall into three basic categories, with historians who came of age before Pearl Harbor holding the most positive assessments of Nye and the investigation. Progressives Charles and Mary Beard wrote approvingly of the munitions committee, finding that it "injected realistic knowledge into the consideration of dynamic forces shaping foreign policies," especially regarding the importance of economics. Historian Merle Curti found the inquiry "ably conducted by Senator Nye and his colleagues. . . . The investigation had brought home to the reading public the idea that war preparedness was not only a racket but an ominous threat to the well-being of the plain people."[5]

The investigation fell into historical disrepute after World War II when it became increasingly identified with Senator Nye, isolationism, and appeasement. Although some historians have challenged the fairness and accuracy of the term *isolationism*, after Pearl Harbor it came to be used to describe a group of policy positions that called for the United States to stay out of European wars. The so-called isolationists might be better described as unilateralists. When Hitler declared war on the United States, the effort to keep out of the European war clearly failed, and those who had said America should not stay out found their reputations on the rise. The interventionists, who had called for greater American involvement with the Allies, took on the title of internationalists. By the early 1940s, their leaders, sometimes with the support of Franklin Roosevelt, argued that isolationism was "subversive" and "tantamount to sabotage." Harvard president James Conant predicted that "isolationism will be as extinct as the volcanoes on the moon." During most of the cold war, he proved to be largely correct.[6]

In the post–Pearl Harbor period the munitions investigators took on a new coloration and, rather ironically, replaced the arms makers as the bad guys. Speaking before the House of Representatives in March of 1942, Congressman Thomas Winter argued that due to the Nye committee "practically every munitions factory was closed" and the country left without needed weapons to fight the enemy in World War II. The truth about the Nye committee became an early casualty of the war, for no munitions plants closed because of the arms investigation. By the early 1950s, Alger Hiss, who served as a legal counsel to the committee, stood accused of aiding America's cold war enemy by passing to the Soviet Union military information used in the munitions investigation. During a time when the United States stood committed to a global system of alliances to contain the Soviet Union and communism, the unilateralist ideas held by most Nye committee members came to be viewed with skepticism. Harry Truman, who had supported the committee as a freshman senator, now called it "misdirected" and misleading.[7]

Most historians during the 1950s and early 1960s took a "realist" approach to diplomatic issues and downgraded the contributions of Nye and the munitions committee, considering them as dangerous at worst and naive at best. Ellis N. Livingston, writing in 1953, found the committee to be biased and concluded that it accomplished little aside from promoting widely held prejudices. He compared some of the committee's actions to McCarthyism. By the later 1950s, Dexter Perkins denounced Nye's charge that bankers and munitions makers had drawn the United States into World War I. Selig Adler took one of the harshest positions in 1963, finding that "the list of Nye's egregious errors of judgement is too long for full enumeration." One year later, James Martin viewed the investigation as a manifestation of 1930s liberalism, and he blamed the liberals for World War II. Writing in 1965, Robert A. Divine called Nye's charges about the munitions makers "crude," and in 1966 Manfred Jonas found that Nye "had none of the earmarks of the constructive legislator though many of the carping critic."[8]

The rising influence of "New Left" views of diplomatic history, associated with William Appleman Williams, led to some less negative assessments. Paul Birdsall, writing in a book edited by Williams in 1956, agreed with the realists in criticizing Nye's views toward bankers and arms makers. He did allow, however, that the "committee has given us invaluable data." Wayne S. Cole, in a biography of Nye published in 1963, found the senator's views to be more complex than "the oversimplified descriptions of the committee's 'thesis' in most history textbooks." The strongest endorsement of the committee came from Paul A. C. Koistinen, who in 1970 found it foreseeing the "full blown 'industrial-military complex' of World War II and the Cold War years." He offered favorable assessments of the investigation, praising its "most impressive reports," clear perception of the basic questions, and care in avoiding allegations of a conspiracy. Nearly twenty years later, Walter LaFeber defended Nye and noted that the senator "thought the entire American system, not just a few 'Merchants of Death,' was at fault."[9]

Wiltz took a realist approach and discounted the committee's work as "odd gospel" within the first one hundred words of *In Search of Peace*. Efforts to control the munitions trade and prevent war profiteering were among the "nostrums of the 1930s," a period when Americans stood ready to support the most impractical plans for preserving the peace. Thus, depression-era Americans overlooked the committee's failures that were so apparent to Wiltz. He saw the committee promoting a "national distraction during a critical period" in American history. The limited sophistication of the people matched well with the attributes of Nye, who was intellectually shallow and a "rather typical midwesterner." A 1964 review in the *Journal of American History* called Wiltz's book "calm" and "dispassionate."[10]

The questions Wiltz posed in researching for *In Search of Peace* reveal his disposition and allow for doubt concerning the objectivity of his study. In 1958, he wrote to Irénée Du Pont, who had testified before the committee, and asked such leading questions as "Did you feel that the committee was unfair or abusive in its treatment of witnesses?"; "Did you feel that by innuendo the committee attempted to distort the evidence exhibited and the testimony given by witnesses?"; "Did you feel that the munitions investigators were consciously trying to discredit the American business community?"; and "Did you feel that the investigation was seriously damaging American warmaking potential, American foreign relations, and American overseas commercial relations?" None of the questions pointed toward any positive outcome from the munitions investigation.[11]

Wiltz again wrote on the Nye committee in 1975 and provided a post–Vietnam War perspective. He still saw its foremost achievement in the disproving of the merchants of death thesis, particularly in regard to World War I. The triumphant certainty of internationalism, evident in the earlier book, had, however, been challenged by the Vietnam experience. Wiltz found the committee's leading liability in its strengthening of isolationism, but he added that this was "assuming that isolationism was bad for the country and for the world at *that* time," a qualifier which had hardly seemed necessary in 1963. Wiltz's tone softened as well, with the nostrums becoming notions. Nye's intellect in 1975 looked narrow and undisciplined rather than shallow, and instead of a "typical Midwesterner," he now seemed an "ordinary" one.[12]

Wiltz's treatments of the munitions investigation suffer from several limitations. In depicting Nye as a one-dimensional character, in essence a stereotype of a rural midwesterner, Wiltz created a figure easy to ridicule. By focusing on the "merchants of death," Wiltz emphasized the most sensational aspect of the munitions inquiry while obscuring much of the more intricate work of the committee. "The Munitions Committee made a mighty effort to prove that arms makers were merchants of death," he wrote, but in reality the death merchants more often appeared in Wiltz's writings than in the hearings and reports of the committee. Wiltz made a mighty effort to tie the Nye committee to the "merchants of death," using the term over thirty-five times in *In Search of Peace*.[13]

As Richard D. Burns noted, Wiltz's "characterization of the mid-1930s as a period when national leadership was distracted . . . undoubtedly stems from the temperament of the 1950s." Focusing on the "merchants of death" and writing from a realist perspective within an isolationist versus internationalist framework, Wiltz diminished the scope of the munitions investigation. He organized *In Search of Peace* both topically and chronologically, an approach that made it difficult to consider the Nye committee's relation to intellectual, cultural, social, and political developments. Wiltz neglected to consider the complex ways in which these forces evolved and interacted with the munitions inquiry. The America of 1936, when the investigation ended, was fundamentally different from America as it had been when the committee started its work in 1934. The arms inquiry represented ideals from America's earlier heritage, and it deserves careful and respectful treatment. For Wiltz and many other realist historians of the cold war era, however, the idealism of the Nye committee looked hopelessly odd and out of place.[14]

Most historians have closely connected the munitions investigation with isolationism, a linkage that appeared in writings from the 1950s through the 1990s and from both "realist" and "New Left" orientations. Selig Adler, writing in 1957, found the committee's role in promoting isolationism to be so strong that it was "destined to leave a strong imprint upon the course of American history." Robert A. Divine saw the investigation as an isolationist exercise in his 1962 book, *The Illusion of Neutrality*. Wiltz, writing in 1975, found the committee's most negative effect in its contribution to the isolationism of the 1930s. Wayne S. Cole, who showed more sympathy for the committee, judged it the "high point for isolationist strength" in his 1983 study *Roosevelt and the Isolationists*. Walter LaFeber wrote in 1989 that the inquiry formed a key element of the isolationist movement. Historians writing in the 1990s viewed it in the same way. Michael E. Parrish called it the "high tide of isolationism," and Patrick J. Maney and Robert David Johnson both considered the committee to be an isolationist phenomenon.[15]

Viewing the munitions committee within the context of isolationism and internationalism not only separated it from other historical developments of the 1930s but also complicated analysis of Franklin D. Roosevelt's relationship to the investigation. Historians have found the president's attitude ranging from zealous support to wary distrust. Accounts from the 1950s and 1960s generally found Roosevelt providing little leadership in regard to the investigation. James MacGregor Burns wrote in 1956 that FDR played a passive role in relation to the committee, a view shared by Adler, who in 1957 found Roosevelt giving support "halfheartedly." Wiltz devoted little of *In Search of Peace* to examining the role of FDR. By the 1970s and 1980s, however, historians were writing of a more involved president. Robert Dallek argued in 1979 that Roosevelt supported the committee and encouraged it to consider international solutions to the arms traffic problem. By 1989, Burns clearly displayed the newer view. In *The Crosswinds of Freedom*, he abandoned the passive FDR in favor of one who "strengthened the isolationist cause by virtually joining it" and he cited the Nye committee as an "egregious case in point . . . Roosevelt was no innocent bystander." Kenneth Davis, writing in 1986, also found an involved president, but instead of joining the cause he saw the committee "from the first regarded with a suspicious eye, a wary dislike, by Franklin Roosevelt." Patrick J. Maney, writing in 1992, saw Roosevelt steering a middle course, supporting the isolationist munitions investigation to balance his internationalist policies toward Latin America, free trade, and the World Court.[16]

A new and more comprehensive interpretation of the Nye committee emerges when its history is considered in a context expanded beyond the limits of isolationism and internationalism. Growing isolationist sentiment certainly played a role in the history of the munitions investigation, but the extent of that role has been so strongly emphasized that other factors have gone barely noticed. Most Americans of the interwar years were not hostile or opposed to an active foreign policy, but they were largely indifferent. Diplomatic historian Warren F. Kuehl, after analyzing editorial opinion from thirty newspapers of the supposed midwestern heartland of isolationism, concluded that the isolationist mood may never have dominated. In fact, Kuehl found that in the years between the world wars "amazing campaigns emerged which were based on the realization that it was essential to convey the reality of internationalism to citizens." With the strength of isolationism more properly assessed, the munitions committee can be broken free from the confining stage of the isolationism versus internationalism debate. Evaluating the committee's role in U.S. history becomes more complicated, requiring consideration of not only the 1930s foreign policy debate but also of the historiographical, intellectual, social, cultural, and political developments of the interwar years.[17]

The munitions investigation grew in part from a historical debate in the 1920s and 1930s over America's role in World War I. Some Americans believed that the country had made a great mistake in joining the Great War, while others believed that the mistake had come in not joining the League of Nations in 1919. Some in the first group suspected that munitions makers and bankers had pushed the country into war, a view supported by revisionist historians such as Charles A. Beard and Harry Elmer Barnes. They argued that financial factors had drawn the United States into the war more fundamentally than did moral concerns or violations of neutrality. Revisionist historians expanded on thoughts expressed at the time the United States joined the war. Senator George Norris, Republican from Nebraska, told fellow senators that banks making loans to the Allies had joined with the munitions companies to develop "the greatest propaganda that the world has ever known" and "now demanded that the American citizens shall be used as insurance policies to guarantee the safe delivery of munitions of war to belligerent nations. The enormous profits of munitions manufacturers, stockbrokers, and bond dealers must be still further increased by our entrance into the war."[18]

The assertion that munitions producers fomented wars had already been popularized in the decades before World War I by socialist propaganda and the Christian Social Gospel movement. Walter Rauschenbusch, a leading minister of the Social Gospel, concluded in his popular 1907 book, *Christianity and the Social Crisis*, that the "rapacity of commerce has been the secret spring of most recent wars." He wrote of "how few wars have ever been fought for the sake of justice or the people; how personal spite, the ambition of military professionals, and the protection of capitalist ventures are the real moving powers; how the governing classes pour out the blood and wealth of nations for private ends and exude patriotic enthusiasm like a squid secreting ink." Five years later, Rauschenbusch published *Christianizing the Social Order*. He sharpened his focus on arms makers and wrote that the "big interests that build dreadnoughts and manufacture ammunition are a very powerful factor in keeping the nations armed to the teeth in times of peace . . . rarely, if ever, is any war fought in which private interests are not the real force demanding war."[19]

Presidents Theodore Roosevelt and Woodrow Wilson accepted some of this logic and tried to rein in the armaments makers. Roosevelt considered pushing for reduced armament expenditures during the Second Hague Peace Conference in 1907, but he was advised that the action would spur strong opposition from the world's munitions makers. Wilson proposed at the Paris Peace Conference to end the private manufacture of armaments, but he could not overcome French resistance to his plan. The Covenant of the League of Nations proclaimed that "the manufacture by private enterprise of munitions and implements of war is open to grave objections" and called for study of "how the evil effects attendant upon such manufacture can be prevented."[20]

The Nye committee's approach to the munitions industry thus stemmed from Roosevelt and Wilson's progressivism as well as from Rauschenbusch's Social Gospel. Rauschenbusch believed the Kingdom of God could be approached on earth and saw humanity rapidly coming closer to it during his time. America's entry into the war to end all wars and make the world safe for democracy provided hope for bringing the world nearer to the ideals of God's Kingdom. For Rauschenbusch, however, the war proved to be unbearable because his German heritage made it difficult to completely support the Allies. As a result, his patriotism was questioned, vandals attacked his property, and his health deteriorated.

He died in June of 1918, his final days soothed by thoughts of his eldest son, Stephen, who was serving as an army ambulance driver in the war. Sixteen years later, Stephen Raushenbush joined the munitions inquiry as its chief investigator.[21]

For most Americans, the armistice in November of 1918 brought joy and relief. The next year brought layoffs in the war industries, strikes, race riots, and the Paris Peace Conference. Wilson secured British and French agreement to form a collective security organization, the League of Nations, but failed to get the U.S. Senate to ratify U.S. membership. In 1920, American voters overwhelmingly rejected Democratic candidates James Cox and Franklin D. Roosevelt, who called for the United States to join the league, and gave 61 percent of the popular vote to Republicans Warren Harding and Calvin Coolidge. The election results effectively closed off the issue of American membership in the League of Nations.

By this time, historians were researching and writing the history of World War I. Had it been a war to enrich bankers and munitions makers, as Norris asserted, or a moral war to crush German barbarism and make the world safe for democracy, as Wilson maintained? Historians lined up on both sides of the question. Many liberal intellectuals, including John Dewey and Charles Beard, had supported American entry into the war in 1917. A number of historians, including Carl Becker, produced propaganda material for the U.S. government during the war. In the aftermath of the Paris conference, Beard, Becker, and other historians and intellectuals had their wartime attitudes challenged by revisionist writers on the war. Initial accounts of the war subscribed to what Beard called the "Sunday-school theory," with the innocent Allies being suddenly attacked by the guilty Central Powers. Germany's barbaric use of the submarine then forced America to fight on the virtuous side. In 1924, Harry Elmer Barnes rejected the "Sunday school theory" and found that Russia and France had instigated the war. He suggested that supporters of Wilson and intervention had been wrong and perhaps deceived into joining the war. Writing in *American Mercury*, Barnes concluded that the United States fought not "to make the world safe for democracy, but to protect our investment in Allied bonds, to insure a more extensive development of the manufacture of war materials and to make it possible to deliver our munitions to Allied ports."[22]

Other historians defended Wilson's idealism and the moral correctness of the U.S. entry into the war. Becker and Beard, however, supported Barnes's revisionism. In the early 1930s, Beard argued that Wilson led the country into war to protect U.S. global commerce and failed to fully consider the national interest. The United States stumbled into the war. He found it "highly doubtful whether the United States would have entered the World War 'in defense of democracy' if American nationals could have sold munitions and supplies as freely to the Central Powers as to the Allies, and if the Germans had not preyed upon American commerce." Beard recommended the suspension of trade with belligerents during future wars so that decisions regarding national policy would not be unduly influenced by commercial interests and motivations.[23]

The debate among historians formed one strand of the iconoclastic intellectual environment of the interwar years. Another strand consisted of Reinhold Niebuhr's challenge to the liberal Social Gospel of Walter Rauschenbusch. Had Rauschenbusch lived to see the postwar world, he would have been both gladdened and saddened. The League of Nations and the 1928 Kellogg-Briand Pact, which outlawed war, seemed to show humanity moving toward the Kingdom of God. Capitalism seemed able to meet the needs of American workers, led by the examples of Samuel Insull, who provided generous benefits to his employees, and Henry Ford, the "Good Businessman" who founded the doctrine of high wages and low prices.[24]

By the time the Nye committee began to function, however, the Social Gospel beliefs that supported its approach to the munitions makers were under challenge from Reinhold Niebuhr. From his ministry at the Bethel Evangelical Church in northwest Detroit, Niebuhr watched closely the actions of Henry Ford, and what he saw failed to support the Social Gospel vision. Niebuhr drifted toward the political left, joined the pacifist Fellowship of Reconciliation, and ran for Congress as a socialist in 1932. After the election, which he lost overwhelmingly, his *Moral Man and Immoral Society* appeared in bookstores. In attacking many aspects of the Social Gospel, Niebuhr challenged the belief that business interests fomented war. He wrote that "neither is it true that modern wars are caused solely by the modern capitalistic system with its disproportion of economic power and privilege." Nations, as large groups, would naturally be self aggrandizing.[25]

Moral Man and Immoral Society set Niebuhr apart from the mainstream liberal Protestant groups that had led the American peace reform movement for over 100 years. Many pacifist organizations of the 1920s and 1930s had strong ties to liberal Protestant leaders, and these organizations tirelessly promoted their agenda. Their work helped bring about the Kellogg-Briand Pact and the munitions investigation. Before the Nye committee held its first hearing, however, the liberal Social Gospel view of businessmen and munitions makers instigating war drew criticism from Niebuhr.[26]

Of the pacifist groups, the U.S. section of the Women's International League for Peace and Freedom most actively promoted the munitions investigation. The WILPF had evolved from a wartime conference called by Jane Addams and Carrie Chapman Catt. Nearly 3,000 delegates approved a platform that advocated nationalization of munitions manufacture, limitation of armaments, and organized opposition to militarism. They established the Women's Peace Party and elected Addams as its chairperson. In 1919, the party became the U.S. section of the WILPF, an organization that represented women of nineteen countries. Addams served as international president. The U.S. section located its headquarters in Washington in 1921, by which time membership had climbed to over 1,300.

Strenuous efforts to promote pacifistic ideas, including a twenty-three city speaking tour, spurred growth to about 6,000 members by 1924.[27]

In that year Dorothy Detzer became the executive secretary of the organization, a position she would hold for over twenty years. More than any other individual, Detzer held responsibility for the creation of the Nye committee. She grew up in a middle-class Indiana family during the 1890s and early 1900s, reaching adulthood during World War I. Her introduction to the peace movement came during the war as she worked at Jane Addams's Hull House. After the war Detzer carried out relief work in the Soviet Union, and upon returning to America she secured the position with the WILPF. Focusing her energy on lobbying government officials, she helped in naming a woman to the American mission to the 1932 Geneva Disarmament Conference. No woman had ever served in such a capacity for the United States, and Detzer's success showed not only her energy and ability but also the problems often encountered by women of the 1920s and 1930s who attempted to take an active role in international affairs. She found the State Department to be initially unreceptive to breaking precedent, but officials finally asked the various women's organizations to "get together" and agree on a particular woman. "To the officials it seemed wholly irrelevant and illogical for us to ask if the men all had to get together, too," she dryly noted, but the women's groups did as requested.[28]

Detzer met with less success in getting the Democrats and Republicans to include peace statements in their 1932 party platforms. For Detzer the failure "was not surprising as one of the most important members of the Republican Party was Pierre Du Pont, and the secretary of the Democratic National Committee was Mr. Rascob [sic]." John Raskob had close ties to Pierre Du Pont and to General Motors, which during the interwar years was largely owned by Du Pont interests. Both Du Pont and General Motors played important roles in supplying America's needs for military materials. Detzer would soon employ her lobbying skills to bring the munitions investigation into being and expose the arms makers who blocked her efforts for peace.[29]

During the interwar years, while increasing numbers of women like Detzer entered public spheres that had previously been the reserve of men, the progressive leaders who had energized the pre–World War I debate were unable to unify around common positions. Many of their followers deferred to the managerial and financial experts who had led the nation to victory in the war. Some voluntary associations, like the WILPF, struggled to generate public interest and work out plans for action, perhaps planting the seeds for future reforms. Calls for social insurance for the elderly, prohibition of child labor, and unemployment compensation coexisted with pleas for peace and disarmament. When the Great Depression forced millions of Americans to reconsider their convictions, such groups found larger audiences willing to listen to their messages. For the WILPF and many other progressive organizations, FDR's election in 1932 meant "the day of harvest was at hand."[30]

For rural progressives, such as Gerald Nye, America's transformation from an agricultural nation to an urban and industrial one caused special anxiety and cultural stress. The 1920 census showed that for the first time over half of all Americans lived in cities and towns, and poor farming conditions during the interwar years stimulated an ongoing migration away from rural areas. The cultural action happened in the cities, from Babe Ruth's home runs to Al Capone's speakeasies, from *The Jazz Singer* to the Dempsey-Tunney fight. Writers like Sinclair Lewis and H. L. Mencken ridiculed small-town life. The tension between the older, rural, white Anglo-Saxon Protestant views and newer, urban, often immigrant and Catholic views appeared in the literature and in debate over prohibition and immigration restriction. In the 1928 election, urban ethnics moved toward the Democrats and Al Smith, but prosperity led most voters to support Hoover and the Republicans.[31]

 Rural Americans could count on Gerald Nye for leadership in their confrontation with the city. Having grown up in Wisconsin, Nye followed the path of his father and entered the newspaper business after graduating from high school in 1911. His editorials supported most of Wilson's New Freedom, and, like his urban progressive counterparts Beard, Becker, and Dewey, the rural progressive Nye supported American entry into World War I. In 1916, he left Iowa and moved to North Dakota, where nearly 90 percent of the population was classified as rural. The largest city, Fargo, claimed a population of about 20,000. The vast and lonely Dakota plains offered a fertile environment for a man of Nye's ambition and ability.[32]

While the agricultural discontent of the Populist movement had subsided in most of the nation by the twentieth century, North Dakotans continued to nurse grievances against powerful railroads and agricultural interests. The Nonpartisan League promoted a program similar to that of the earlier populists, calling for state ownership of terminal elevators, flour mills, and packing houses. League-backed candidates often won statewide races, and by the end of the war Nye had aligned his newspaper with the league's platform. In 1924, he received the league's support in an unsuccessful bid for Congress. The league fared better with its choice for governor, A. G. Sorlie, and when shortly after the election one of North Dakota's Senate seats became vacant, he appointed Nye to fill it. The thirty-two-year-old Nye made his first trip east of Chicago to take a seat in the U.S. Senate.[33]

Nye brought the ideas of the Nonpartisan League and the values of his own rural background with him to the nation's capital. His views represented a continuity with America's past, stretching back past William Jennings Bryan to Thomas Jefferson. Historian Wayne S. Cole noted that Jefferson, Bryan, and Nye "glorified the farmer and the rural way of life" and "shared an antipathy for moneylenders and creditors, and blamed those who controlled such sources of wealth for the farmer's difficulties." Jefferson, Bryan, and Nye wanted to end the favoritism toward urban businessmen that put rural farmers at a disadvantage. In foreign policy, all held traditional nineteenth-century views that criticized Great

Britain and generally opposed American imperialism outside of the Western Hemisphere as well as U.S. involvement in European wars. Nye, however, supported Wilson's protests to Germany after the *Lusitania* sinking, while Bryan considered the response to be too harsh and resigned as secretary of state. Ten years later, Bryan died shortly after defending creationism in the 1925 Scopes Monkey Trial. Nye's arrival in Washington that same year helped fill the void felt by rural Americans upon the death of the "Great Commoner."[34]

Nye quickly generated headlines when his seating in the Senate caused controversy due to questions over Sorlie's power to make the appointment. Regular, or Old Guard, Republicans saw little to gain by seating the progressive Nye, and Democrats gave him stronger support when the Senate voted forty-one to thirty-nine to seat its newest, and second youngest, member. Nye received support from western progressive Republicans, including George Norris of Nebraska, William Borah of Idaho, Hiram Johnson of California, and Robert La Follette, Jr., of Wisconsin. Two years later, the public spotlight again focused on Nye as he presided over the final phases of the Teapot Dome investigation in his role as chairperson of the Committee on Public Lands and Surveys. In 1927 and 1928, he supported the McNary-Haugen bills that called for subsidized farm exports, although he believed such a program would only begin to address the problems of American agriculture.[35]

In the 1928 election Nye endorsed Herbert Hoover, probably more from dislike of the city-born Al Smith than from strong feelings for his own party's moderately progressive candidate. Smith sometimes went out of his way to provoke rural Protestants and may have earned Nye's enmity. The two men exchanged angry public charges during the Teapot Dome hearings in 1928 when Nye inquired about possible connections between Smith and Harry Sinclair. After the election, Nye supported the Agricultural Marketing Act of 1929, but, believing that high tariffs hurt farmers, he opposed the Hawley-Smoot Tariff in 1930. In that year he also led another investigation, this time as chairperson of the Select Committee on Senatorial Campaign Expenditures that looked into political "dirty tricks" and skullduggery.[36]

By then, the economic depression overshadowed other issues and helped shape a public environment receptive to an investigation of the armament companies. As Americans watched unemployment rise by millions and farm prices collapse, the experts and business leaders in whom they had placed their faith seemed unable to provide answers. The 1931 Wickersham commission report on prohibition, for example, featured eleven separate conclusions from the eleven commission members. Writing in the later 1930s, journalist Frederick Lewis Allen concluded of the report that "the puzzled citizen could be sure of only one thing: that the supposed enlightened device of collecting innumerable facts and trying to reason from them to an inevitable conclusion had been turned into a farce." Some historical experts, too, began to express doubt. Carl Becker, speaking in his role as president of the American Historical Association, delivered "Everyman His Own Historian" in 1931. History was an "imaginative creation, a personal possession," he noted, concluding that the "history written by historians . . . is thus a convenient blend of truth and fancy, of what we commonly distinguish as 'fact' and 'interpretation.'"[37]

If reason proved to be unreliable, perhaps Americans could reject it and embrace tradition. But tradition did not fare well, either. One of the most enduring visions in American history, one held dear by Franklin Roosevelt as well as Gerald Nye, was of the small family farm, but falling commodity prices in the early 1930s led to a steep rise in foreclosures and increased farm tenancy. The death throes of the Jeffersonian dream brought extreme pain in agricultural areas such as North Dakota. For Americans like Nye, and to some extent even those like Roosevelt, the depression came because the country had strayed from the Jeffersonian path. Nye wanted to battle the bankers and industrialists who overpowered the small farmer. Roosevelt proposed moving people out from the cities and back to the countryside. Reinhold Niebuhr, looking forward rather than backward, led efforts to organize the landless agricultural laborers.[38]

With the experts disagreeing, reason failing, and tradition crumbling, the puzzled citizen found little solace from leaders in business and government. Samuel Insull's empire of electricity companies collapsed in 1932. Leading figures from Wall Street testified before the Senate's Pecora committee and admitted to a variety of unethical activities. President Hoover told Americans that prosperity waited just around the corner, but farm foreclosures mounted, unemployment rose to frightening dimensions, and bank failures steadily climbed. Some individuals, including Senator Nye, viewed the lack of purchasing power as a chief cause of the depression, but for many Americans it was easier to personalize the cause of all the troubles. Greedy and unethical financiers and businessmen, who had enjoyed praise during the high-flying 1920s, were scorned and vilified during the depressed 1930s.[39]

These same elites had been identified by Barnes, Beard, and Becker as the profiteering instigators of U.S. involvement in World War I. Artistic and literary works that depicted the Great War as meaningless mass murder for the soldiers in the trenches further stoked the bitterness of depression-era Americans toward their business and financial leaders. Ernest Hemingway's *A Farewell to Arms* and Erich Maria Remarque's *All Quiet on the Western Front* presented the war as futile and senseless slaughter. Remarque's book was a best seller in 1929, and the film version of the following year drew millions of viewers.[40]

In 1932, the bloody finale of the Bonus March underlined the contrast between the poor common soldiers and the rich war profiteers. Army Chief of Staff Douglas MacArthur, who had felt revulsion at the profiteering of World War I, gave the veterans a bitter welcome when about twenty thousand assembled in Washington to demand early payment of a bonus. MacArthur used a force of infantry, cavalry, and tanks to disperse the veterans and their families. At the end of the ordeal, two veterans and one child were dead. The headlines, photographs, radio reports, and newsreels of the Bonus March accentuated messages of the war's costs and unfairness and reinforced antipathy toward big business and big finance. The arms makers and bankers had grown rich while the fighting men suffered, much as the unscrupulous speculators of the 1920s had enriched themselves and left the workers and farmers in poverty.[41]

The American Legion, representing hundreds of thousands of veterans, took aim at the war profiteers during the interwar years and called for legislation to control or eliminate war profits. In response, the Hoover administration established a War Policies Commission to recommend ways to mobilize more efficiently and reduce inequalities. Chaired by Secretary of War and American Legion member Patrick J. Hurley, the twelve-member commission included Democratic Congressman John McSwain of South Carolina and Republican Senator Arthur Vandenberg of Michigan. Their report called for wartime price controls and high tax rates on extraordinary wartime profits. Vandenberg, acting with legion support, called for a congressional review of the commission's findings but no action had been taken by the end of 1933. Vandenberg, Hurley, and McSwain would all become involved with the Nye committee's activities in the middle 1930s.[42]

The next moves on war profits would come during the Roosevelt administration. FDR tapped into the resentments toward businessmen and bankers in his inaugural address when he placed primary blame for the depression on the "unscrupulous money changers" who had abandoned the right to lead. The president promised "direct, vigorous action," and many of those who would be leading figures in the munitions investigation made important contributions to the success of the early New Deal. FDR's first one hundred days in office saw a special session of Congress enact over a dozen pieces of major legislation, including the National Industrial Recovery Act that created the National Recovery Administration (NRA) and the Agricultural Adjustment Act that brought about the Agricultural Adjustment Administration (AAA). Bernard Baruch, a future nemesis of the Nye committee, influenced FDR's appointments to important posts, including the selection of Hugh Johnson to lead the NRA. The New Deal drew early support from most segments of American society, including business and financial leaders. A coalition of Democrats and progressive Republicans like Nye and La Follette helped push FDR's proposals through Congress.[43]

Despite reservations, Nye supported the AAA and the NRA. He believed farm problems would be better resolved by monetary inflation and easy credit, but he also realized that many of his constituents benefitted from AAA payments. The program proved to be detrimental, however, to tenant farmers and sharecroppers who were forced off the land when AAA subsidies pushed out of production acreage they previously tilled. Efforts by Niebuhr's followers to aid the landless farm workers were supported by some AAA officials, including Alger Hiss, who later took part in the munitions investigation. Senator Nye paid little attention to the AAA, instead focusing on the NRA and its regulatory codes. He believed that the codes protected big business at the expense of smaller companies and protested to Hugh Johnson. Meetings with Johnson and Roosevelt led to the creation of the National Recovery Review Board, which in May of 1934 issued a report supporting some of Nye's criticisms.[44]

While Nye saw the New Deal harming small business, some powerful business leaders, including those in the armaments industry, sensed an antipathy toward big business and finance. The National Industrial Recovery Act legitimized collective bargaining rights for workers, a position that many business leaders found repugnant. At the end of 1933, FDR tried a gold-purchasing scheme to lower the value of the dollar and thus encourage exports. Many conservative financial leaders believed in the sacredness of the gold-backed dollar and were aghast at Roosevelt's heresy. Some of his own Treasury Department officials opposed the policy. Al Smith, whom FDR had nominated for president in 1928, denounced the "baloney dollar." The president kept going with the policy into early 1934, though it seemed to do little economic good. At least the administration was doing something in a time when most Americans demanded action.[45]

Roosevelt's political antennae sensed a split with conservative financial and business leaders as early as October of 1933, when he told several cabinet officials that bankers were conspiring to stop the New Deal. In November, FDR wrote to Robert W. Bingham and noted that "inevitable sniping has commenced, led by . . . the Mellon-Mills influence in banking and certain controlling industries." At the same time he received a letter from Edward House, who had advised Woodrow Wilson, that warned of plans for a meeting at which Al Smith, Newton Baker, Carter Glass, and other conservative Democrats would protest FDR's policies.[46]

The Du Ponts, America's leading munitions makers and a certain target for any investigation of the armament industry, marched at the front of those opposed to Roosevelt. Pierre S. Du Pont, chairman of the board of the E. I. Du Pont de Nemours & Company, initially supported FDR in the 1932 election. Most Du Pont family members, however, backed Hoover. In 1933, Pierre received appointments to the NRA's Industrial Advisory Committee and to the National Labor Board (NLB), but by 1934 he and other Du Ponts began to voice opposition to the administration. In the Du Pont Company Annual Report for 1933, released in January of 1934, company president Lammot Du Pont criticized Roosevelt's monetary policy. The *New York Times* summarized the comments under the headline, "Administration Is Scored." The rift between the administration and the Du Ponts widened in March when Pierre Du Pont filed the first dissent to an NLB decision. He opposed the extension of collective bargaining agreements to employees who did not belong to the bargaining unit, an issue of significance to thousands of workers at Du Pont and General Motors. Pierre subsequently resigned from the NLB and the Industrial Advisory Board. The New Deal's critics were few in number, however, as common men and women lined up with Roosevelt against the corrupt moneychangers and greedy businessmen who received blame for both the Great Depression and the Great War.[47]

For many Americans, U.S. involvement in World War I looked like a huge mistake from the perspective of the early 1930s. The results of America's last effort to make the world safe stood starkly in the foreground with unpaid war debts, antiwar novels and films, and the Bonus March. In the background were Japanese aggressions in Asia and Italian and German military threats in Europe. Organizations that followed the pacifistic Social Gospel and viewed the armaments makers as threats to peace stepped up their efforts, and in 1932 the Women's International League for Peace and Freedom called for a federal investigation of the munitions industry. As the excitement of the emerging New Deal enveloped Washington, Dorothy Detzer set to work on what would be her greatest lobbying achievement.[48]

The history of the munitions committee unfolded amid the many tensions of middle 1930s America. In the political realm, the munitions-making Du Ponts and their conservative allies confronted FDR and the liberals. From a cultural perspective, Nye and rural Americans felt threatened by the rise of the city and its foreigners and moneychangers. Intellectual life found Walter Rauschenbusch's Social Gospel idealism challenged by Reinhold Niebuhr's realism, while historians wrestled with conflicting interpretations of World War I and even questioned the existence of objective truth. In terms of social policy, progressive associations, led more frequently by women, countered conservative prescriptions developed mainly by men. Disagreement between isolationists and internationalists over foreign policy formed another issue of the period, but not the only one important to understanding the munitions investigation. Many of these tensions intersected in the Nye committee, making it something more than a national distraction.

Chapter 2

The Formation of the Munitions Committee, August 1933 to August 1934

Dorothy Detzer took her campaign for a munitions investigation to Capitol Hill and contacted twenty U.S. senators, but she found only Norris and La Follette much concerned with the issue and neither was willing to sponsor the resolution. Norris said he was too old, while La Follette maintained that he was too busy. She reported several senators saying, "You can't do anything to beat the munitions industry, its ramifications are too wide," and that sponsoring the legislation would be "political suicide." Detzer twice asked Nye to sponsor the resolution, but he showed little enthusiasm for attacking the munitions merchants. Detzer maintained her optimism. In August of 1933, she wrote to historian Mary R. Beard and predicted that the munitions inquiry would take place.[1]

The National Recovery Administration, with its code-making authority, offered another avenue for regulation of domestic arms makers. Detzer suggested in late 1933 that the munitions code authority committee include State Department munitions specialist Joseph Green, League of Nations Association leader Raymond Fosdick, and a representative appointed by the president. Finding some State Department support for the idea, Detzer asked FDR to appoint a special committee to "watch the munitions code . . . as it relates to the export and import, manufacture, and control of arms for the purposes of war." Roosevelt liked the proposal, but the administration decided not to pursue it after NRA chief Hugh Johnson expressed opposition. Unsuccessful in her attempt to employ the NRA in controlling the munitions industry, Detzer continued to search for a senator to sponsor the munitions investigation.[2]

Shortly before Christmas she met with Norris and went over a list of all ninety-six senators. He crossed off the names of those he thought unsuitable. Some were too closely tied to munitions interests in their states, some were up for re-election in 1934, and others were not able enough. At the end of the process, only Nye's name remained. His state had virtually no economic dependence on the munitions industry. He was youthful and energetic and did not face the voters again until 1938. He had competently played leading roles in previous Senate investigations. Perhaps most important of all, he believed in the issue. In early January, Detzer approached Nye for the third time and overcame his reluctance. With Norris's backing, he agreed to sponsor the proposal.[3]

With many characteristics in common, Nye and Detzer formed an effective professional relationship. Both were midwesterners working in the nation's capital, and they were close in age and educational experience. Each generously credited the other, with Nye noting that Detzer's contribution to the investigation was "not to be in any degree discounted." Detzer described Nye as a "skillful and shrewd parliamentary tactician." The two differed in other ways. Nye sometimes felt inadequate and never became completely comfortable in his role as a senator, while Detzer possessed more self-assurance and enjoyed the limelight generated by the munitions inquiry. Drew Pearson and Robert Allen, in their column "The Washington Merry-Go-Round," named Detzer "Woman of the Year" for 1935. She remembered "the meteoric popularity usually associated with channel swimmers and sweepstakes champions. The role of lady lioness was quite new and highly entertaining to me." She also became a target for critics of the investigation. In the summer of 1935, Republican Senator L. J. Dickinson alleged that Detzer held socialist views, and, after Pearl Harbor, one congressman called her "the most notorious woman Communist in the United States." Dickinson's attack troubled her. Soon afterward, she wrote a friend that she "wouldn't trust Senator Nye not to repudiate me if he got into a jam!"[4]

Detzer and Nye worked to draft a resolution acceptable to the many people interested in the munitions investigation. Nye met with Joseph Green at the State Department on 17 January 1934 and sought help in drafting the resolution. Green agreed to assist but noted that his personal action did not signify departmental approval. Detzer expected senate opposition to the measure and worked to find a balanced proposal that would both pass and assure a potent inquiry. The final draft concisely stated the aims: "That the Foreign Affairs Committee be and is hereby authorized and directed to investigate the activities of individuals and corporations in the United States engaged in the manufacture, sale, distribution, import and export of arms, ammunition and other implements of war." To the frustration of Detzer, Nye hesitated to submit the resolution, telling her that "the psychological moment for putting it in had not yet come."[5]

The proper timing came on the afternoon of 8 February when Nye offered the resolution for consideration. Detzer expected intense opposition, but instead the resolution was accepted without protest and assigned to the Foreign Relations Committee, where chairman Key Pittman of Nevada would control its fate. Nye explained to Detzer that the right moment had come because none of the senators who might have opposed the resolution was on the floor. With Nye's absence on 1 March, Pittman transferred the resolution to the Military Affairs Committee. Detzer thought this move threatened the resolution because "the members of that committee were predominantly and vigorously military minded." She feared they would stop the investigation before it started or would conduct the inquiry themselves and "whitewash the most important facts."[6]

Nye and Detzer's resolution touched off a flurry of activity. State Department officials sought to work out a policy line, and at a 20 February news conference, Secretary of State Cordell Hull wanted Congress to lead on the matter. Speaking off the record, he said he was "endeavoring to show genuine interest in the investigation . . . from every angle in which everybody would be interested." In Wilmington, Delaware, Du Pont officials reacted to the proposal for a munitions investigation. K.K.V. Casey, Du Pont sales director, talked in mid-February with Military Intelligence officials at the War Department. Casey hoped military officials would express their concern to the State Department so that "at least they will be familiar with the situation and the possible disadvantages from the viewpoint of the Army."[7]

While the State Department and the Du Pont corporation reacted to the resolution, Detzer sought its implementation. She organized a conference of supporters to devise a strategy for passing the resolution. The group decided to link the Nye resolution with Arthur Vandenberg's American Legion-backed resolution that called for a review of the War Policies Commission. They asked for a select committee to conduct the investigation because they wanted it to be out of the hands of the Military Affairs Committee. Nye and Vandenberg accepted the recommendations, and on 12 March Nye submitted Senate Resolution 206. Morris Sheppard of Texas, chair of the Military Affairs Committee, responded positively, and the full committee favorably reported the resolution on 19 March. The Committee to Audit and Control the Contingent Expenses of the Senate, chaired by South Carolina Senator James F. Byrnes, endorsed it on 2 April with a recommendation that funding be cut from $50,000 to $15,000.[8]

That media interest in the armaments issue increased in the spring of 1934 was a good omen for Nye and Detzer's resolution. *Fortune* magazine, a generally conservative and business-oriented publication, included the article "Arms and the Men" in its March issue. *Fortune* rejected a conspiratorial view of the munitions industry, noting that "if the armament business were conducted by an outlawed band of international gangsters, the problem would be simple to define. The difficulty is that precisely the opposite is the case. The armament business is a part of the most essential industries of industrialized nations—steel and chemicals." Not only a few capitalists but also tens of thousands of workers and their families had linked their livelihoods to the armaments industry. To build demand for their products, armament makers constantly publicized war scares, lobbied governments to build up defenses against neighboring states, and bribed officials to get contracts. *Fortune* suggested nationalization as the simplest solution to the problem, but "to do that, the State would have to take over most of the essential industries of modern life." While the article strongly criticized the activities of the leading European arms makers and their leaders, it also recognized that armament and disarmament were complex issues that defied easy answers. Nye entered the article into the *Congressional Record*, and it reached a wider audience in May when a condensed version appeared in *Reader's Digest*.[9]

Two books critical of the armaments industry reached store shelves at around the same time. *Iron, Blood and Profits: An Exposure of the World-Wide Munitions Racket*, by George Seldes, and *Merchants of Death: A Study of the International Armament Industry*, by Helmuth C. Engelbrecht and Frank C. Hanighen, asserted that arms manufacturers encouraged conflict and stirred up animosities. Both books received favorable reviews, and *Merchants of Death* became a Book-of-the-Month Club selection in April. Interested Americans could easily learn about the activities of the international arms merchants, including the U.S. based Du Pont corporation that merited its own chapter in *Merchants of Death*.[10]

The rather unlikely duo of progressive Senator William Borah and conservative businessman Henry Ford added to the chorus criticizing the arms industry. Borah blasted munitions makers during a 5 March 1934 Senate debate on naval construction, saying their political influence made armament reductions difficult. Two future members of the munitions investigation joined the debate, with Senator Bennett Clark of Missouri interjecting that naval expansion bills were "invariably accompanied by propaganda as to the possibility or probability of a war." Senator Homer Bone of Washington asked Borah about nationalization of the munitions industry. Borah finished his speech by saying that the efforts of arms makers "to foment discord . . . among nations, all that such profits may be made and enlarged reaches the dead level of human depravity." Two days later, in a speech covered by the *New York Times*, Ford said that "if we could get rid of the approximately 100 men responsible for war in this world the people would enjoy peace." The mounting criticism and public pressure drew attention from Du Pont officials, who in May ceased discussions with European gunpowder producers because "a formal agreement among manufacturers would cause the loudest and most violent criticism and put us in a very disagreeable position. We would be accused of joining together to foment wars, increase armament, etc."[11]

The growing anti-armament sentiment did not attract a majority of the senators. The WILPF found that forty-five senators opposed S.R. 206 and only twenty supported it. Twenty-nine were uncommitted. When questioning of the uncommitted senators showed that twenty-two of them would back the position taken by the Roosevelt administration, Detzer went to see Cordell Hull. The secretary of state talked positively of the investigation but told her that administration policy would depend on the attitude of the president.[12]

FDR had experience in dealing with the munitions makers from his service as assistant secretary of the navy during the Wilson administration. In that role, Roosevelt had refused to count on the patriotism of suppliers to ensure fair prices and instead relied on his own assistant, Louis Howe, to ferret out the facts behind navy bids and contracts. Roosevelt, Howe, and Navy Secretary Josephus Daniels often suspected collusion among bidders on contracts. When American steel manufacturers turned in identical bid prices for armor plate on a new battleship, Roosevelt negotiated a lower price with a British manufacturer that led the domestic firms to lower their bids. Efforts to obtain cheaper coal opened bidding to many new companies, but some of the firms helped by FDR's actions provided poor quality coal and he ended up in an uncomfortable session before the House Naval Affairs Committee. When the navy received bids on patrol boats, Roosevelt wrote Daniels "that at least half of these bidders cannot be called responsible firms with adequate equipment for the work." Such problems never led Roosevelt to conclude, however, that government arms manufacturing should replace private companies. He believed that government-owned plants should complement the private sector, setting a baseline for prices during peacetime and augmenting production during wartime.[13]

The political aspects of a munitions inquiry could hardly have escaped consideration by a master politician like Franklin Roosevelt. American Legion interest provided a strong incentive for Roosevelt to support S.R. 206. He had demonstrated his respect for the veteran's organization when, shortly before his inauguration, he spoke to American Legionnaires in Miami. It was one political speech FDR probably never forgot, for moments afterward a would-be assassin fired several pistol shots at him. FDR's willingness to appeal to the legionnaires made good political sense. With over 800,000 members of voting age, the legion formed a powerful interest group during the interwar years. Important business leaders and former military officers controlled the group's affairs, and secretaries of war and their assistant secretaries were usually active members.[14]

Roosevelt's decision on S.R. 206 came just as big business and big finance completed their break with the administration, a coincidence that may have affected his choice. On 9 February, the day after Nye submitted his original resolution, FDR called for regulation of the stock exchanges, a move that more than any other generated opposition from the business community. The president of the New York Stock Exchange organized leaders of finance and industry to campaign against the bill. Congressman Sam Rayburn, co-sponsor of the bill, called the opposition "the most powerful lobby ever organized against any bill which ever came up in Congress." The battle climaxed in mid-March, with FDR accepting some compromises in a new bill drafted on 20 March. Roosevelt stood firm with the provisions of the new bill and, after it made its way through the legislative process, signed the Securities and Exchange Commission Act in June.[15]

Corporate executives at Du Pont, America's leading munitions maker, had already broken with the administration and in March took their first steps toward forming an organization to combat the New Deal. Robert R. M. Carpenter, a Du Pont vice-president, complained to John Raskob of how "Negroes on my place in South Carolina refused work this spring, after I had taken care of them and given them house rent free and work for three years during bad times, saying they had easy jobs with the Government. . . . A cook on my houseboat at Fort Myers quit because the Government was paying him a dollar an hour as a painter." Raskob sympathized with Carpenter's plight. He called for the "du Pont and General Motors groups, followed by other big industries, to definitely organize to protect society from the suffering which it is bound to endure if we allow communistic elements to lead the people to believe that all business men are crooks, not to be trusted, and that no one should be allowed to get rich." Raskob took up the idea with Jouett Shouse, executive chairman of the Democratic National Committee from 1929 to 1932.[16]

Within the context of New Deal politics, a munitions inquiry not only appealed to rank-and-file American Legionnaires but also virtually guaranteed negative publicity for many of the industrialists and financial leaders opposed to administration policy. The Du Ponts in particular would be a leading target for any probe of the industry, and Roosevelt understood the kinds of problems they could cause. When FDR ran for vice-president in 1920, the Democratic presidential nominee, James G. Cox, accused Coleman Du Pont of working to defeat the Democrats and the League of Nations. By the spring of 1934, Pierre and Lammot Du Pont were displaying their unhappiness with the administration. The Pecora investigation was drawing to a close, and S.R. 206 offered another opportunity to focus public attention on the "unscrupulous moneychangers," and this time on perhaps the most unscrupulous of all—the munitions merchants.[17]

In mid-March, as the battle over the Securities and Exchange Commission Act reached its boiling point, the administration endorsed S.R. 206. On 17 March, the *Detroit News* described a tentative plan to form a special munitions investigation committee. Morris Sheppard and Marvel Logan, both members of the Military Affairs Committee, would hold two of four Democratic seats. Sheppard would chair the investigation, with Republican members to include Nye and Vandenberg. The tentative proposal met the expectations of Cordell Hull, and the State Department announced its support for the investigation on 19 March, the same day the Military Affairs Committee reported on S.R. 206. Hull later remembered that he and FDR reluctantly acquiesced to popular support for the resolution. "In the Executive Branch it was evident that no one could withstand the isolationist cyclone. The mere hint of an investigation had met with wide acclaim. . . . The President and I felt that our only feasible step was a sort of marking time. There was no hope of success and nothing to be gained in combating the isolationist wave at that moment." Pessimistic reports from the Geneva Disarmament Conference added to Hull's distress over armament and munitions issues. According to Detzer, however, Hull expressed a favorable attitude toward the munitions inquiry when they met in March.[18]

Hull appreciated public concern about the munitions traders and took steps to protect the government from criticism. When the U.S. consulate in Dublin inquired about promotions of American arms, Hull answered on 26 March that "it is of the utmost importance that representatives of this Government should avoid any action which might conceivably be interpreted as associating this Government with the promotion of the international traffic in arms." On the same day, Detzer and twenty-one other pacifist leaders encouraged Roosevelt by letter to give official and public support to the munitions investigation.[19]

Administration backing increased senatorial support for S.R. 206, and in a 10 April radio speech Nye confidently predicted an investigation that would "let people know how they are made monkeys of by profit-sundry, soulless madmen who are making lunatics of the people of the world by their incessant propaganda for ever-larger appropriations." Two days later Nye and Vandenberg maneuvered to get the resolution passed during debate on a tax bill. Nye offered an amendment that called for personal income above $10,000 a year to be taxed at a 98 percent rate during wartime. After Nye spoke for over an hour, Vandenberg rose and delivered a long talk in support of the amendment. He discussed the "intriguing influences of an international munitions lobby" and said the Nye and Vandenberg resolution would enable Americans to learn "whether this malignant influence is in any degree persuasive within our own United States." Finance Committee chair Pat Harrison, anxious to pass a tax bill, spoke with Nye and Vandenberg and learned that several days of speeches on the tax amendment were planned. Harrison suggested that the debate be interrupted for a vote on S.R. 206. If it passed, he wanted Nye's tax amendment to be referred to the munitions investigation committee. Nye and Vandenberg accepted the proposal, and upon Harrison's urging Nye asked for unanimous consent. "My heart sank," Detzer remembered as she watched from the gallery. "I was desperately anxious to have the investigation authorized, but we were still short five votes." But no senator objected.[20]

There was no dramatic roll call vote and no senators decried the death merchants. With administration approval, S.R. 206 passed almost by accident. Clearly, administration opposition would have killed the munitions resolution, if not within the Military Affairs Committee then certainly on the floor. Why did the Roosevelt administration support S.R. 206? FDR had a genuine interest in establishing effective governmental controls over the armaments industry. His service in the Navy Department during World War I gave him firsthand knowledge of the problems involved in dealing with private military suppliers. As president, he used the National Labor Board to gather information on private shipbuilders. He told Hull that he favored national regulation of munitions manufacturing. Domestic political considerations also made the munitions inquiry attractive. Not only would it please American Legionnaires and pacifist organizations, but also it would expose unsavory practitioners in the munitions industry who were also enemies of the New Deal, most notably the Du Ponts. Finally, FDR and Hull had every reason to expect Morris Sheppard or some other Democrat to chair the committee and protect the interests of the administration. The argument that an internationalist-minded president caved in before overwhelming isolationist pressure cannot be dismissed, but FDR's decision six months later to confront the isolationists and push for U.S. membership on the World Court weakens such assertions.[21]

With the resolution passed, Vice-President John Nance Garner appointed a special committee of seven senators to investigate the domestic armaments and munitions industries, report on the need for stronger governmental regulation, review the work of the War Policies Commission, and study the merits of "a Government monopoly in respect to the manufacture of armaments and munitions and other implements of war." Garner asked Nye and Vandenberg to recommend four Democrats and three Republicans. After conferring with other senators, Nye and Vandenberg submitted the names of Sheppard, Bennett Clark, Homer Bone, and James P. Pope to represent the Democrats and W. Warren Barbour and themselves for the Republicans. Detzer may have influenced the selection of members to the munitions investigation. In a June 1934 memorandum covering the history of the WILPF munitions campaign, she noted that the "committee which was finally chosen by the Vice-President . . . was no accident, nor was the choice of the chief investigator." Garner approved the list. Walter George, a Democrat, replaced Sheppard before the committee began its work. This was an important development because Sheppard, according to press reports, was to chair the investigation.[22]

FDR praised Garner's leadership of the Senate in April of 1934, but the vice-president's choices for the munitions committee offered little to cheer the Roosevelt administration. Of the Democrats, only Pope consistently supported the New Deal. A former mayor of Boise, Idaho, he was elected to the Senate in 1932. He had close ties to pacifist organizations and hoped to use his influence as a senator to promote peace. His support for the League of Nations and collective security measures made him one of the most internationalist-minded leaders of the party. Nye and Vandenberg wanted him on the committee to provide balance to their own unilateralist opinions, and he was the only outspoken internationalist who appeared on their list.[23]

Homer Bone of Washington was, like Pope, a freshman senator in his early fifties from the Pacific Northwest. His unilateralist foreign policy views contrasted sharply with Pope's internationalism. His father had been taken prisoner during the Civil War, and his mother had lost two brothers in the conflict. She believed that "war was man's chiefest insanity," and her son embraced similar views. He believed nationalization of munitions plants would be a major step toward peace. A progressive Republican earlier in his career, Bone ran as a Democrat in 1932. Groups that called for far-reaching economic change, led by the Commonwealth Builders, supported his campaign and were largely responsible for his victory. Bone represented a variant of West Coast radicalism that included Upton Sinclair's "End Poverty in America" and Francis Townsend's pension plans. The Roosevelt administration prudently maintained a distance from such extreme programs. Bone was not a reliable New Dealer.[24]

Bennett Clark, for personal and policy reasons, distanced himself from the administration. His father, former Democratic Speaker of the House Champ Clark, had sought the Democratic presidential nomination in 1912. Although he received an absolute majority of the delegate votes, he failed to reach the two-thirds majority that party rules demanded. FDR, an enthusiastic Wilson supporter, organized a timely convention demonstration that some credited with stopping a surge toward Clark. Bennett Clark entered the Senate in 1933 and enjoyed close friendships with leaders from his father's era, especially southern conservatives like Garner, Harrison, Byrnes, and Carter Glass of Virginia. Glass openly broke with the New Deal early on and became a leading critic, and Clark's voting record placed him not far behind. The Missouri senator voted against both the NRA and AAA in 1933.[25]

Walter George became a senator in 1922 when he filled the seat left open by the death of Tom Watson, the former Populist. George's twelve years of Senate experience made him the committee's senior member. He held conservative and internationalist views, and Nye and Vandenberg wanted him on the committee for ideological balance. Although the son of a tenant farmer, George had strong ties to business interests. He socialized with officials of the Georgia Power Company and the Atlanta-based Coca Cola Company, and his attitude toward the New Deal closely followed the views of business. He supported much of the "100 Days" legislation but began to oppose administration proposals more frequently by 1935. He later became a leading critic of the New Deal, causing FDR to back a rival candidate in the 1938 Democratic primary. When George joined the munitions investigation in 1934, however, the administration had no reason to view him as a political opponent.[26]

Of the Republicans on the committee, Nye most often supported New Deal legislation. Hoover had not inspired Nye in 1928, and the situation was much the same four years later. While running for re-election himself in 1932, Nye refused to support the Republican presidential nominee. Though he offered some positive remarks regarding FDR, he stopped short of a public endorsement. Some of Roosevelt's programs did not fully satisfy Nye and other progressive Republicans, who often called for the administration to do more and criticized the New Deal from the left. From FDR's perspective, however, Nye may have been more reliable than Democrats like Clark, George, and Bone.[27]

Arthur Vandenberg, co-sponsor of S.R. 206, provided leadership for conservative Republicans in Congress during the New Deal. He opposed the NRA, AAA, and Tennessee Valley Authority, but he did not allow himself to be perceived as a reactionary. He supported the Securities and Exchange Commission bill under consideration while the munitions investigation formed. Some contemporaries had a difficult time in assessing Vandenberg's positions on issues, and the same has been true for historians. Historian C. David Tompkins wrote that "Vandenberg did not share most of Nye's isolationist views," but Wayne S. Cole found that "both had been fervent isolationists." Another historian concluded that in the munitions investigation Vandenberg "established himself as a leading isolationist." Vandenberg had much in common with Nye. Both had worked in the newspaper business, both had been appointed to the Senate in the 1920s, and both were from the upper Middle West. In equally important ways, however, they differed. Vandenberg's home state included much heavy industry and many sizable cities, and the Michigan senator did not champion the cause of the farmer in the ways that Nye did. Unlike the sometimes ill-at-ease Nye, Vandenberg enjoyed orating, leading one critic to remark that he "addressed people in conversation as if he were in a public hall."[28]

The third Republican on the committee, W. Warren Barbour, represented New Jersey, a heavily industrialized state. A millionaire who owned manufacturing facilities, he had entered the Senate in 1931. Barbour stood much closer to Vandenberg's conservatism than to Nye's progressivism, though he occasionally voted for administration reform proposals. He understood the importance of the munitions industry in his state. In July of 1933, he asked Roosevelt to postpone personnel cuts at the Picatinny Arsenal in Dover that threatened 800 jobs. Four months later, he wrote to the president concerning modernization and expansion of the air force, noting that "representatives of the Aviation Industry in New Jersey, having large payrolls, have inquired of me as to what funds will be expended by the federal government." The headquarters of the New York Shipbuilding Corporation, a major navy contractor, was in Camden, New Jersey.[29]

A majority of the committee members had joined the Senate within the previous three years, but there had been opportunities for all to assess each other during floor debates and through service on standing committees. Bone, Clark, Nye, and Vandenberg sat on the Territories and Insular Affairs Committee. George, Pope, and Vandenberg held seats on the Foreign Relations Committee, while Clark, Nye, and Vandenberg served on the Commerce Committee. No other standing committee included more than two senators from the munitions committee. Bone sat on the Naval Affairs Committee, an area of concern for the investigation, and he and Pope were members of the Agriculture and Forestry Committee.[30]

Almost everyone expected a Democrat to chair the investigation. Democrats controlled sixty seats in the Senate compared to only thirty-five for the Republicans, and committee chairmanships routinely went to majority party members. Furthermore, Garner's role in appointing the committee allowed him to discuss the chairmanship with prospective Democratic members. But the vice-president left the choice to the committee members, and when they met on 23 April, Clark nominated Nye, Bone seconded, and no one objected. Nye was surprised, for he had expected Clark to get the position. Pope later said the senators believed the choice of Nye would affirm their support for a nonpartisan inquiry.[31]

At the State Department, Hull failed to share Pope's equanimity. "Had I dreamed that an isolationist Republican would be appointed I promptly would have opposed it," he later wrote. Hull blamed Garner and Senator Pittman for what he called a "fatal mistake" and a "blunder of major proportions." Despite his reservations, Hull on 27 April promised Nye the "most cordial cooperation of the Department" as well as his own personal support. He put Joseph Green "at the disposition of the Committee at any time" when it might desire his assistance.[32]

One of the first important decisions involved the selection of a chief investigator. The committee wanted to get the investigation started quickly, and within days of becoming chairperson Nye had a line of applicants crowded into his office. Making her way through the crowd to keep an appointment with Nye was Detzer, who believed the choice of chief investigator would be crucial to the success of the investigation. She learned the committee planned to come to a decision on the following day and that Nye had a person in mind. After she raised concerns about the applicant, Nye asked her to suggest someone. Detzer seized the opportunity and organized a lunchtime meeting to discuss prospects for the position. Present were Florence Boeckel of the National Council for Prevention of War, Pat Jackson of the Nonpartisan League, and William T. Stone of the Foreign Policy Association. When Jackson suggested progressive activist Steve Raushenbush, Detzer and the others responded with immediate enthusiasm.[33]

Detzer saw in Raushenbush "a first-class intellect, and the proficiency of an experienced investigator. . . . But it was not only Steve's training and equipment for the job which made me respond so quickly and enthusiastically to Pat's suggestion. In his fearlessness, and in his passion for human progress, Steve was carrying on the crusading social gospel of his famous father, Walter Raushenbush [sic]." Jackson set out to locate Raushenbush, who was "somewhere in Pennsylvania," while Detzer teamed up with Jeannette Rankin of the National Council for Prevention of War and contacted the senators on the munitions committee. Rankin, who had voted against U.S. entry into World War I and would later cast the sole vote against the declaration of war on Japan, talked with Barbour, George, and Pope. Detzer met with the others. She found Nye and Clark receptive and Bone enthusiastic. Vandenberg warned her not to "send us any wild-eyed radicals," but he agreed to meet Raushenbush the following day with the rest of the committee. After being reached late in the night, Raushenbush drafted an outline for the investigation on a brown paper bag while riding the train from Harrisburg to Washington. He got the job. "Apparently the plan (presented to the committee later that morning) impressed them," Detzer later wrote. Her lobbying abilities were once again impressive, and she noted that "within twenty-four hours after we had initiated our Raushenbush campaign, no other candidate was considered for the job."[34]

As the eldest child in his family, Stephen Raushenbush had enjoyed a particularly close relationship with his father. Leading an investigation of the munitions industry allowed him to act on his father's teaching that the drive for profits was the underlying cause of war. Raushenbush's investigators could examine the role played by bankers and munitions makers in leading the United States into the Great War and perhaps validate the theories of fellow progressives like Senator George Norris and historian Charles Beard. He might also defend his father's heritage from the realist attacks of Reinhold Niebuhr if investigators found evidence to support the Social Gospel beliefs about arms makers. The investigation might expose the interests that led the United States into the war and brought so much misery to his father and millions of others.

The thirty-eight-year-old chief investigator assembled an able staff to conduct the research. Calvin Nichols and Ben T. Moore, who served with Raushenbush in the Washington office, analyzed field reports from investigators and prepared material for questions during the hearings. Donald Wemple managed the committee's New York City office. Because many of the munitions companies and banks were headquartered there, the majority of investigators operated out of Wemple's office. Robert Wohlforth, whom Detzer introduced to Nye, guided research on the munitions trade. Wohlforth had been researching the munitions industry for several years, and in March of 1934 he published "Armaments Profiteers: 1934," in the *Nation*. Floyd LaRouche led the investigation of the shipbuilding industry, Lawrence Brown directed research into the Wall Street banks, and Josephine Joan Burns studied State Department documents. A large number of individuals, some of them assigned to the committee from federal relief programs, worked for the munitions committee. As with any large organization, personnel conflicts and problems occasionally developed. Investigators had to be relied upon to keep information confidential and not to use it in their own books and articles.[35]

Later accusations that Alger Hiss misused committee information made him the most notorious staff member of the munitions investigation. The facts as to how and why Hiss joined the munitions investigation in July of 1934 are confusing. Technically, Hiss continued working in a policy-making capacity for the AAA until the summer of 1935. He maintained that Bone and Pope, who knew of him through their work on the Agriculture and Forestry Committee, arranged for the AAA to loan his services to the investigation. Jerome Frank, Hiss's superior at AAA, remembered that either AAA staff member Gardner Jackson or Detzer recommended Hiss to the committee. Jackson recalled that another AAA staff member, Lee Pressman, suggested to him that Hiss join the munitions investigation. The record shows that Nye asked the Agriculture Department to detail Hiss to the munitions investigation, and the acting general counsel agreed to the request during Frank's absence.[36]

Hiss's relationship to the munitions investigation took on political importance during the early cold war years. In August of 1948 the House Un-American Activities Committee heard testimony from Whittaker Chambers, a former member of the Communist party, that implicated Hiss in pro-communist espionage activities against the United States. Chambers said Hiss took confidential State Department documents from munitions committee files and passed them on to him. Hiss denied the charge, but acknowledged having known Chambers in 1934.[37]

The Hiss-Chambers case produced sensational headlines within the context of the early cold war, and officials involved with the munitions investigation took sides on the matter. Nye, in a 1960 interview, said that he believed Chambers. Joseph Green, who worked closely with Hiss and the munitions committee, refuted Chambers and said the munitions investigators never received secret documents or originals of any documents. In fact, however, the committee did receive confidential documents and had agreements with the State Department concerning the uses of such materials.[38]

For those looking for a communist conspiracy, the murkiness of the story allowed them to see what they wanted. Pressman played the crucial role. He had befriended Hiss while both studied under Felix Frankfurter at the Harvard Law School. He had been involved with the Communist party for years, and as a high-ranking AAA official he recruited like-minded people to the agency. From the conspiratorial perspective, Pressman brought Hiss to the AAA and then had him assigned to the munitions committee so the communist underground could gain access to secret records of munitions manufacturers. Hiss then manifested his loyalty to the communist cause by giving confidential material to Chambers.[39]

Speculation concerning how and why Hiss came to the committee is augmented by further mystery about his departure from the Agriculture Department. Hiss had a large role in writing an agency opinion that made it illegal for certain landowners to remove tenants. AAA chief Chester Davis opposed the policy and considered Hiss, Pressman, and several others who worked in the agency's legal department to be insubordinate. In February of 1935, Davis fired everyone involved except Hiss. Why Hiss escaped remains unclear. For anticommunists of the early cold war, Hiss's effort to restrict property rights looked suspiciously un-American, the kind of behavior to be expected from a communist agent who passed military secrets to the enemy.[40]

Although Hiss's role later became an issue of particular interest, for Raushenbush and the senators he filled one position in an organization charged with a very important task. Another part of the organization consisted of an advisory council made up of Dr. Manley Hudson of Harvard University, Dr. Harold Moulton of the Brookings Institution, and John T. Flynn, a writer for the *New Republic* who had worked in the Pecora investigation. The advisory council met with munitions committee members on 5 June 1934 to plan the investigation. Raushenbush argued that the $15,000 appropriated by the Senate would not allow for a thorough inquiry. Nye wanted a stronger case for additional funding. By the following day, a "Revised Outline for the Committee's Work" had been prepared and called for research into five areas: the international activities of domestic arms companies, the procurement policies of the U.S. government, the "influence and operations" of armaments companies, arms control, and wartime taxes on munitions and military supplies.[41]

Endorsements of the investigation came from many directions during the early weeks of work, with the most important and one of the strongest coming from Franklin Roosevelt. In an 18 May message, he showed little of Hull's apprehension about an isolationist investigation led by a Republican. Roosevelt said he was pleased to learn of the munitions inquiry, recommended that it receive "the generous support of the Senate," and directed executive branch departments "to cooperate with the committee to the fullest extent." He called the activities of munitions makers a "serious source of international discord. . . . The peoples of many countries are being taxed to the point of poverty and starvation in order to enable governments to engage in a mad race in armaments which, if permitted to continue, may well result in war. This grave menace to the peace of the world is due in no small measure to the uncontrolled activities of the manufacturers and merchants of engines of destruction." FDR did not surrender to isolationism in proposing a solution to the problem, but rather called for ratification of the 1925 Geneva Convention for the Supervision of the International Trade in Arms and Ammunition and in Implements of War, noting that the munitions problem "must be met by the concerted action of the peoples of all nations." Within one hour of reading FDR's message, Key Pittman reported to the Senate that the treaty had a unanimous recommendation from the Foreign Relations Committee.[42]

Norman Davis, chairman of the U.S. delegation at the Geneva Disarmament Conference, followed Roosevelt's message with a speech to the conference on 29 May. He stated that "production and traffic in engines of death, and the profits resulting therefrom, must be controlled or eliminated. Those who have a sordid financial interest in fomenting international suspicion and discord, which in turn increases the demand for what they have to sell, must be put in a position in which they do not have the power or the incentive to do so much evil." The Roosevelt and Davis statements illustrate how the administration used the "merchants of death" analysis. They agreed with former Secretary of State Frank B. Kellogg, who in May wrote to Nye that there was "no question whatever that the world munition manufacturers are adding their influence and in every way trying to prevent disarmament." In June, Eleanor Roosevelt joined those calling for control and regulation of the munitions industry.[43]

FDR offered further encouragement when he met with committee members for the first time on 6 June. According to Assistant Secretary of State J. Pierrepont Moffat, FDR talked favorably about "clipping the wings of the arms manu-facturers" and even suggested abolishing air forces. He offered to give the committee copies of all correspondence between himself and Davis concerning disarmament. The president's support may have helped in the Senate, for one week after the meeting Nye's request for an additional appropriation of $35,000 was approved. The action brought funding for the investigation up to $50,000, the amount originally requested in S.R. 206. Five days later, Congress adjourned after one of the most active legislative periods in American history. The "100 Days" legislation, the Securities and Exchange Commission Act, and the munitions inquiry were among the congressional achievements. "It's been a grand session," FDR wrote to his vice-president, "greatly due to all of your help."[44]

Looking forward to the off-year elections in November, Roosevelt ended June with a fireside chat and asked Americans if they were "better off than last year." Then he began a cruise through the Caribbean and Central America and on to the Pacific Northwest. With the president out of town and Congress in adjournment, the midsummer produced few headlines regarding the arms investigation. The National Education Association convened in Washington and called for "prohibiting profits on the manufacture and sale of munitions and other war equipment." The munitions committee opened its New York office with an initial staff of twenty researchers sifting through thousands of documents from companies involved in the munitions business. Wohlforth informed Nye that investigators were "striking more pay dirt all the time." Senator Nye predicted on 25 July that the inquiry would expose "startling facts." He said that the munitions makers wanted the investigation to be stopped, an assertion supported by the actions of Irénée Du Pont. The *New York Times* published excerpts from a letter written by Du Pont in which he argued that attacks on munitions makers would "weaken the defensive power of the capitalistic countries" against Russian communist aggression.[45]

Roosevelt's cruise, meanwhile, was a tremendous success. When he landed in Oregon on 3 August, he started his campaign to boost Democratic chances in the upcoming election. He travelled by train across the northern plains, through Montana, North Dakota, and Minnesota, seeing the effects of drought and the huge dust storms that had started in the spring. Roosevelt saw hope and courage in the faces of the struggling farmers. "Coming across the continent the reception was grand," he wrote to Garner, adding that "so far as having the people with us goes, we are just as strong, perhaps stronger, than ever before." Roosevelt appeared with Nye at a campaign stop in Devil's Lake, North Dakota on 7 August. Acting upon FDR's request, Nye introduced the president to an audience of 35,000 people. Roosevelt then honored the political adage that all politics is local and focused his comments on the weather rather than the munitions makers. Afterward, Nye introduced Eleanor Roosevelt to the crowd.[46]

The Devil's Lake appearance represented the high point of the Roosevelt-Nye relationship. Nye had supported much of the New Deal and could do more for FDR in the future. While the munitions committee's election of Nye as chairman may have upset Hull's foreign policy considerations, it offered unexpected possibilities for Roosevelt's domestic political fortunes. In five weeks, a Republican would lead the investigation of FDR's most active opponents, the Du Ponts. In thirteen weeks, voters would show their opinion of the New Deal.

Chapter 3

The Roosevelt Administration, the Du Ponts, and the First Munitions Hearings, August 1934 to December 1934

On 8 August, one day after Roosevelt and Nye stood together in North Dakota, Douglas MacArthur expressed concerns about the munitions inquiry and the delicate issue of private documents. In a letter to Nye, he noted that Du Pont and other U.S. companies had procurement plans with the War Department which, if made public, would reveal to potential enemies important information about American preparedness and strategic planning. He also wrote Raushenbush regarding the confidential nature of Army Air Corps records. The State Department took an interest in protecting sensitive documents as well and on 8 August completed an agreement that allowed Joseph Green to prevent publication of some materials. The agreement covered neither documents from other government departments nor records of private corporations.[1]

MacArthur also wrote to Lammot Du Pont, mentioning company files related to munitions production and stressing the need to maintain secrecy. Du Pont proceeded to stamp company documents with the notation that "upon instructions of the War and/or Navy Department, this document is entrusted to Mr. Donald Y. Wemple, for use by the U.S. Government only." The MacArthur–Du Pont correspondence linked a man FDR thought to be one of the most dangerous people in America with the leading critics of his administration. During the summer of 1934, MacArthur and several of the Du Ponts were further linked in a supposed plot to form a fascist army and carry out a Mussolini-style march on Washington. General Smedley Butler, former commandant of the Marine Corps, testified in late 1934 before the House Un-American Activities Committee and named MacArthur and the Du Ponts among those involved. James Van Zandt, national commander of the Veterans of Foreign Wars, corroborated Butler's testimony. The plot, however, appeared to consist of little more than a few scattered conversations.[2]

While a military coup against the Roosevelt administration never materialized, an organized political attack did. John Raskob and Jouett Shouse, both closely tied to the Du Pont corporate empire, pursued their campaign to defend America against attacks from "communistic elements." They organized the Liberty League, a conservative pro-business group. The Du Ponts, America's leading munitions makers and a chief target of the munitions investigation, formed the heart of the league, which received up to 60 percent of its funding from Du Pont sources. Irénée sat on the board of directors, and Pierre served on the League's national executive committee. Raskob and Alfred P. Sloan, of General Motors, were members of the national advisory council. Shouse served as president and in that capacity met with Franklin Roosevelt on 15 August. He told FDR that the league had two basic goals, both educational: to teach respect for human and property rights, and to teach the need for government to promote private enterprise and protect property rights. Shouse assured Roosevelt that the organization would be "absolutely non-partisan in character." The president, perhaps playing the role of the fox more than that of the lion, listened to Shouse's presentation and agreed to issue an endorsement of the league. Roosevelt realized that the league represented his political opponents, and his earlier support for the munitions investigation now paid a handsome dividend. He had in his corner a double-barreled attack that would rip into the organization before it had a chance to get off the ground.[3]

FDR shot off one barrel on 24 August, two days after the league's initial press conference, when he offered a rather dubious endorsement of the organization. "An organization that only advocates two or three out of the Ten Commandments may be a perfectly good organization," he told reporters, "but it would have certain shortcomings in having failed to advocate the other seven or eight." He claimed to have "laughed for ten minutes" after reading a news report that the "speculative fraternity in Wall Street regards the new American Liberty League as a direct answer from Heaven to their prayer." FDR had made his point. "I don't believe that any further comment is necessary after this," he concluded for the press. But he provided additional remarks in private letters, calling the Liberty League the "Apoplectic Losers League" and noting the involvement of the Du Ponts.[4]

The blast of the other barrel came from the Nye committee and aimed at the league's heart. Only two days after Shouse met with FDR, committee investigators began searching through Du Pont company records. With the investigation barely started, Nye attacked the Du Ponts. In a 27 August speech at the Chicago World's Fair, he noted the "greediness of the dominant industrialists and financiers" in the munitions business. The dominant American company easily stood out. "During four years of peacetime the Du Ponts made only $4 million. During four years of war they made $24 million in profits," Nye said. He scoffed at Irénée Du Pont's charge that criticism of the arms companies aided the communist cause. "Naturally, Du Pont sees red when he sees these profits attacked by international peace," Nye concluded.[5]

Less than a week later, Nye spoke over the CBS radio network and again struck at the Du Ponts. He cited the profits made by seven U.S. businesses during World War I and noted that the Du Pont family dominated four of the profiteering companies—Du Pont de Nemours, Atlas Powder, Hercules Powder, and General Motors. With the hearings due to start on 4 September, Nye looked toward the outcome. He mentioned the creation of a Peace Department to balance the War and Navy Departments, the establishment of a "government monopoly or control over the primary items entering into the conduct of war," the restriction of trade with belligerents, and legislation to end war profiteering. The proposal for a government monopoly over military supplies posed a direct threat to Du Pont interests and ran directly against the basic principles of the Liberty League. Press reports suggested that a majority of munitions committee members favored strict government regulation over armaments production.[6]

As the hearings drew near, concerns mounted over what would be revealed and who might be named. Aiken Simons, in charge of export sales for Du Pont, met with Joseph Green on 28 August to ask that certain documents related to China be kept confidential. A Du Pont memorandum indicated that some officials of the Chinese Embassy in Washington supported a faction in conflict with the recognized Nanking government. As the officials in question were supposed to represent the Nanking government, publication of the memorandum would compromise their positions. Colombian officials expressed concern that publication of information about U.S. military exports to their country would allow potential enemies to know the extent of their preparedness. When Green took the latter question up with Raushenbush, the chief investigator replied that munitions companies were behind the Colombian protests because they wanted to "hide the fact that they have been selling exactly the same types of arms and munitions at different prices to the governments of different American Republics."[7]

The hearings opened in an increasingly tense international arena, with Japanese aggression in Asia of particular concern for Americans during the summer of 1934. In August, the heads of Royal Dutch Shell and Standard Oil of New Jersey suggested to State Department officials that the United States threaten to embargo oil exports to Japan. Cordell Hull demurred, but the question of exports to Japan would not go away. At the end of August, Senator Pope said the munitions committee would investigate U.S. shipments of scrap metal to Japan. In September, the Japanese told American officials that they would terminate the Washington Naval Treaty in December, opening the way for an unrestricted naval armaments race in the Pacific.[8]

The hearings began on Tuesday, 4 September. Following the outline scripted in June, the committee opened with a probe into the global activities of American armaments companies. The first witnesses represented the Electric Boat Company, which would later become part of the General Dynamics Corporation. Their three days of testimony uncovered many issues the inquiry would delve into over the following year and a half, including the high profits from international arms deals, the reliance on bribery to facilitate overseas sales, the antipathy of munitions merchants to peace and disarmament efforts, and the relationship between American armaments companies and the executive and legislative branches of the United States government.

The senators' general approaches emerged during the first set of hearings. Nye demonstrated a restrained demeanor, particularly when contrasted with his earlier talk about the greed of "soulless madmen" as a cause of war. Bennett Clark provided the most pointed questioning and engaged in verbal sparring with the witnesses. Homer Bone focused on the catastrophic consequences of modern total war. To the extent that any senator sided with the witnesses, Republican W. Warren Barbour provided that support. His state, New Jersey, was home to the Picatinny Arsenal and New York Shipbuilding's Camden yard. Arthur Vandenberg missed the first two days of hearings but would become deeply involved as the investigation proceeded. Democrats Walter George and James Pope maintained low profiles while Electric Boat officials testified.

The combination of exorbitant profits and unseemly bribery led quickly to questions about a mysterious munitions middleman, Sir Basil Zaharoff, who in 1917 received a large commission from Electric Boat on vessels built for Spain. Company president Henry Carse advised Zaharoff on how to avoid U.S. income taxes on his $1.3 million in commissions from Electric Boat and other American sources during 1917. Electric Boat then paid Zaharoff over $750,000 in additional commissions from 1919 through 1930. Carse linked Zaharoff to Woodrow Wilson, testifying that the former president "gave Sir Basil his confidence and advised with him" during the Paris Peace Conference. Zaharoff provided a tantalizing subject, useful for generating interest in the hearings, but ultimately little could result because he lived outside the jurisdiction of the committee. Joseph Green noted earlier that Zaharoff had "always been able to surround himself with an air of mystery and all sorts of myths have rolled up about him which have taken the place of accurate knowledge of his life and activities." The munitions hearings did nothing to alter his assessment.[9]

Electric Boat's activities in South America provided evidence to support uncomplimentary views toward armaments manufacturers. Clark's questioning showed that Electric Boat stimulated demand with commissions and bribes, tried to disguise their sales, and viewed peace efforts with disdain. While questioning Lawrence Spear, a vice-president of Electric Boat, Clark zeroed in on the use of bribery to secure foreign contracts. Spear conceded that "you could not do business with South America without paying a good many commissions. I do not know whether it was bribery or not. I have heard of some cases of direct bribery." Electric Boat worked hard to close sales with Chile and Peru. Clark asked about a sale to Peru that the company intended to camouflage "to avoid any complaints being raised in Washington by the Colombian authorities, which might prevent delivery of the vessels." Clark introduced a 1928 letter in which Spear complained that it was "too bad that the pernicious activities of our State Department have put the brake on armament orders from Peru by forcing the resumption of formal diplomatic relations with Chile."[10]

The Electric Boat testimony also revealed extensive connections between the U.S. government and the international munitions business. Numerous communications named navy officers as supporters of Electric Boat's sales efforts. One memorandum said that the navy considered sending a fleet of submarines to South America to generate publicity for the company. Clark asked about an instance in which an admiral served as "a go-between for the purpose of negotiating a loan which would be used by Peru for armament purposes." In another case, the company paid for a voyage to Europe by the wife and son of an admiral who served as chief of the American Naval Mission to Peru.[11]

The outline of what would later be called the "iron triangle" of interest groups, legislative committees, and executive agencies emerged early in the hearings. Nye queried Carse about a 1928 letter in which Electric Boat Vice-President Sterling Joyner "successfully managed campaign for candidate Rules Committee, which is most important to us, when any legislation is up." The next year, Joyner wrote Carse when the congressional session ended and noted that "all of our legislative efforts have borne fruit. The Cruiser bill is passed, the submarine appropriations have been passed . . . we succeeded in getting our claim through, and we expect to receive payment at two o'clock this afternoon or early tomorrow morning." The claim action brought $3 million to the company, plus $700,000 in bonds held by the government. According to Joyner, navy officials thanked Electric Boat for helping pass legislation supported by their department. Joyner worked with John Q. Tilson, congressman from the district that included Electric Boat's shipyard in New London, Connecticut. The Navy Department assured Tilson that two submarine contracts would be assigned to Electric Boat.[12]

The committee next turned its attention to the Driggs Ordnance and Engineering Company. Louis Driggs, company president, generated headlines with his accounts of a highly competitive business environment. Company documents criticized tactics used in Turkey by representatives of the Vickers armament firm of Britain, calling them "the dirtiest opponents here. They have almost an entire embassy in number working for them and use women of doubtful character freely." More sensational was a telegram asserting that English King George V "intervened" with the Polish ambassador on behalf of Vickers for a contract being sought by Driggs and others. The accusation itself tarnished the king's reputation, but Clark went for more. He asked if the royal family held stock in Vickers, if "the King was playing his own game, or just playing salesman." Driggs's answer expressed the grim reality of the 1930s: "I think he was just helping get them out of the depression."[13]

The questioning of Driggs led to considerations of modern national defense. In wars of movement with mass armies, the distinction between offensive and defensive weapons could sometimes be hard to define. When Driggs described anti-aircraft guns as defensive material, Clark suggested the gun could be "used just as easily by an offensive army against defensive aircraft as by a defensive army against offensive aircraft." Nye noted that Electric Boat officials called submarines defensive weapons. As the testimony drew to a close, Bone compared some armaments makers to mass murderers, prompting Driggs to ask how to distinguish "between something that is fine for national defense and may win a war for your country, and mass murder?" Nye's response still resonates through American debate on military policy generations later. "That depends entirely on what you term an adequate national defense," he said. "Does national defense mean that people should go to all corners of the earth to wage war?"[14]

Testimony of officials from the American Armament Company, an export company founded by a former Driggs salesman, reinforced concerns generated by the Electric Boat inquiry. Allegations of bribery to secure business in South America surfaced again when American Armament president Alfred Miranda was asked about a letter he received from a British firm that noted how "arms deals are not usually done without some officials getting 'greased.'" Miranda said the Europeans often used such practices but that his company used "cleaner" methods. Bone quickly produced Miranda's reply to the British company in which he wrote that the "remarks anent greasing the wheels that make the deals go around are very true and we fully appreciate that very often oil must be added to your quotations." Like Electric Boat, American Armament established close ties with key U.S. Navy personnel. Miranda's brother managed a stock market account for Commander James H. Strong, and Miranda wrote in a 1933 letter that "Strong and I are very, very good friends" and that "he will do everything possible to throw the business our way."[15]

Alger Hiss took on a high profile for the first time in the hearings when he questioned officials from the Curtiss-Wright Export Corporation. Hiss established the financial interests involved in Curtiss-Wright, noting the influence of the Du Ponts, and proceeded into some of the same issues discussed in earlier testimony. Bribery in the South American munitions trade surfaced again when the corporation's Latin American sales representative, Clarence Webster, admitted that the payment of commissions to government officials amounted to a "very polite" way to handle corruption. Hiss asked about efforts to sell aircraft to all sides in South American conflicts. After Colombia purchased Curtiss-Wright planes, Webster worked to get Peru to buy more planes in order to start an arms race among the Latin American nations. As Peru bought additional equipment, Colombia would need to add to its air force to maintain superiority. Similar opportunities arose with a dispute between Bolivia and Paraguay over possession of the Chaco region. Bolivia had Curtiss-Wright planes that "created a real menace to the Paraguayans, as well as a deep fear." If a war broke out, it would become "absolutely necessary for Paraguay to find the money for the purchase of aircraft and other munitions." Webster wanted to keep Curtiss-Wright business with Paraguay quiet since the Bolivians would "raise 'merry hell' if they believed that we were dealing with their enemies."[16]

Webster's sales efforts provided a merchants of death flavor to the hearings. Hiss introduced a February 1933 letter in which Webster assessed the situation in South America as one where "the real activity is just beginning. . . . National pride and stubbornness will not permit these countries to quit until they blow up through absolute bankruptcy, and while the show is going on, it is our job as distributors of munitions to get our share." Unfortunately for the arms marketers, the show did not run for very long. Another letter, written to a Curtiss-Wright agent from Frank Jonas, sales representative for the Du Pont–controlled Remington Arms Company, described the situation in December of 1933. "The Paraguay and Bolivia fracas appears to be coming to a termination, so business from that end is probably finished," Jonas lamented. "We certainly are in one hell of a business, where a fellow has to wish for trouble so as to make a living, the only consolation being, however, that if we don't get the business someone else will. It would be a terrible state of affairs if my conscience started to bother me now." Jonas testified one week later.[17]

The Curtiss-Wright hearings shed more light on the connections between the government and the munitions manufacturers. Not surprisingly, the Department of Commerce promoted the products of the U.S. munitions makers. The U.S. Navy also helped by issuing a letter of recommendation for Curtiss-Wright aircraft to support sales efforts in Argentina. The company drafted the letter for the navy. Hiss asked about a 1932 letter that portrayed Douglas MacArthur as a promoter of U.S. munitions firms. According to the letter, representatives of Curtiss-Wright and other American companies talked with MacArthur about "the business which we are carrying on with the Turkish authorities, and, apparently, he talked up American military equipment to the skies in discussions which he had with the Turkish general staff." The hearings brushed close to the Roosevelt administration when press secretary Stephen Early was mentioned in connection with Curtiss-Wright's effort to get its name shown in a newsreel of James Doolittle flying stunts in one of the company's airplanes.[18]

Publication of company documents detailing individual actions created problems when those implicated disputed the record. MacArthur wrote directly to Nye and disclaimed having ever discussed American military equipment with Turkish officials. Former Secretary of State Frank B. Kellogg refuted testimony that he had ordered the U.S. ambassador to Spain to assist in the sale of submarines. The hearings created problems for the State Department when foreign governments objected to charges of corruption among their officials. Sumner Welles, assistant secretary of state for Latin American affairs, informed Hull of the negative effects in Argentina, Chile, and Paraguay. Hull received a "very sharp protest" from the British over the allegation concerning King George V and arms sales to Poland.[19]

Rumors of Hull's unhappiness with the munitions committee surfaced shortly after the hearings started, and Assistant Secretary of State R. Walton Moore assured Nye on 7 September of the department's "sympathy" with the investigation. Four days later, Hull met with committee members during a recess in the hearings. Afterward, he issued a statement that neither the U.S. government nor the committee wished to offend any foreign governments or their officials. He also released a letter from Nye stating that inclusion into the record of documents from American companies was not meant to imply that such documents were true and accurate.[20]

Foreign governments also made their concerns clear to the munitions companies. Hull learned that Chile, in retaliation for publicity generated by the investigation, would reject U.S. bids for aviation materials. The U.S. consul general in Mexico City wrote about the negative impact the hearings had on American munitions sales in that country. In late September, the president of the New York Shipbuilding Corporation, Clinton L. Bardo, questioned whether it would be "worth our while to waste any time in endeavoring to get South American business" due to the disclosures of the committee.[21]

When the hearings disrupted American foreign relations, Hull considered denying the committee access to State Department records. He directed the department's legal advisor, Green H. Hackworth, to study the question. Hackworth concluded that the secretary could decline to furnish documents to Congress "when, in your opinion, it is to the best interests of the Government to so decline." Among the records that concerned the State Department were those related to the Chaco dispute. Sumner Welles warned Hull that "if any facts are now brought out and made public purporting to show that this Government, through its approval of prior loans made to Bolivia, facilitated the purchase of arms and munitions by Bolivia, for use by Bolivia in the Chaco War, the effect upon continental opinion will be bad and might be disastrous in Paraguay at this crucial moment." Hull continued to provide documents in spite of departmental concerns.[22]

Mid-September was not a good time for the Roosevelt administration to confront the munitions committee. The elections were only seven weeks away, and the Du Ponts were just taking the stand for questioning. FDR had not forgotten about either. Soon after the Du Ponts began to testify, Roosevelt received a letter from a former government official who investigated munitions companies' claims to the U.S. government at the end of World War I. After reading that one of the claims "involved the Du Pont Company, and some things I learned about this particular claim was such that it would not look well in print," FDR sent the letter to his secretary, Marvin MacIntyre, with instructions to get the facts. The Justice Department followed up on the matter but found nothing substantial.[23]

The munitions committee brought out plenty of facts to satisfy FDR's desire to discredit the Du Ponts. Pierre, Irénée, and Lammot began their testimony on 12 September. Six additional officials of the corporation, including Felix Du Pont, testified over the next three days as the committee inquired into the activities of America's leading munitions maker. Bone began the questioning and had no problem establishing that the Du Pont corporation earned huge profits during World War I. Du Pont common stock paid out 458 percent of its original value in dividends during the war, and the price of the stock increased 374 percent. As a result, Du Pont was able to acquire a 25 percent share of General Motors for $47 million. The company's annual report for 1918 discussed the figures and concluded that it would be "difficult to imagine a more satisfactory financial result, especially in view of that fact that the liquidation of the balance of the military powder investment as it stands today cannot materially alter the conditions above recited." The latter part of the statement referred to the fact that wartime sales to Allied powers were made at prices high enough to amortize quickly the plants built to fill the orders.[24]

Bone questioned the Du Ponts about the 1916 annual report which complained that the "United States Government has made our stockholders victims of excessive taxation." The Du Ponts themselves were the major stockholders in the corporation. Irénée explained that a retroactive munitions tax fell almost entirely on the Du Pont corporation and he questioned the need for such a tax prior to U.S. entry into the war. He argued that the company's profits from twenty years of military powder sales to the U.S. government "were wiped out by a tax in a single year during which the Government did not contribute anything to us, except protect us from invasion." Pierre took a more diplomatic approach on the tax issue, noting that there "was no great complaint. . . . The stockholders naturally were not very much concerned about it. They made extremely good profits." Irénée averred that with hindsight the criticism probably should not have been in the report, but he still "would not say that no harm was done." The attempt to portray Du Pont stockholders as victims provided an ironic twist to the hearings. Money poured into their pockets from the sale of munitions used on the battlefields of Europe, and over 8 million of the war's true victims lie buried in cemeteries.[25]

Nye showed that the company had paid out over $16 million in bonuses during the war years. He then queried the Du Ponts about their acquisition of General Motors stock. He asked Pierre if "your success, your increase in assets, your increase in the general business you have done is traceable very directly to the war?" "To the profits made during the war, exactly," Du Pont replied. But later in the day, under questioning from Vandenberg, Irénée stated that the company "did not make any profit during the war and paid more in taxes than we made in profits." Shortly afterward, he contradicted himself in saying that the company had made "enormous profits during the war" because of increased efficiency.[26]

Irénée proved to be the most combative of the Du Pont brothers, defending the company at every turn and occasionally sniping at the senators. When questioned about a letter describing a plan to circumvent a U.S. embargo on arms shipments to Bolivia and Paraguay, Irénée responded that if the Du Pont agent "had as much brains as you have he would not have retained a copy of the letter at all." He argued that Du Pont powder shipments to Britain and France in 1915 and 1916 saved the United States from becoming a German colony. He ridiculed the idea of nationalizing the armaments industry, saying that selling the plans to Pearl Harbor would cause less damage to national security. He said the munitions investigation would weaken national defense.[27]

Evidence of close links with the federal government prompted Bone to ask if Du Pont acted as a "semi-official agency of our Government," but Irénée would concede only that "the War Department and the Navy Department look on us as a material aid." He noted that company officials were U.S. citizens bound to support their government. K.K.V. Casey testified that Du Pont took no action abroad without first ensuring that the War and Navy Departments had no objections, but he later admitted that the company sometimes failed to inform the government of its foreign dealings. Felix Du Pont clarified Casey's statement, specifying that the company informed the executive branch of "every move that we make with regard to sales to foreign governments," but it also acted without consulting the agencies on questions not directly connected to such sales. Casey maintained, however, that the company did not act against the expressed views of the U.S. government. "I do not know of my own knowledge, anyway, that any manufacturer has ever tried to conform to the wishes of his government any more than we have," he concluded.[28]

Pope produced a letter showing that not all company officials shared Casey's respect for U.S. policy makers. Aiken Simons, in charge of Du Pont export sales, had written in December of 1932 about "the attempts of Mr. Hoover and the 'cooky-pushers' in the State Department to effect embargoes on munitions sent out of the country." Pope asked about the meaning of the "rather 'luscious' term 'cooky pushers,'" but Casey said he had never before heard the expression. Pope asked if Secretary of State Henry L. Stimson had been a "cooky pusher," or even President Hoover, but Casey declined to speculate. Simons could not testify due to illness, but his letter had been sent to the president of Federal Laboratories, Incorporated, a company the committee planned to investigate. More would be heard about the "cooky pushers" later.[29]

The questioning sharpened on the third day of Du Pont testimony. Raushen-bush tried to show that Du Pont encouraged sales to all sides in military disputes around the world, starting with questions about the Chaco War between Paraguay and Bolivia and quickly moving to the war in Manchuria between Japan and China. He asked if Du Pont had been "securing cheaper powder for Japan on one side and giving bribes to China on the other." Lammot Du Pont denied the charge. Clark then took the lead, bearing down on the issues in his typical manner. His questioning brought out evidence of a meeting between Felix Du Pont and a representative of the Nazi German military staff. He asked Lammot if it was "really helpful, in your opinion, to the peace of the world, to have a bunch of private munitions manufacturers working and jockeying around to arm anybody who has money to spend for arms?" "No, sir," the Du Pont president replied. Toward the end of the session, Bone asked about government ownership of munitions plants, a volatile topic for the leaders of the Liberty League. Irénée emphatically argued that the private sector operated with greater efficiency than the government. He blamed the government for the depression and discussed the Liberty League. "I question if we have a democratic form of government today, and my reason for joining the Liberty League was, I think, our Constitution is on the verge of going into the scrapbasket," he explained.[30]

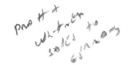

At the end of their testimony, Lammot thanked Nye for "the courteous reception we have had," but he admitted that "we may have appeared a little nettled at times." Pierre voiced his gratitude to the committee and asked if "instead of waiting for 20 years before we have these reunions we might have them once or twice a year?" Nye, perhaps surprised, responded "Like this?" "Yes, like this," Du Pont replied. "Do not let us wait 20 years, but have one every year. We will not need so much time to rehearse." Pierre Du Pont would not have long to rehearse before he enjoyed a reunion with the munitions committee. He and other Du Pont officials would testify again within ninety days.[31]

Some U.S. officials did not share Pierre's enthusiasm for the munitions investigation. On 12 September, the chief of Naval Intelligence met with Undersecretary of State William Phillips and discussed "the injury which the Committee was doing to the Navy Department in the methods of its attacks upon the Du Ponts and other manufacturers." Around the same time, Hull and Commerce Secretary Daniel Roper met with committee members in an effort to protect secret reports on German rearmament and confidential information about a bribery case that involved the son of Argentina's president. The secretaries stressed that publicity for either situation would not serve the interests of the United States. Speaking off the record to reporters on 20 September, Hull said the investigation put the government in a difficult position because of the allegations concerning officials of other countries.[32]

Witnesses that followed the Du Ponts provided their own information about German rearmament and bribery in South America. Hiss questioned officials from the Pratt & Whitney Aircraft Company and the United Aircraft Exports (UAE), Incorporated. Pratt & Whitney was acquired in 1929 by the United Aircraft & Transport Corporation, a conglomerate that included the Boeing Aircraft Company and the Chance-Vought Corporation and also held interests in Northup Aircraft and Sikorsky Aviation. UAE handled the export business for subsidiaries of United Aircraft & Transport. Nye cited figures showing that UAE had increased sales to Germany by 500 percent from 1933 to 1934. Shipment of 176 Pratt & Whitney engines, usable in military applications, accounted for the majority of the orders. Pratt & Whitney negotiated a licensing agreement with Bavarian Motor Works (BMW) that allowed the latter to use its engine designs. Nye produced a May 1933 letter that said German aircraft factories had doubled and tripled their number of employees in the months since Hitler came to power.[33]

After the Pratt & Whitney and UAE testimony, officials of Federal Laboratories, Incorporated, took the stand. Included among their number was the committee's most colorful witness, Frank S. Jonas, author of the letter calling munitions sales "one hell of a business." Jonas served as a sales representative for Federal Laboratories, the Remington Arms Company, and other concerns. His communications with agents working in South America reflected the image of the unprincipled arms dealer and munitions merchant. In a 1932 letter Jonas discussed how "unsettled conditions in South America has been a great thing for me. . . . It is an ill wind that does not blow someone some good." For Jonas, the ill wind led to orders for bombs from Bolivia, Brazil, Colombia, Ecuador, and Peru. In another episode, Jonas received word from Federal Laboratories that Paraguay and Bolivia were on the verge of war. He reported back that he "immediately took a plane to Washington and visited both the Paraguay and Bolivia Legations. Unfortunately for us, however, it looks as if the trouble they are having is going to be settled amicably." Bone's reading of the letter prompted laughter from those present in the hearing room. In another case, Jonas told his operative in Sao Paulo that "according to the *New York Times* the lid is off in Brazil, so get busy and see if you cannot stir up something." Later, Jonas offered to act as an intermediary in a scheme to run guns to Brazilian revolutionaries. "I wish I had had all my letters destroyed," he commented wistfully as his testimony neared conclusion. But Nye appreciated the correspondence. "You seem to be one of the few who have entered somewhat into the spirit of this investigation," he noted. "We do appreciate, Mr. Jonas, what you have done."[34]

The first set of hearings came to a close on Friday, 21 September. Questioning of officials from Lake Erie Chemical Company generated testimony similar to that of Jonas earlier in the week. U.S. Ordnance Engineers, an export company for Lake Erie Chemical, competed directly with Federal Laboratories in the South American market. Sales agent Ferdinand Huber failed to match the pithy quotes served up by Jonas, but he did call munitions sales a "shady business all the way through" and pronounced that Jonas was "crooked." Clark spiced up the hearing by citing the company's catalog description of phosgene gas as "the most practical and economical gas for the production of quick death . . . if heavily gassed, men will be dropping dead like flies within a few hours."[35]

After fourteen days of questioning business representatives, the committee brought two government officials in to testify before the recess. Ernest Tupper of the Department of Commerce provided statistics on U.S. exports to Japan, Germany, and several South American countries. Nye interpreted the figures to show that munitions exports were rising while overall exports were falling. The last witness, Stephen Hamilton, deputy collector of customs for the port of New York City, testified to the difficulty of regulating arms exports. Even during the depression, a minimum of 3,000 export declarations came to his office every day. He said weapons could be exported without interference if packed in crates and purposely mislabeled, and that his office would not learn of errors or misrepresentations on cargo manifests unless the goods were returned to the United States. After listening to Hamilton, Nye suggested that "the Commerce Department is unable to know what the truth really is." Hamilton agreed.[36]

On that uncertain note, the first phase of hearings came to a close. Nye summarized the findings. "The facts uncovered here have had the tendency to paint a rather sordid picture of the industry and many who have had contact with it. Some instances have been encountered which find the traffic in arms and ammunition weaving its way through governments and official public positions both at home and abroad. Much testimony and much evidence taken into the record reflects upon governments and their officials. . . . Some, indeed too much, corruption has been so far proven," he concluded. He adjourned the hearings until 4 December, following the upcoming congressional elections.[37]

Nye's mention of government involvement in the munitions trade foreshadowed future problems with the Roosevelt administration. Although allegations of bribery had been limited to foreign officials, testimony frequently implicated U.S. officials from the War, Navy, and Commerce departments in promoting the munitions trade. Some military officers stood accused of having conflicts of interest due to their relationships with arms companies. The committee also discovered that Elliott Roosevelt, one of FDR's sons, had been involved in a deal to send Fokker planes from the United States to the Soviet Union. When Anthony Fokker wanted out of the contract, the company's U.S. representative considered enlisting FDR's assistance. He noted that if knowledge of the contract "should come into the hands of certain politicians it would cause a great deal of embarrassment to the administration." Fokker replied cryptically by telegram that a "telephone threat father will work." Whether such a threat was made cannot be determined from the record. Clearly, however, the investigation discomforted people close to the administration as well as business leaders opposed to the New Deal.[38]

In September, Roosevelt made several important decisions that affected his future relations with the committee. Assistant Secretary of State R. Walton Moore wrote to the president about neutrality policy and outlined a proposal that "would, by tending to discourage war profiteering, greatly minimize the risk of the United States being drawn into a conflict." On 25 September, Roosevelt sought Hull's recommendations for neutrality legislation. FDR also approved a State Department request to push for U.S. membership in the World Court. On 30 September, FDR took aim at the upcoming elections and made his second, and last, fireside chat of 1934. He attacked the Liberty League without naming the organization. "I am not for a return to that definition of liberty under which for many years a free people were being gradually regimented into the service of a privileged few," he told his radio audience.[39]

In the fall of 1934, the president seemed to draw no particular connections between the munitions inquiry, isolationism, and his future foreign policy agenda. He did not mention the investigation when seeking Hull's advice on neutrality policy. His decision to seek World Court membership flew in the face of the supposed isolationist cyclone whipped up by the munitions committee. In October, he met with Henry L. Stimson for a wide-ranging discussion of foreign affairs. Stimson's memorandum of the talk covered numerous issues, including U.S. concern about Japanese naval expansion, but it made no mention of any discussion about the Nye committee. There was a belief in Washington that the investigation had largely completed its work. Perhaps Roosevelt was aware of this and presumed that the committee would not much affect events in 1935.[40]

Nye and Raushenbush, however, had other ideas. Nye announced plans for an upcoming lecture tour and then spoke over the radio on 3 October. Labeling the arms business an "unadulterated, unblushing racket," he said that the committee "listened daily to men striving to defend acts which found them nothing more than international racketeers, bent upon gaining profit through a game of arming the world to fight itself." He called for eliminating the private manufacture of munitions and establishing a 98 percent tax on individual income over $10,000 a year during times of war. Raushenbush wrote Nye in mid-October about the importance of maintaining media interest. He saw timing as a key element, believing that "if we get into the constructive end of things before the investigation has gone as far as it should that certain forces will say 'take these few little bills and call off the dogs.'" Efforts by Nye and Raushenbush to publicize the investigation received support from the Women's International League for Peace and Freedom, which used the committee's findings to mobilize peace-minded voters.[41]

In early November, Raushenbush again wrote to Nye and reflected on lessons to be drawn from the first round of hearings. He wanted to focus future testimony around a few main points and allow the hearings to "shape up into a preliminary for constructive action far more effectively than if we simply continued on, somewhat at random, into the companies' ways of conducting business." He asked Nye to contact former Secretary of State Kellogg about testifying. Raushenbush's note came only three days before the 1934 congressional election.[42]

The 1934 elections formed round one of Franklin Roosevelt's battle with the Du Ponts and their Liberty League. As he optimistically expected, FDR came out a big winner. Before the voting, Democrats held a solid majority of sixty seats in the ninety-six seat U.S. Senate and controlled over two-thirds of the House of Representatives. On election day voters took the highly unusual step of increasing congressional numbers for the party controlling the White House. Democrats picked up thirteen seats in the House and nine in the Senate. A few days after the landslide, Garner wrote to FDR that "it was your individuality more than any other one thing that caused this great expression of confidence." Roosevelt agreed with Garner's assessment. Historian Charles Beard viewed the results in ideological rather than personal terms, hearing "thunder on the left" from the voters. Journalist Arthur Krock called the election "the most overwhelming victory in the history of American politics."[43]

With the election over and the Liberty League effectively wounded, much of the political service the Nye committee could provide for Roosevelt had been performed. The administration quickly moved to take control of the munitions issue, and on 13 November Hull proposed an international convention to regulate the manufacture and trade in munitions. Delegates in Geneva had been working for a disarmament treaty since 1932 but had made little progress toward a comprehensive agreement. Hull wanted an agreement to control at least the production and shipping of munitions, even if disarmament could not be achieved. Later in the month, Green met with Nye and Raushenbush to seek their support for the administration's action. Green believed Nye favored more radical measures, but the senator endorsed the proposal. Green criticized a recent Nye speech and hoped the senator would be less inflammatory in future public appearances.[44]

The State Department was not alone in trying to restrain Nye and the committee in the weeks after the election. On 20 November, Secretary of War George Dern informed Nye that the Remington Arms Company and the Winchester Repeating Arms Company would not turn over defense plans to the committee. Departmental officials would instead testify during an executive session. On the same day, the Commerce Department prevented testimony from Douglas Miller, the U.S. commercial attaché in Berlin. Assistant Secretary of Commerce John Dickinson said the president had made the decision, but Raushenbush was miffed by the department's handling of the affair. Eight days later, Roosevelt rebutted questions from journalists about administration resistance to Nye committee inquiries. Committee investigators charged the Justice Department with withholding information, and news accounts reported that other agencies were opposed to continuing the inquiry.[45]

The Du Ponts, scheduled to testify again in December, also wanted to limit the scope of the public hearings. On 3 December, Lammot Du Pont wrote to Nye concerning disclosures that might jeopardize the public interest. When Nye curtly requested more details, Lammot replied apologetically that the government, and not his company, could better determine the public interest. K.K.V. Casey visited Joseph Green at the State Department and brought with him a copy of Lammot's first letter. Green said the department could do nothing about Lammot's request.[46]

Two days earlier, on 1 December, Green was approached by Colonel John M. Noonan. Noonan said he and his associates wanted to "break up the investigation," which they saw as a ruse to build support for Nye and Vandenberg as presidential candidates in 1936. He claimed to have stopped a similar inquiry led by Henry Cabot Lodge after World War I, and he said he would consult with Roosevelt and James Farley to end the investigation. Green attached little significance to Noonan's talk. Perhaps it only added to the sense of building intrigue as the next round of hearings drew close. The story of the supposed plot to march on Washington that involved the Du Ponts, MacArthur, and numerous other prominent Americans appeared in the 3 December 1934 issue of *Time*.[47]

That the munitions investigation might further tarnish the Du Ponts was underlined in a 4 December letter from Senator Hiram Johnson to President Roosevelt. Johnson sarcastically described Liberty League activities in California, where Pierre Du Pont had spoken to league supporters. "Du Pont, in the sacred precincts of one of our most exclusive clubs, aroused his auditors to a pitch of frenzied enthusiasm when he inveighed against the iniquities of the bonus," Johnson reported. "The glorious affecting picture of a self sacrificing patriot who, with even handed justice furnished munitions to every country for shooting down the youth of the world, preaching against any payments to those who escaped his impartial activities, entranced our 'best people.'" The next round of hearings would bring Du Pont out of the exclusive club and again put him on the front pages of the nation's newspapers. Roosevelt would leave the munitions committee alone until it finished with the Du Ponts.[48]

Chapter 4

Examining the Du Ponts,
December 1934 to January 1935

Witnesses for the Du Pont interests testified for thirteen of the fourteen days of munitions hearings in December of 1934, and some committee members relished the opportunity to malign the leaders of the Liberty League. Led by sharp and tough questioning from Clark, Vandenberg, Hiss, and Nye, the investigation sometimes stained the reputation of the Du Ponts. The committee examined the overseas activities of the Du Pont organizations, their role in the procurement of military supplies, their behavior during World War I, and their relationships with the executive and legislative branches of the U.S. government. Franklin Roosevelt initially let the hearings take their course as his leading critics were pilloried.

Du Pont activities in China formed a starting point for the December hearings. During the 1920s, the company sought to end a U.S. embargo on munitions shipments to China, and Clark wondered why the request came not from the Chinese government but from "somebody who wanted to make money from shipping them munitions." K.K.V. Casey, director of Du Pont smokeless powder sales, proposed bypassing the embargo by shipping through neutral countries. Clark showed that, in spite of the embargo, U.S. exports of arms and munitions to China increased sevenfold from 1932 through 1934.[1]

Clark repeatedly baited Irénée Du Pont, as when he described the differences between them. "In other words," he told Irénée, "you approach the subject of war from a viewpoint that regards the war as a situation out of which there may be made two or three hundred million dollars of profits and come out with a whole hide. On the other hand, I entered the war, with three boys, without any prospect of making any money out of it, but who might be considered in the position of becoming cannon fodder. Therefore, we look at it from a diametrically opposite viewpoint." Clark provoked the combative Irénée more than once and sometimes used such instances to humble the powerful businessman. "I would like to disabuse your mind of the idea that your are running this investigation," he told Du Pont. "You are merely a witness before the committee."[2]

Clark concluded that the munitions manufacturers were "a primary cause of war" and backed his view by reading a broker's promotional letter touting current investment opportunities in war materials. "While one may regret the social side of warfare, the business possibilities are so tremendous that they may not be overlooked," investors were told. Then, in a sentence that nearly defined Du Pont, the letter added that many "great corporations that paid dividends of astounding proportions during the decade following the World War laid their foundations on the production of war material, long before America entered the conflict."[3]

Irénée rebutted Clark and argued that munitions makers were the same as other entrepreneurs. He argued that Du Pont's efficiency held the price of gunpowder down during a time when prices for most everything else went up. He believed that the "real profiteers on war are not the powder manufacturers. The real profiteers, the ones who did not have to do any additional work, but got two and sometimes three times the price of their product, are the raw-material manufac-turers, essentially the farming group." Du Pont's attempt to portray farmers as war profiteers drew a quick response from Nye, who noted that wartime efforts to increase flaxseed production had contributed to the "dust bowl" storms that started in 1934. The farmer's work to increase earnings during the war led to eventual disaster for many in agriculture, while Du Pont's profits allowed its expansion into many new industries. Du Pont's references to agriculture raised important questions, however, about how far governmental controls would have to extend in order to prevent profiteering.[4]

Vandenberg disagreed with Irénée and saw the munitions industry as a special case. He brought out the irony of promoting munitions exports in order to maintain a viable domestic armaments manufacturing base during peacetime. He asked if the United States was not "in the anomalous position of being forced to let the other fellows have the advantages which we had obtained for ourselves, in order to keep our munitions manufacturers going, so that we can take advan-tage of the same progressive steps?" "I think that is stating it a little crudely," K.K.V. Casey answered.[5]

Vandenberg generated some heated exchanges when he asked about Du Pont involvement with German rearmament and possible violations of the Versailles Treaty. Irénée Du Pont resented some of the questions, while Lammot Du Pont disavowed responsibility for the statements made in company correspondence. Casey reported German violations of the Versailles Treaty armaments limits as early as 1926, but he indicated that stopping the problem would be difficult due to commercial ties between European munitions makers. The State Department knew of the violations, too, but believed European governments would do little to stop them because German arms exports produced money to pay war reparations.[6]

Alger Hiss led questioning into the Du Pont's construction and operation of a World War I powder-making facility known as "Old Hickory," which the committee presented as a case study in profiteering. The committee built a strong case. The War Department negotiated with Du Pont during 1917 and 1918 to contract for the plant, offering a $1 million guarantee with final figures to be determined after the war, but the company turned down the offer. Hiss produced a November 1917 letter in which Pierre Du Pont wrote that "we cannot assent to allowing our own patriotism to interfere with our duties as trustees." Du Pont wrote that no other company had the expertise to meet the War Department's requirements and defended the "propriety of the seemingly high charge of 15 percent commission which may amount in maximum to $13,500,000."[7]

Hiss introduced a War Industries Board (WIB) report from late 1917 that found "the price demanded by the du Ponts for construction, service, and operation is utterly out of scale with any possible service they can render," and led board chairman Bernard Baruch to withhold approval of the Old Hickory contract. The WIB dealt with production and allocation of military materials during World War I, but Baruch did not have authority to stop the War Department from signing the contract with Du Pont. Army officials argued that the plant was needed as soon as possible, so War Secretary Newton Baker met with Pierre Du Pont and agreed to the company's terms. Baker told Du Pont that the company would generate between $13 million and $30 million in profits from the contract and that he "could not conceive of services of anyone being worth such a price."[8]

As it turned out, the war ended before the plant became fully operational and Du Pont reported a profit of $1.96 million on Old Hickory. Hiss showed, however, that the government had borne nearly all risk associated with the venture and that Du Pont's profits represented a return of over 39,000 percent on capital invested. Pierre Du Pont heatedly challenged Hiss's "ridiculous statement," and Irénée sardonically suggested that Du Pont "made a bad mistake in overcapitalizing" and could have earned 200,000 percent on the investment. Much of the discussion focused on what risks Du Pont might have faced, and Pierre and Irénée mentioned employee embezzlement and insurance company bankruptcies as instances in which the company could have been liable.[9]

Hiss delved more deeply into Old Hickory and showed that Du Pont subsidiaries received subcontracts that profited the parent corporation. The Du Pont Engineering Company signed the contract for Old Hickory, and it earned a one dollar profit on construction of the plant. Subcontracting costs, however, were passed on to the government, and profits to subcontractors went largely unregulated with the federal government doing little independent auditing of the project. Over $4.5 million was spent on cotton linters and hull shavings bought from E. I. Du Pont de Nemours and from Du Pont American Industries. Most of the paint came from the parent corporation. Forty-one Chevrolet cars were purchased, and Du Pont owned a one-quarter interest in General Motors, the parent company of Chevrolet.[10]

Hiss went on to show that while Du Pont's profit on construction of the plant was limited to one dollar, one subcontractor netted over $1 million in fees. He added subcontractor costs to the Du Pont profit on operation and noted that the

government had paid out over $3 million in fees to build and operate Old
Hickory. Pierre Du Pont again angrily reacted to Hiss's line of reasoning, calling
the statement "almost a falsification of the record." Hiss responded that Du Pont
had come close to falsifying the record by stating in company literature that Old
Hickory's construction had been "undertaken at a profit of $1." Clark defended
Hiss and noted that it had not been asserted that Du Pont made large profits from
building the factory, but only that the government had paid out over $1 million
in construction fees. For those following the hearings in the news media, Hiss's
tough questioning developed a picture of the Du Ponts putting profiteering before
patriotism. This was the picture Franklin Roosevelt wanted to the public to
see.[11]

The essential question about Old Hickory was whether Du Pont's expertise and
services were worth what the government paid. Pierre Du Pont defended Old
Hickory profits by comparing his company's services to those provided by a
physician to a needful patient. John E. Wiltz, in *In Search of Peace*, appreciated
Du Pont's comparison and found it unfortunate that newspapers did not place
more emphasis on it. Du Pont's argument, and Wiltz's acceptance of it, calls for
some consideration. The skills acquired by a doctor over many years of arduous
specialized training differed from the assets inherited by the Du Pont brothers.
The Old Hickory negotiations took place during a national emergency, with U.S.
forces fighting in a declared war. It would be highly irresponsible for an
emergency-room doctor to refuse to use his or her knowledge to save a patient,
demanding first a fully agreed upon price. In the case of Old Hickory, the patient
offered a $1 million minimum payment for assistance, but Dr. Du Pont refused
to begin treatment.[12]

By the afternoon of Monday, 17 December, Old Hickory had been pretty well
dissected and discussion turned to mobilization plans for future wars. The Du
Ponts, as major figures in the plans, continued to testify and were joined by
Lieutenant Colonel C. T. Harris from the War Department. Harris made clear the
extent of mobilization necessary for modern war when he said that over 12,000
plants were involved in the department's plan. The report of the War Policies
Commission (WPC) formed the starting point for questioning. The War Department, acting on WPC recommendations, drafted contracts for immediate use
should war break out. Lengthy negotiations that delayed production, such as had
taken place with Old Hickory, might thus be avoided. The department failed,
however, to form a consensus on profit margins. The WPC, backed by the War
Department, wanted a 6 percent profit on military contracts during times of war,
but some industrial leaders thought the figure to be too low. Pierre and Irénée
Du Pont expressed reservations about the 6 percent figure and suggested that it
would curtail research and development. Pierre guardedly endorsed the figure but
noted that "it is very difficult to lay down a rule that will apply to everyone. I
do not see how the rule could apply to things such as farm products."[13]

Wages and salaries also came under government regulation in the contracts,
leading Clark to ask if bonuses were also covered. When Harris said they were

not, another debate ensued between Irénée and Clark. Again their difference in perspectives became evident, with Clark talking of "men in the front-line trenches frequently working 24 hours a day, without any incentive," while Du Pont believed that "the best investment we made during the war was in our bonus plan." Irénée doubted, however, that the bonus plan could be used effectively in the army. Pierre disagreed and said he could not "imagine how the Army would fail to improve in its operation if there was a system of reward for success, financial as well as honors. Some people are appealed to more by honors than money, and frequently the reverse is the case." He added that patriotism during a time of war would overwhelm other considerations and lead individuals to give their best effort in all possible ways. "It was certainly apparent when we joined the war, how everybody joined in in every way," Pierre concluded, perhaps forgetting earlier testimony that showed him refusing to forsake shareholder profits in the interest of patriotism.[14]

Clark and Hiss probed further into the wartime contracts and the 6 percent profit limit, asking about how costs would be established upon which to base the percentage of profit. Harris noted that of the 12,000 plants involved in the mobilization plan, two-thirds were assigned to the Quartermaster Corps to produce the same materials made during peacetime. He expected no major problems in securing contracts in such cases. The War Department allocated 1,000 plants to ordnance production. Clark drew out differences between arms makers and other suppliers as far as war profiteering was concerned. "You might send troops into battle in overalls if you did not have the proper uniforms," he noted, "but it is very hard to send them in without powder." The necessity of munitions supply could allow one contractor "to hold up the whole prosecution of the war, as the du Ponts did with the Old Hickory plant." Hiss argued that the tremendous volume of contracts would make it nearly impossible for the government to validate the cost figures supplied by manufacturers. Harris agreed that there was a "possibility of the Government being gypped."[15]

The War Department wanted the chief executive to hold broad powers to control the resources of the country during a time of war. The scope of the modern military-industrial complex again became evident when Clark pointed out that the department's proposed legislation would allow the president to name printer's ink and other items necessary to the press as essential commodities and thereby require newspapers to have a license in order to use them. Lieutenant Colonel Harris agreed that the president would probably be able to censor the press.[16]

More than material resources were involved in modern total warfare, and the committee also considered conscription of capital, labor, and even knowledge during wartime. The War Department legislation allowed plants to be seized by the government if necessary, but the expertise to operate the facility could not be easily conscripted. Harris testified that an organization like the Du Pont Engineering Company, contractors for Old Hickory, would be difficult to conscript. Clark, as usual, provided the quick riposte: "You take men to carry a gun and get jabbed up with bayonets without any consultation or negotiations or haggling." Harris, however, saw no easy way to circumvent the government's reliance on the manufacturers. "I do not think we can fight a war unless we can depend on industry to meet us in fair agreements," he concluded.[17]

Hiss developed another aspect of the procurement issue when he showed how some industries continued to reap profits after the war by repurchasing surplus materials from the government. Companies lobbied the government to hold surplus items from the open market, and they often were able to buy back at much lower costs what had been sold to the government at inflated prices during the war. Hiss cited congressional reports that found packers buying 15 million pounds of surplus meat that some military officials believed could have been sold to the general public at a price 20 percent higher. The War Department withheld 200 million cans of vegetables from the market as part of an agreement with the Canners' Association. Leather goods were similarly handled, and the report concluded that the government would receive not more than 15 percent of the "cost value of its surplus leather goods."[18]

Some companies contracted to build plants for the war effort with the expectation that they would repurchase the facilities at greatly reduced prices after the armistice. When the war ended, the government formed committees to quickly dispose of surplus properties. In the ensuing negotiations, the companies were represented by "shrewd business men, well versed in their line and were more than a match for the comparatively inexperienced members of the settling boards." Hiss's questions showed that control of war profits might require legislation covering all sorts of industries during both war and peace.[19]

The testimony on procurement issues revealed a multitude of linkages between the armament makers and the government. The committee found numerous instances of close cooperation between the Du Pont companies and government officials and agencies. Nye asked about Du Pont efforts to limit action at the 1925 Geneva Disarmament Conference. Herbert Hoover, who headed the Department of Commerce during the 1920s, brought together leaders of various munitions companies to discuss their concerns about U.S. disarmament policy. The Du Pont representative found Hoover striving to protect the munitions makers and concluded that "the interests of the du Pont Co. and our customers will be properly looked after." Another participant expressed relief that "there will be no result from the Geneva conference." Probably little would have been accomplished by the Geneva Conference under any circumstances, but the testimony showed the Du Ponts and other munitions makers, as well as some government officials, hindering disarmament. K.K.V. Casey later noted that the "net result of this conference does not appear to be disadvantageous to the munitions manufacturers."[20]

The munitions committee examined other cases of governmental assistance to the Du Ponts. Pope asked about an incident in which Du Pont informed an admiral of an impending embargo resolution in the House of Representatives. According to a company memorandum, the admiral acted immediately to get "appropriate action to have the bill opposed on the floor of the House." Clark asked about army relations with the company, including an instance where a general instructed a major to "find a way" to meet a Du Pont request in spite of "grave doubt" about legality. In another case, the War Department gave Du Pont officials inside information about a competitor's bid for gunpowder-making machinery offered for sale by the government. Du Pont acquired the machinery, leading Clark to wonder if "it is not bad practice for the War Department to be telling one perspective bidder a bid they expect from another prospective bidder." Vandenberg asked about a War Department gunpowder order with specifications "intended to insure procurement from the du Pont Co."[21]

Cozy relations between the military departments and Du Pont formed one part of the story. Some Du Pont officials were wary of the less disciplined legislative branch, where the actions of hundreds of representatives and senators proved difficult to anticipate and control. In a 1919 letter, K.K.V. Casey criticized a company policy that would "give Representatives in Congress just the ammunition they are looking for to attack us, and we will be accused of being traitors, of giving away Government secrets, etc." Clark asked about another letter in which Casey wrote of a "shortsighted" Congress that would "not make appropriation to order material to keep our business alive. . . . The Army and Navy would spend money for this purpose if they could get it; and because they cannot, they are doing all they possibly can do, and that is to help us make sales to other nations. This is our country and not the country of Congress." Clark questioned Casey's conclusion that Du Pont had a greater claim on the country than did Congress. Irénée also found Congress to be shortsighted, telling the committee that "you people here have not the least apprehension of what the chemical industry has in store for humanity, and what it has already accomplished." Most senators probably did not share Irénée Du Pont's vision of the future, which predicted discovery of a chemical that would replace sleep and allow people to work and be active for twenty-four hours a day.[22]

Nye turned to a letter that asserted that Du Pont had a senator "fixed" for a vote on dye tariffs. R. M. Carpenter, the recipient of the letter, denied doing active legislative work for Du Pont, but a variety of committee exhibits revealed otherwise. A letter written by Carpenter to Irénée Du Pont recommended opening a Washington office to deal with sales to the government. He suggested that the "man in charge of the Washington office could be a man thoroughly capable of looking after legislation, in fact the sales office would be a good hiding place for the legislation if it were necessary to have one." Clark asked about the "hiding place," with its intimation that Du Pont would have some secrets to hide. Carpenter said there was a typographical error and the term should have been "hiving place," which he called a place to "hold out." "There was no reason why we should hide anything," he added. Irénée saw it differently. "It reads 'hiding place.' That is what I understood it to mean. That is one reason I jumped on it," he said. After the committee considered several other pieces of correspondence, Nye concluded that Carpenter had been involved in legislative activities. "I do not blame you for thinking that," the former Du Pont vice-president answered. "Some of these letters certainly look it."[23]

The committee also focused attention on the Du Pont–controlled Remington Arms Company and its connections with the War and Navy departments. The questions covered a variety of mundane matters, but taken together they illuminated the web of the interwar military-industrial complex. Nye inquired about the *Army and Navy Journal*, a publication produced by former military officers, and asked if Remington believed its purchases of advertising would influence military decisions. The company offered a complimentary rifle to an Army officer, leading the committee to wonder if the action constituted a conflict of interest. A Remington letter said that the War Department had acted on the company's request to oppose gun control legislation in Massachusetts. Robert Wohlforth, the committee's assistant chief investigator, asked about a letter in which the War Department expressed "extreme regret" over a loss suffered by Remington Arms on defective ammunition and proposed buying some of it to help the company. Wohlforth considered the offer to be "very solicitous," but Egbert Hadley, technical director of Remington Arms, called it equitable. K.K.V. Casey's testimony pretty well summarized the close relationship between Du Pont interests and the military agencies. When Du Pont bought control of Remington Arms, Casey advised officials of the newly acquired company to consider themselves "a subdivision of the War Department."[24]

Wohlforth showed that the munitions companies did not always treat the government with a solicitous attitude. In the late 1920s, a study of comparative costs between various private munitions manufacturers and U.S. government arsenals found the government production about one-third cheaper. Although the government shared information about its costs with the private manufacturers, the companies refused to give their data to the government. Wohlforth introduced various letters from War Department officials that called for the arsenals to share their information with only those companies willing to return the favor. He concluded that the War Department expected to get such information, but Hadley disagreed. "If you will change the word 'expect' to 'hope' I will agree with you," he responded. In any event, War Department officials were unhappy when their hopes or expectations went unrealized. Wohlforth reviewed earlier testimony on government assistance to the munitions companies and pointedly contrasted it to the companies' unwillingness to cooperate with the government.[25]

On Thursday, 20 December, the munitions committee exposed the Liberty League to the American public as the Du Ponts testified for the final time. Irénée again offered provocative testimony, at one point drawing on his sense of history to assert that there was "only one way to really wage war, and that is to have an absolute monarch at the head. Caesar found that out, and Napoleon." When Pope asked if the United States should immediately create an absolute monarch in order to better prepare for war, Du Pont responded that "we are too close to that already." Further questioning about Du Pont lobbying activities led to the Liberty League. Nye introduced letters exchanged between R. M. Carpenter, retired Du

Pont vice-president, and John Raskob during the spring of 1934 that criticized the Roosevelt administration and discussed founding an organization to "protect society" from the excesses of the New Deal. The *New York Times* reported the letters in a front page story.[26]

By the afternoon of 21 December the committee had thoroughly documented many of the difficulties involved in mobilizing for a modern total war. The necessity of organizing thousands of plants and factories, securing tens of thousands of workers, and providing huge amounts of raw materials, all in a rush while under threat of attack, formed a daunting task. Toward the end of the day Hiss asked about amortization of wartime munitions plant construction, finally wearing out Lieutenant Colonel Harris. "Mr. Hiss, you have convinced me we should never go to war. It is too much trouble," he concluded. Harris ended the day by reading an official statement of the War Department concerning munitions production. Military leaders were less concerned with profiteering than with production. "It is conceivable that a war might be conducted with such great regard for individual justice and administrative efficiency as to make impossible those evils whose existence in past wars is well known," wrote department officials. "It is also conceivable that the outcome of a war so conducted might be defeat. In all plans for preparedness and policies to be pursued in event of war it must never be overlooked that while efficiency in war is desirable, effectiveness in mandatory."[27]

At 4 p.m., Nye adjourned the hearings of 1934. As the star witnesses, the Du Ponts testified more than half of the days the committee met. While hardly exposed as evil death merchants and instigators of bloodshed, it seemed to be apparent that money and profit dominated their thinking about war. As company records showed, Du Pont placed the financial interests of shareholders above other considerations, and most of the shares were held by the Du Pont family. On occasion the Du Ponts expressed disdain toward the committee. Pierre's asking in September to have hearings again soon so the brothers would not have so long to rehearse provided one example. Irénée's admonition that the senators were ignorant about the chemical industry was another. He occasionally blew smoke rings from his pipe during the hearings.[28]

The December hearings satisfied few of the participants. Raushenbush occasionally grew frustrated, writing to Nye on 18 December to accuse the Du Ponts of evading questions about legislative lobbying. Du Pont representatives were also frustrated. The most notable example was Pierre Du Pont's angry reaction to Hiss's questions on Old Hickory. After the Du Pont hearings adjourned, K.K.V. Casey visited Joseph Green at the State Department and accused the committee of sensationalizing the hearings by using documents out of context. Casey also told Green about reports that "the President is opposing the continuance of the Committee's activities."[29]

Casey's sources may have been well placed, for in December circumstances called for Roosevelt to gain control of the investigation. When the munitions committee tarnished the image of the Du Ponts, it served the political purposes of the president. Content with a Pecora-like investigation of big businessmen taking place during the 1934 election campaigns, FDR initially let the munitions hearings take their course. Questioning of the Du Ponts, however, was ending. At the same time, the investigation was becoming a liability for the president. The discovery of numerous links between the munitions companies and government officials led to questions about executive branch policy. Reports that the munitions investigation would end in December had been wrong, and the next phase of the hearings would examine the shipbuilding industry. Negotiations for a new naval treaty with Japan were concluding in failure, making 1935 a poor time to disrupt American shipbuilders. FDR wanted an expanded U.S. fleet. He was concerned about domestic opposition to naval shipbuilding, a movement that could be fanned by the upcoming hearings.[30]

On 13 December 1934, President Roosevelt moved to gain control over the issues raised by the munitions committee. He announced the formation of a special committee to study war profits legislation and appointed Bernard Baruch and former NRA chief Hugh Johnson to head it. The war profits question formed a key part of the Nye committee's reason for being, particularly due to Vandenberg's desire for a review of the War Policies Commission recommendations. S.R. 206, the resolution that created the munitions investigation, had been passed during debate over raising income taxes in times of war, and the committee planned to investigate the war profits issue in the spring.[31]

Nye and other committee members sensed in Roosevelt's action an effort to outflank the munitions investigation. "It is amazing to me," Nye told reporters, "that efforts would now be made to seem to check and halt the work of our committee. . . . If this is an attempt to halt the investigation, it is not the first one we have encountered during the late weeks." Vandenberg, Clark, and Pope vowed to press forward with the inquiry. A few days later, Nye, Vandenberg, and Clark announced their intention to introduce their own war profits legislation. Meanwhile, supporters organized to defend the investigation. At the headquarters of the Women's International League for Peace and Freedom, Dorothy Detzer sent telegrams urging state leaders to make their continuing support for the inquiry known to FDR. "Conference called yesterday by President on war profits is known to be move to stop further appropriations for continuing munitions hearings," she warned. She also wrote to Roosevelt and encouraged him to back more funding for the munitions committee.[32]

Roosevelt's naming of the Baruch-Johnson committee garnered support from what was for him an unusual source. Leaders of the business community applauded the effort, with *Business Week* writing that FDR's move "takes the punch out of the inquisition by the two Republican senators, Nye and Vandenberg, steals the show, saves the War and Navy departments some embarrassment regarding their relations with munitions makers and forestalls the Senate committee's recommendation for nationalization of the industry." *Business Week*, in singling out Nye and Vandenberg while ignoring the more acidic and confrontational Clark, focused unwarranted attention on the Republicans who had, in effect, become traitors against a most powerful interest group in their party. Given a choice between Roosevelt and the Nye committee, conservative business leaders leaned toward the former. Unfortunately for them, the Baruch-Johnson committee failed to derail the munitions investigation.[33]

Roosevelt met with Nye on 26 December and used his personal charm to overcome the senator's concerns about the Baruch-Johnson committee. Earlier in the day, Nye had spoken with Joseph Green and expressed dissatisfaction at FDR's action. After talking with Roosevelt, Nye telephoned Green to say that the meeting had been "eminently satisfactory" and that the president supported an additional appropriation for the investigation. The Baruch-Johnson committee never actually functioned, although South Carolina Congressman John McSwain, chair of the Military Affairs Committee, introduced war profits legislation based on Baruch's ideas when the 74th Congress convened on 3 January 1935. The munitions committee, meanwhile, sought an additional $100,000 appropriation. Raushenbush sensed a movement in the Senate to tie further funding to the development of legislative recommendations by April, which he believed would have "the effect of shutting off further investigation." He urged John T. Flynn, a member of the committee's advisory council, to draft quickly a war profits bill to counter any proposals of the Baruch-Johnson committee.[34]

On 10 January, Clark and Bone asked the Senate for a $100,000 appropriation, and four days later Pope spoke in favor of the request. The Senate approved a $50,000 appropriation on 17 January with the understanding that additional funding could follow. Fortified with more money, the committee planned for what would become its most sensational area of inquiry: American bank financing of Allied military purchases in World War I. The banking hearings remained far in the future, however, and the committee knew it would need more funding and continued public support to get there. Investigators remained sensitive to the importance of good press coverage. One wrote to Raushenbush on 18 January that he had found a witness who would provide "plenty of fireworks" and "the proper headlines."[35]

Roosevelt's support for more funding could not conceal the fact that the investigation was moving in a different direction from the administration. An 8 January brief prepared to guide the shipbuilding inquiry concluded that the "Big Three" shipbuilders—Bethlehem Shipbuilding Company, New York Shipbuilding Corporation, and Newport News Shipbuilding and Dry Dock Company—engaged in collusive bidding on naval contracts. It discussed a "partnership" between the navy and the companies and noted that "naval officers have close social and business relations with shipbuilders." The brief also referred to "innumerable instances of Senators and Congressmen receiving favors from shipbuilders." Nye talked to reporters about the links between the arms makers and the government in early January and spoke to the Senate concerning the issue on 15 January. As historian Wayne S. Cole noted, by 1935 "Nye and his committee wanted to restrain *both* business and government in the name of peace." Roosevelt's support for the munitions investigation had never been based upon a desire to restrain the government or embarrass navy officers.[36]

Another fault line between Roosevelt and Nye formed along the World Court issue. The president had in September of 1934 assented to State Department proposals to push for Senate ratification of U.S. membership in the World Court. The plan quickly ran into a roadblock in the person of Senate Foreign Relations Committee chair Key Pittman. In late 1934, he was locked into a disagreement with the administration over an issue close to his heart, American silver policy. Pittman was not overly enthusiastic about the administration's stand on the World Court, either, and he refused to take leadership on the resolution. At a White House meeting on 5 January 1935, Senate Majority Leader Joseph Robinson agreed to lead the effort. Passage of the World Court resolution required approval by a two-thirds majority, or fifty-nine votes. Robinson believed opponents would at most total twenty votes, not enough to block the measure. After the Foreign Relations Committee voted fourteen to seven to recommend the resolution, Senate deliberation began on 14 January. Hiram Johnson, a progressive Republican who held nationalist views, led the Senate opposition and made the essential argument of those opposed to the resolution. He believed that U.S. membership in the World Court would restrict American freedom to act in global affairs. After two weeks of debate his side won, with only fifty-two senators voting for World Court membership. Thirty-six voted against it, including Nye and Bone from the munitions committee.[37]

The usually optimistic and amiable Roosevelt showed uncharacteristic bitterness after the Senate defeat, suggesting that World Court opponents were "willing to see a city burn down just so long as their own houses remain standing in the ruins." In a letter to Robinson the day after the vote, FDR wrote that if the opponents "ever get to Heaven they will be doing a great deal of apologizing for a very long time—that is if God is against war—and I think He is." After the cabinet discussed the Senate defeat, Interior Secretary Harold L. Ickes noted FDR's "showing of willingness to hurt those who brought about his defeat." In early February, Roosevelt wrote Henry Stimson and noted that "I have an unfortunately long memory and I am not forgetting either our enemies or our objectives." With Nye among FDR's "enemies," the Roosevelt-Nye relationship had deteriorated seriously since the two men shared the stage in Devil's Lake, North Dakota, six months earlier.[38]

Roosevelt's sharp reaction to the World Court defeat stemmed from his pessimistic appraisal of global events. In Europe, the Geneva Disarmament Conference recessed in June of 1934. An attempted Nazi coup in Austria during July was followed in October by the assassination of the king of Yugoslavia and the foreign minister of France. The president wrote William E. Dodd, U.S. ambassador to Germany, in August and expressed his gloom. "I too am downhearted about Europe," he noted, "but I watch for any ray of hope or opening to give me an opportunity to lend a helping hand. There is nothing in sight at present." Roosevelt and State Department officials saw the World Court defeat as a turning point in American foreign relations. FDR wrote to Stimson that the "people are jumpy and very ready to run after strange gods. This is so in every other country as well as our own." He believed that the United States would "go through a period of non-cooperation in everything" for at least the next year. Dodd attached even greater significance to the World Court vote and predicted that it would convince Hitler that the United States would do nothing to stop Nazi aggression. War would result. Some government officials found Dodd's argument to be extreme but also believed that FDR held similar views.[39]

In early 1935, the president found himself wavering before the forces of isolationism. FDR's ill feeling toward World Court opponents involved the munitions committee because Nye and Bone had voted against the administration. By the fall of 1935, Roosevelt would link the committee more closely with isolationism. But contrary to the assertion that FDR succumbed to isolationist fervor or joined the isolationist movement in supporting the munitions investigation, the record shows that the closer he linked it with isolationism, the more he opposed it. The World Court defeat motivated the president much as did the later Supreme Court defeat of the NRA. International events demanded attention, but before Roosevelt could act he needed to gain control over foreign policy and to do this he had to reign in the troublesome Nye committee. He made his first attempt by naming the Baruch-Johnson committee, touching off a whirlwind lobbying effort from supporters of the munitions committee. He would have to find a less obvious approach in 1935. Political reality called for the tactics of the wily fox rather than those of the courageous lion.

Problems the investigation created for Roosevelt's State and War departments gave the president more reasons to act. In mid-December, military officials met with several members of the committee to discuss the importance of maintaining secrecy for national security information. In preparation for hearings on the war profits question, the committee sought information on wartime industrial mobilization plans. Douglas MacArthur, who had been concerned about secrecy throughout the munitions inquiry, now spoke directly to Nye and Raushenbush. He saw a "danger of military secrets being divulged" if the plans were discussed in public hearings. With the committee suitably warned of the potential danger, War Department officials agreed to allow the senators to decide how the data would be used.[40]

Hull experienced ongoing problems with unauthorized disclosures of State Department information that complicated U.S. relations with foreign governments. Joseph Green, who was responsible for giving department approval on the committee's use of diplomatic records, kept a close watch to see that confidential materials were not revealed. In early February, he called on Raushenbush to point out Clark's use of unauthorized documents. A subsequent meeting with Raushenbush, Nye, and Vandenberg resulted in an apology to Hull for "what may appear to have been gross betrayal of the splendid confidence which we have enjoyed with and through you and your office." Nye added that greater care would be exercised in the future, but the problem was never resolved to Hull's satisfaction.[41]

The War Department shared Hull's concerns about confidential information. Of equal or greater concern to military officials, however, was the committee's focus on nationalization as a means to control the armaments industry. During the hearings, Lieutenant Colonel Harris stressed the department's concern that efforts to prevent profiteering not reduce efficiency of production. After several committee members expressed favorable attitudes toward a government monopoly on the manufacture of munitions, the War Department announced its opposition to the idea. Secretary of War Dern made the department's view clear during testimony before the House Military Affairs Committee in January of 1935, saying that the government manufacture of munitions "would probably remove any objectionable features that may have developed in connection with the munitions industry, but the result might at the same time be detrimental to national defense."[42]

The Du Ponts also opposed government ownership. A company memorandum introduced during the hearings argued that state-owned arms factories would hinder disarmament because workers would elect legislators committed to operating the plants at full capacity. Using France as an example, the memo noted that "while socialist deputies with their liberal doctrines cry for disarmament, any attempts on the part of the French War Department to close down the government factories are bitterly opposed by these same deputies on the basis that it would throw voters out of work." Unmentioned in the Du Pont analysis was that workers in privately owned plants might also vote for representatives pledged to keep the arms factories humming with government contracts. Regardless of the arguments offered by Nye, the military departments, or the Du Ponts, nationalization did not present a serious concern for the Roosevelt administration. The 74th Congress would never endorse such a radical idea.[43]

In addition to all the other considerations, the upcoming presidential election forced FDR to assess the political repercussions of the munitions investigation. In mid-February, Roosevelt wrote to Edward House and surveyed the field of candidates for 1936. Among the six people he listed as opponents were Nye and Vandenberg. One week later, FDR wrote to Hull and attached an unsigned memorandum that addressed war profits and how the munitions committee might use the issue against the administration. The memorandum, attributed to Bernard Baruch, argued that weapons exports provided a means to "test killing implements and a nucleus for a war-time munitions industry by maintaining an export market for instruments of death. Of course, it is absolutely indefensible and we could not be put in a position of excusing it. If the Nye Committee should anticipate in reaching this conclusion it would put the Administration in an embarrassing position." The memorandum concluded that this was "what the Nye Committee is now doing, and obviously intends to do, to embarrass the Administration." Embarrassing the Du Ponts was one thing, embarrassing the administration another. FDR's honeymoon with the munitions committee was over.[44]

Chapter 5

Shipbuilding and War Profits: Discovering the Impact of Total War in Modern Society, January 1935 to April 1935

While Roosevelt watched the World Court resolution go down to defeat, the munitions committee on 21 January opened its 1935 hearings into the shipbuilding industry and war profits legislation. Officials from the New York Shipbuilding Corporation, the Newport News Shipbuilding and Dry Dock Company, and the Bethlehem Shipbuilding Company, collectively called the "Big Three" shipbuilders, testified first and answered questions about profiteering, lobbying tactics, and bidding procedures. Officials of smaller shipbuilding companies testified later, after the committee considered the war profits issue. In studying shipbuilding and war profits, the committee explored the roles played by various businesses and industries associated with military production and noted the importance of labor unions, the media, and especially the government. Committee members spent little time trying to show that armament companies fomented war. By the end of the 1935 hearings, they had moved far beyond such suspicions to consider the implications of a large and encompassing military establishment.

The committee had little trouble showing that the shipbuilders used a variety of questionable means to increase profits for their companies and incomes for themselves, with witnesses frequently unable to explain their actions with much precision. Questions about former Treasury Secretary Andrew Mellon's interest in New York Shipbuilding provided a starting point. He had been a large stockholder, and in 1916 American International Corporation bought the company in a deal that provided him with approximately $7.5 million in New York Shipbuilding bonds. The Treasury Department promptly argued that American International had paid nearly $3 million too much for the company, overvalued the assets acquired, and then tried to recoup some of the money through tax breaks from exaggerated depreciation on the inflated assets. The statute of limitations lapsed, however, before any final action could be taken.[1]

The Mellon episode identified two major problems for the committee, problems that had emerged during the 1934 hearings. First, if top government officials turned out to be munitions profiteers, the hope for government action to restrain the arms makers was misplaced. Second, if many cases turned out to be as complicated as the New York Shipbuilding/American International transaction, the average person would probably be unable to understand what happened. Depreciation of overvalued assets hardly formed a topic of interest to forgotten men at the bottom of the economic pyramid, and even experts frequently disagreed on how to handle such complicated and difficult accounting procedures.

The issues did not become any simpler when the committee turned to the "cost plus" contracts negotiated during World War I. The contracts allowed businesses to pass expenses to the government and collect a profit above cost, a procedure that led into a morass of conflicting views on what constituted a justifiable expense. New York Shipbuilding tried to claim income taxes, charitable gifts, Christmas presents, and over $15,000 for tobacco and alcohol expenditures as expenses billable to the government. The government disallowed many of the items, but the company did get salary increases for company officers included in cost figures. The testimony led Raushenbush and Nye to conclude that wartime tax policies needed to be set before war started in order to avoid lengthy postwar litigation. Raushenbush noted that tax collection often came after the "spirit of war or patriotism and so forth" had passed.[2]

A contract from 1920 allowed the company to charge taxes as a cost, creating a situation where, as Clark noted, "the more taxes which were assessed against you, the more money you actually received from the Government." The contract also allowed the company to include stock dividends as an expense. Raushenbush showed that when the contract was made, a member of New York Shipbuilding's board of directors, P.A.S. Franklin, also served the government's Emergency Fleet Corporation. Franklin was a "dollar a year" man, one of a group of business and professional men who served the government for minimal compensation during the war. Later, according to Raushenbush, New York Shipbuilding gave Franklin "a reward, or tip, or whatever it is, for his services to the corporation, in the form of allowing him to buy treasury stock out of the treasury for $1, which, a little later, was worth, under option, $30." Clark could not resist asking if Franklin used "the same dollar he got from the Government."[3]

The committee found similar situations in the other large shipbuilding companies. Newport News Shipbuilding and Dry Dock Company contested its World War I tax liabilities, arguing that it had $20 million invested in its plant instead of the Internal Revenue Service allowance for only $3.8 million. The matter remained in dispute until 1931, when both sides agreed to assess the capital investment at a level close to other comparable shipbuilders. Bethlehem Shipbuilding tried to list expenditures for liquor, a yacht, foreign advertising, and trap-shooting tournament fees as costs for the government. The government disallowed over $2 million of the claims, but auditing the shipbuilder's operations proved expensive. Raushenbush noted that it cost over $700,000 to audit three of the company's facilities and concluded that "it cost the Government an awful lot to make those $2,218,000 savings." Comptroller F.A. Shick offered a confusing defense for the company's policy, stating that "naturally they were in our expense there" although "it was not our policy or idea of trying to get these items into cost."[4]

Nye asked whether executive salaries and bonuses formed a legitimate component of cost and cited the $2.8 million in bonuses received in 1917 and 1918 by Bethlehem Shipbuilding president Eugene Grace. Shick testified that bonuses were not figured into cost on the World War I contracts. Bethlehem stockholders authorized the bonus policy on 3 April 1917, the day after Woodrow Wilson asked Congress to declare war on Germany. While Grace said the bonus system "was not created for the purpose of making an unusual effort during the war period at all," the timing allowed for unusually high levels of executive compensation.[5]

Bone probed into possible conflicts of interest, showing that one Bethlehem officer served on the War Industries Board as a "dollar a year" man and continued to receive a company bonus at the same time. In another case, a major stockholder in the company served as chairman of the wartime Emergency Fleet Corporation. Bone produced a 1923 government report that concluded that the "Bethlehem contracts were unconscionable and against public interest." When Grace could not answer questions about a resulting lawsuit, Bone expressed his frustration. "It is an astounding thing how many big executives have come before us and have no knowledge of the affairs of their company," he said. "This is a major thing, involving many millions of dollars." Later, Grace could not answer basic questions about the steel producers that supplied his company.[6]

The committee also examined each company's lobbying activities. Investigators found several documents in the files of New York Shipbuilding that showed that former company president Clinton L. Bardo had been an active lobbyist for his firm, but he was reluctant to testify. He knew from firsthand experience that his ties to the munitions industry could bring personal discomfort. In June of 1934, an Episcopalian minister in Camden, New Jersey, had attacked him as a "munitions racketeer" and called New York Shipbuilding officers and directors "truculent, swashbuckling militarists." Bardo answered the charges in a six-page letter, parts of which appeared in the *Camden Courier-Post*. In another letter, he blamed the committee's early hearings for diminished business prospects in South America for his company and other munitions makers. While the munitions investigation may have had nothing to do with his decision, he submitted his resignation from the presidency of New York Shipbuilding on 18 October 1934.[7]

Bardo believed that the hearings were being conducted in a biased manner. Starting his testimony with a prepared statement, he criticized the committee for holding "ex parte" hearings where witnesses had no opportunity to be represented by counsel and were not allowed to explain the meaning of the various exhibits. "From the most innocent transactions inferences and innuendos are drawn intended to induce the newspapers to print and the public to believe that sinister influences have dominated the shipbuilding industry," Bardo said, adding that "the fifth amendment to the Constitution and laws pertaining to self-incrimination were adopted to protect citizens against inquisition of the character I refer to." The criticism did not slow the hearing.[8]

The committee probed into Bardo's efforts to stop a Reconstruction Finance Corporation (RFC) loan to Gulf Industries, a newly formed potential competitor based in Pensacola, Florida. New York Shipbuilding wanted Jersey City Mayor Frank Hague to "do everything possible to scotch the plan." Hague, a powerful machine-style political boss, dominated New Jersey politics and held an interest in the matter due to the fact that New York Shipbuilding built its ships in New Jersey. Bardo took his concerns about the RFC loan to New Jersey Governor A. Harry Moore, a Hague confidant, who then contacted Postmaster General James Farley. Farley handled patronage matters for Roosevelt and in that capacity worked closely with Hague. Moore also wrote to FDR, and the president responded in a brief note that "we have no intention of acquiring shipyards." Raushenbush pointed out that an RFC examiner had initially approved the loan to Gulf Industries, but the agency overruled the recommendation and denied the request. The munitions investigation implicated the Roosevelt administration in some suspect actions, but it could provide only limited circumstantial evidence. Roosevelt placed special emphasis on friendly relations with the Hague machine, perhaps creating a political motive to interfere with RFC policy making.[9]

Bardo may have focused his efforts on mayors and governors because of his low regard for members of Congress. "Judging the Congressmen from my experience with them last winter, it would be useless to furnish them with a statement of this length," he wrote in a 1928 letter regarding cruiser construction. "There is not one in 100 of them who would take the time to read it, and not more than this proportion have the brains and the intelligence to correctly understand it if they did." After reading the letter in the hearings, Raushenbush asked Newport News president Homer L. Ferguson if it represented "the attitude of shipbuilders generally about Congress?" Ferguson did not get to answer because Nye asked that the letter be read a second time. When Raushenbush said that more details on the letter had been requested from the navy, Nye dryly added that the committee wanted information "as to the cruisers, and not the intelligence of the Members of Congress."[10]

Later testimony from officials of a smaller shipbuilder, United Dry Docks, Incorporated, provided more details on lobbying and an example of what would later be called the "revolving door" between government and business. The company employed a Washington lobbyist who had previously served with the United States Shipping Board for seven years. Joseph W. Powell, president of the company, stayed in close contact with the legislative branch by sharing a Washington apartment with his congressman, Anning S. Prall of New York. In a 1933 letter to United Dry Docks' insurance broker, Powell noted that Prall "has been extremely helpful to me in all of our Washington business. His son, Bryan W. Prall, is in the insurance business . . . you will have to help him to a slice of our business somewhere or other."[11]

In another case, a congressman on the House Naval Affairs Committee asked the company to hire an unemployed sheet metal worker. A company memorandum suggested that the man be hired because "a member of the House Naval Committee may be very useful to us in future dealings with the Navy." Later testimony showed that the company enjoyed good relations with the navy without help from Congress. A navy officer assisted in preparing estimates for a 1933 cruiser bid, giving the company what he described as "information that otherwise might not be available." The officer had been posted as an inspector at the Bethlehem shipyard, a bidding competitor, while providing his services to United Dry Docks.[12]

William S. Newell of Bath Iron Works, another of the smaller shipbuilding companies, testified on his effort to influence Maine newspapers toward favoring naval expansion. Newell sent accounts of Japanese naval construction to Guy Gannett, owner of several newspapers, and suggested that the Maine congressional delegation be made aware of the story. Gannett acted quickly and instructed his editors to write editorials supporting a larger navy. He promised Newell that he would send copies of the articles to Maine's representatives in Washington. Nye, a one-time newspaper editor, recalled that just before he voted on navy bills he often read a "great deal in the papers about trouble with Japan. How many of these annual scares of trouble with Japan have you and others interested in the munitions game played up?" Newell said the instance under discussion was the only such effort of which he had any knowledge.[13]

Homer L. Ferguson, president of Newport News Shipbuilding, discussed his company's relations with shipbuilding lobbyist William B. Shearer. Shearer's activities at the 1927 Geneva Naval Conference had generated controversy, and some observers assigned him primary responsibility for its failure. Company documents showed that Shearer was paid by Newport News and other shipbuilders during the conference, and he later asserted that his work served their purposes. In a letter to the shipbuilders, he wrote that "owing to the failure of the tripower naval conference at Geneva, there is now before the Seventieth Congress a 71-ship building program costing $740,000,000." Ferguson denied having any knowledge about Shearer's activities in Geneva.[14]

When the committee later questioned Shearer, he provided few details on his activities at the conference except to say that his work consisted of a "very fast and vicious campaign" financed by U.S. shipbuilders. He proved to be a colorful and combative witness, leveling insults and charges of disloyalty at just about anyone who disagreed with him. Clark asked about a 1929 letter in which Shearer stated that nine senators had ties to the Communist party, but he could find out little about the source of the information. In a written statement addressed to the committee, Shearer said he was persecuted by "practically every

Jewish publisher in New York" and that he had been denounced by Rabbis. He also said that certain Democratic party officials, Wall Street financial leaders, and the *New York Times* persecuted him. When questioned by Nye, Shearer could provide nothing substantial to back up the charges.[15]

Senator Bone asked about a pamphlet, *The Cloak of Benedict Arnold*, which listed Shearer as the author. In one section, titled "Knaves or Fools," Shearer provided a list of names headed by Franklin D. Roosevelt. When Shearer shied away from direct criticism of the president, Bone pressed the question. "Are you so cowardly that you would not indict him, if he required indictment, as a 'Benedict Arnold'? You told us you had lots of courage," Bone said. Shearer rose from his chair. "I have not mentioned my courage, and I do not like the implication about being a coward," he retorted. Nye ordered Shearer back to his seat, creating one of the committee's more dramatic moments.[16]

The most dramatic issue of the shipbuilding hearings, however, did not involve Shearer or lobbying but rather allegations of bid rigging. The committee probed deeply into the cruiser bids of the interwar years and especially into 1933 bids for naval construction financed by $238 million of Public Works Administration (PWA) money. Questioning about the cruiser bids examined whether the navy promised to award contracts to New York Shipbuilding. A telegram from Bardo to Treasury Secretary Mellon mentioned an "understanding" that the contracts were to be awarded to private shipyards, including New York Shipbuilding. Bardo called the word "understanding" an "unfortunate use of language" and denied that any agreement or understanding existed between his company and the Navy Department on the matter. Clark cited a portion of the message that said Bardo's company had invested substantial funds in preparation for the contracts. "You were not in the habit of spending large sums of money on understandings when you did not know with whom the understanding was, were you?" he pointedly asked. Clark wondered why the company went to the treasury secretary about the matter. "Since he had formerly owned control in the New York Shipbuilding Corporation and was still also retaining bonds of it, did that have anything to do with your appealing to him?" he asked. Bardo said the financial ties were not a factor, though he admitted that no other cabinet secretaries were contacted.[17]

Bardo's assistant, George B. Yard, carefully qualified his statements but indicated that Bardo discussed bidding with other shipbuilders prior to submitting bids. Nye asked if the shipbuilders discussed bids over the telephone. "I believe they did, Senator," Yard responded. "Do you not know they did?" Nye pressed. "Yes; I know they did," Yard testified, giving the committee something stronger than circumstantial evidence of collusion among the shipbuilders. Many other witnesses, however, testified that no collusion had taken place. Newport News officials denied Yard's charges, saying that New York Shipbuilding officials called only a few times throughout the course of a typical year and that bids and prices were never discussed in those conversations.[18]

Homer L. Ferguson and eight other Newport News officials collectively fielded questions about their bidding procedures, concentrating on the 1927 and 1929 contracts. When the company received awards for two cruisers in 1927, it had based its bid on an anticipated profit of $1,940,000 from the two ships. The actual profit turned out to be $5.5 million, leaving Ferguson "perfectly amazed that we made so much." Over one-third of what the government paid went to profits for the company. Raushenbush asked why the company, after doing so well, submitted a 1929 cruiser bid that was $488,000 above the 1927 bid. Ferguson defended the 1929 bid, noting that the later cruisers were new designs and contained nearly $350,000 more in materials than the earlier vessels. Additionally, his yard had plenty of business in 1929 and did not necessarily need or even want to contract for another ship.[19]

Raushenbush explored the impact of greater competition on bidding when questioning officials of Bethlehem Shipbuilding, focusing on 1932 when a fourth shipbuilder joined the bidding on a navy cruiser. Although bid prices had generally gone up during the interwar years, in 1932 the Big Three all submitted lower cruiser bids than they had in 1931. Raushenbush showed that Bethlehem estimated the ship would cost $1.1 million less to build, but lowered its bid by over twice as much with a $2.5 million decrease. The committee wanted to know what role the new competitor played in bringing down the bid and getting Bethlehem to accept a smaller profit margin. The company's general manager, S. W. Wakeman, said the depression caused the lower bids. "We had been up here to 4,700 men and we were down here to around 500," he explained. "We simply had to have that contract."[20]

Testimony during the first week of hearings opened the door to an extensive inquiry into the 1933 bidding that took place early in the Roosevelt administration. John P. Frey, president of the metal trades department of the American Federation of Labor, told the committee that Laurence R. Wilder, a former president of New York Shipbuilding, had some ten days prior to the 1933 bid opening predicted which companies would be the lowest bidders for the various categories of ships. Wilder listed his predictions on paper and sealed them in an envelope. After the bids were opened and published in the press, Frey found that Wilder had correctly named the lowest bidders in every category. When he later asked Wilder about the prediction, the former New York Shipbuilding official replied that "I have been in the game myself."[21]

W. A. Calvin, secretary-treasurer of the metal trades department, corroborated Frey's account and related another story involving Wilder and the 1933 bids. After leaving New York Shipbuilding, Wilder became chairman of the board at Gulf Industries. Calvin testified that Wilder had been approached in August of 1933 by a man offering to secure at least $10 million of PWA money for the new company. The man, Axel B. Gravem, wanted $250,000 to pay off a "fixer" who would handle the matter.[22]

The committee questioned Laurence R. Wilder for the first time during a two-hour session on 30 January. He corroborated the testimony of Frey and Calvin, saying that his knowledge about the bidding came primarily from former Gulf Industries' vice-president Thomas M. Cornbrooks. Cornbrooks, in turn, received information from his brother, Ernest I. Cornbrooks, who served as a vice-president at New York Shipbuilding. Wilder described a dramatic late-night Washington, D.C., meeting in July of 1933, where the Big Three argued out who would bid for what among the navy ships. He said the "row was so severe that Mr. [Ernest] Cornbrooks had a heart attack at 4 o'clock in the morning, and was taken out on a stretcher at the Mayflower Hotel." The Big Three came to agreement, however, and determined the low bidders on each type of ship. The companies not seeking a contract then submitted artificially high bids, called "protective bids," and, as a result, there was no real competition. "It is a racket," Wilder concluded.[23]

Thomas Cornbrooks refuted Wilder's claim that information about the bids came from him and denied having any personal knowledge about the alleged late-night meeting. Committee investigator Floyd LaRouche produced the Mayflower Hotel register showing that Ernest Cornbrooks, Clinton Bardo, and top officials from several shipbuilding companies had rented rooms in late July. Thomas Cornbrooks was in Washington at the same time but said he had not known that his brother was also in town. Wilder suspected collusion when the bids were opened, but Cornbrooks did not believe the story and ignored the charges.[24]

The committee next questioned Julia M. Kitchen, Wilder's secretary and the first female witness of the hearings. She corroborated Wilder's account and contradicted that of Thomas Cornbrooks. She clearly remembered Cornbrooks relating the story of the late-night meeting. She also testified that Cornbrooks supplied bidding information to Wilder and that he had said the information came from his brother.[25]

Ernest Cornbrooks supported his brother's testimony on all significant points. He maintained that only officials of New York Shipbuilding were involved in the all-night conference where he prepared estimates of construction costs for the ships, a job made more difficult because the NRA shipbuilding code remained under discussion while the bids were due. Company officials wanted the bids to take code requirements into account, not only for their company but also for other industries that provided materials for the ships. Vandenberg noted that Cornbrooks made detailed estimates on six of the thirty-two ships to be built, and that New York Shipbuilding received contracts on those six and no others. On other ships he made a cursory study of costs and provided an estimate, after which the company submitted unsuccessful bids. Cornbrooks denied knowledge of any bidding arrangement that allowed him to focus on the six ships.[26]

The navy rejected charges of bidding collusion, and Navy Secretary Claude Swanson had reported on 9 August 1933 that he found no evidence to support the allegations. Swanson said the navy rejected Wilder's bid from Gulf Industries because "this company was not in position to undertake construction of the vessels upon which bids were submitted." Swanson provided an alternative context within which to consider Wilder's charges of collusion. Perhaps the accusations amounted to little more than sour grapes.[27]

Wilder also charged that the Roosevelt administration forced the navy to accept the collusive bids. He said some navy officials had been dissatisfied with the 1933 bids and believed that the shipbuilders were asking for too much money. In late July, after officials from the shipbuilding companies met with Swanson, navy officers went to meet with Roosevelt. Four days later, the navy accepted the bids and awarded the contracts. Wilder admitted that his version of the story was mostly hearsay, but he concluded that the navy was "coerced, forced by political pressure into making those awards against its will."[28]

Newport News Shipbuilding officials provided more details on the 1933 bids, with president and general manager Homer L. Ferguson testifying that the companies discussed allocation of naval work before submitting their bids. Newport News Shipbuilding received contracts for two aircraft carriers priced at $19 million each, and Raushenbush produced a memorandum showing that the company bought $180,000 worth of furniture for the carriers several days before the bids were opened. Company officials denied that the action indicated prior knowledge about the allocation and said that the purchase was contingent upon their receiving the carrier contract. Raushenbush noted that the memorandum failed to make clear the conditional nature of the furniture purchase.[29]

William M. Flook, former board chairman of New York Shipbuilding, testified about some of the strongest evidence on bidding collusion. Nye introduced a 22 June 1933 letter from Clinton Bardo to Flook that said the navy had encouraged the shipbuilders to discuss bidding before submitting bids. "I know from my talks with some of the representatives of the Navy," Bardo wrote, "that they are desirous of finding some substantial reasons for awarding this work to the largest possible extent to private yards. . . . There was also expressed to us the desire that the builders themselves should get together and agree as far as we could upon what each would bid and then bid on nothing else." Everyone understood the significance of the Bardo letter. "That is collusion if you ever saw it," Bone concluded. "That makes the Navy a party to the collusion," added Nye. "Collusion is a word of opprobrium," said Flook.[30]

The committee recalled Bardo, who said that he had no direct authorization from the navy to make such a statement. He argued, however, that even though his statement was literally false, practically it was true because the letter conveyed what had come out of a general discussion among the shipbuilders. Senator Pope was dissatisfied with the explanation and asked why the company president lied in a letter to his board chairman. Bardo dismissed the charge and said he had only made "careless use of language."[31]

U.S. Navy rear admirals Emory S. Land and Samuel M. Robinson also testified on the Bardo letter. Land denied that any "such statement was made to Mr. Bardo by any official in authority in the Navy Department." Robinson found it "perfectly obvious from the reading of that testimony, that those shipbuilders had some sort of discussion before these bids were opened," a change from the position stated by Secretary Swanson in 1933. Some navy officers had found the committee's hearings to be persuasive. Raushenbush noted that Bardo remembered discussions among the Big Three and the navy prior to submission of the 1933 bids, but that officials from Bethlehem and Newport News "denied any such discussions, or forgot to remember them." Clark sharply commented that instead of forgetting to remember, the shipbuilders may have "remembered to forget it."[32]

Raushenbush summarized the testimony as the committee neared the end of its study of bids and bidding. He described a process in which "on certain classes of ships everybody admits that one yard has an advantage, and then the other yards corroborate that by doing a relatively small amount of estimating on the jobs on which they do not have the advantage, but they put in bids, and the bids are in there and certainly give the impression of active, intense competition." He said the process protected shipbuilders from scrutiny by the navy and the public. Instead of critically examining the bids, "everybody says, 'Well, here the low bidder is $4,000,000 below the high bidder. Certainly the Government is getting a good bargain.' That might not be at all true," he concluded.[33]

The committee pursued the charge that Axel Gravem had offered to "fix" some government contracts for Gulf Industries in exchange for $250,000. Gravem denied making the offer and disputed the earlier testimony of Calvin, Wilder, and Kitchen. He named his friend and contact in the shipbuilding industry, Arthur P. Homer. The committee recalled Kitchen and learned of Gravem's claim that the "fixer" had already secured two destroyer contracts for Bath Iron Works and received nearly $60,000 for his services. Gravem had said that Homer enjoyed close relations with the president and top navy officials and stressed that "the methods he suggested were the only ones which would produce results." He claimed to be a former official in the Reconstruction Finance Corporation.[34]

Bath Irons Works officials disclosed that their company had worked with Homer. After the 1932 election, he supplied the shipbuilder with supposed "inside information" from the White House and at one point introduced company president William S. Newell to FDR's secretary, Marvin MacIntyre. Company treasurer L. Eugene Thebeau said that Homer called MacIntyre and requested special treatment for telegrams to the president. The testimony supported some of Homer's claims, but Bath officials could not say how the administration responded. Newell minimized Homer's importance, saying that he already knew the top officers of the Navy Department and hardly needed assistance to gain access. Regarding the 1933 bids, Newell did what navy officials told him to do.[35]

Vandenberg noted Homer's service to Roosevelt's presidential campaign. As chair of the marine committee of the finance division of the Democratic National Campaign Committee, Homer wrote fundraising letters that promised FDR would know about all donations. When he talked with committee investigators, Homer stressed his close relationship to the president and maintained that the two men had once been partners in a lobster business. He said that he initiated the idea of spending PWA money for naval construction and used his influence to gain

FDR's support for the proposal. Homer exaggerated the extent of his access to Roosevelt. When Roosevelt had served as assistant secretary of the navy, he seconded Homer's nomination for membership in the New York Yacht Club. Three years later, Homer sent FDR complimentary tickets to the 1916 New York Motor Boat Show. Such interactions hardly placed him within Roosevelt's inner circle. FDR repudiated Homer's fund-raising letters in 1932, saying that they were not authorized and that he did not approve of them.[36]

Clark forced Homer to admit the excessiveness of his claims. Some were at best half-truths, such as when Homer noted his call to Marvin MacIntyre asking that certain "telegrams be segregated from the mass of telegrams and delivered to the President at breakfast. This was done." Clark asked if Homer actually had any knowledge about what happened to the telegrams. "Not the slightest," he answered. The telegrams urged Roosevelt to overrule a decision by the navy to reject Bath Iron Works' 1933 destroyer bid. Homer organized a micro-level military-industrial complex to lobby for the ships, with the governor of Maine, the mayor of Portland, Maine, the bank president in Bath, Maine, and the worker's organization at Bath Iron Works sending the telegrams to the president. According to Homer, he developed the campaign in conjunction with navy officials. When the awards were announced and Bath Iron Works received contracts for two destroyers, Homer took credit and requested $50,000 for his services, but the company refused to pay. Homer's memory proved to be very unreliable and the committee could not determine much based on his testimony. At one point, he could not remember statements he had made two months earlier in an interview with Clark and Vandenberg.[37]

Toward the end of the shipbuilding hearings, the committee heard from more government officials. Captain William G. DuBose, from the Construction Corps of the navy, appeared before the committee on 21 February. He could not answer many of the questions and frustrated some of the senators. Vandenberg wondered "how, in the absence of accurate information respecting private yards costs, the Navy Department is able at any time to determine whether its bids are proper or not, or within a reasonable range." The navy's lack of information about the private yards extended beyond wage scales and the bidding process. After ships were built, the navy took no action to review the legitimacy of cost claims, viewing that as a task for the Treasury Department. The committee offered some reasonable criticisms. Treasury officials, lacking expertise in military affairs, would have difficulty evaluating cost claims, while navy officials simply accepted the shipbuilders at their word. This combination seriously impaired oversight of the shipbuilding companies.[38]

On the following day, the committee questioned Harold L. Ickes, secretary of the interior, about PWA spending for naval construction. In addition to the $238 million navy shipbuilding program, the PWA allocated nearly $40 million for "general naval purposes" and provided the War Department with over $446 million. Close to $100 million of the War Department funds went to "military purposes," with the remainder going to non-military uses, including Corps of

Engineers projects. More than 10 percent of the initial PWA appropriation went for military spending, providing a rough gauge of the importance of the defense sector to the American economy in the early 1930s.[39]

By the end of the shipbuilding hearings, the committee had raised issues central to the nature of the military-industrial complex. That once started it might be difficult to stop was suggested by a postwar decision to build ninety-seven destroyers ordered during World War I. Bethlehem and a subsidiary company built over half the destroyers at a cost of over $90 million. Senator Bone wondered why the navy did not cancel the contracts as work on the ships had not begun when the war ended. "Maybe they did not have confidence the war was actually over," Bethlehem president Eugene Grace offered. "It may be," Bone responded. "It is hard for me to believe, but it may be that the Navy Department had heard vaguely that the war was over, after the armistice." In earlier hearings, Congress had asked navy officials about the decision. Admiral C. J. Pratt responded that "if you start a big machine moving, such as this production is, it takes a certain amount of time before it gets slowed up."[40]

The "big machine" went beyond the armaments industry, as Grace pointed out when asked about how to eliminate war profits. "When you talk of profits and the necessities present to prosecute a war," he said, "you must not narrow it down to just the words 'guns' and 'battleships', but it is everything produced; it is the cigar, the cigarette, the food, the shoes, and everything." A year earlier, *Fortune* magazine said in "Arms and the Men" that armaments production involved "most of the essential industries of modern life." The munitions committee learned that the military-industrial complex of the 1930s involved that and more.[41]

The testimony of John Frey and W. A. Calvin showed that organized labor formed an important component of the emerging military establishment. Calvin noted that the American Federation of Labor (AFL) "gave its full support to legislation leading up to the treaty-strength Navy bill." The organization also supported using the PWA funds for construction of thirty-two navy ships. Raushenbush saw in the AFL's position a "change in the historic policy of the labor groups," and Calvin agreed. He said that the unions wanted to get jobs for their workers, and military spending provided a means to that end. He argued that the United States needed to build 437 naval ships in order to keep pace with Britain, France, Italy, and Japan. The U.S. fleet in 1935 consisted of 377 vessels.[42]

The shipbuilding hearings provided some troubling moments for the Roosevelt administration, but FDR maintained his usual calm and optimistic demeanor as the inquiry wound through February and into March. At a 1 February press conference reporters asked about Arthur Homer, leading Roosevelt to joke about the case. "Almost every night, around half past 5:00 or 6:00 or 6:30, every manufacturer of great wealth and lobbyist drops in on Mac [Marvin MacIntyre] and says, 'Will you put this on the President's breakfast table at 9:30 tomorrow morning?' And Mac says, 'Of course I will,'" the president told laughing reporters. Asked about Laurence Wilder's testimony, FDR went off the record. When he spoke again for the record, he added the comment "Wilder and wilder" for the again laughing journalists. A *New York Times* story on the following day said Roosevelt seemed to be "unperturbed" by the Nye committee hearings.[43]

The president's concern grew, however, as the days of hearings passed. On 23 February, he wrote Hull and requested a meeting to discuss "war profits and kindred subjects." FDR attached the memorandum, previously discussed, which said that the Nye committee "obviously intends . . . to embarrass the Administration." The committee next planned to study war profits, and Roosevelt had already shown his desire to lead on this issue by naming the Baruch-Johnson committee in December. Another troubling sign for FDR came with a broadcast speech by Senator Pope on 3 March. The only reliable New Dealer on the munitions committee, Pope took aim at the executive branch and stressed his surprise at discovering close links between military officials and the munitions companies. Such statements could have been expected from Republicans Nye and Vandenberg or even from Democrats Clark and Bone, but with Pope going in the same direction FDR could rely on none of the committee's senators to protect his military departments from more embarrassing inquiries.[44]

The munitions committee, meanwhile, considered various ideas for controlling war profits, with John T. Flynn heading the effort to develop a proposal. The committee also pressed toward its planned investigation of World War I finance and issued a subpoena for bank records. The subpoena disturbed British Ambassador Ronald Lindsay, who in mid-March expressed his government's concern about the sensitive nature of the information.[45]

After talking with Lindsay, Hull drafted a memorandum to Roosevelt on 14 March. He urged the president not to send arms traffic legislation to Congress because it "would not serve any useful purpose and might result in a head-on collision with the Nye Committee." He recommended that Roosevelt meet with the munitions committee and outlined a six-point agenda. Three items dealt with the arms trade, suggesting that FDR ask committee members to support State Department proposals, that he encourage them to support publicly the U.S. position at the Geneva conference, and that he seek their support for ratification of the 1925 Geneva Convention for the Supervision of the International Trade in Arms and Ammunition. Two points dealt with war profits, recommending that FDR stress the complexity of the issue as well as his own interest in the committee's proposals. Finally, Hull suggested that Roosevelt ask the senators to respect British and French concerns during any public hearings on World War I finance. FDR agreed to confer with the committee, and Hull informed Ambassador Lindsay that the meeting was planned for 18 March.[46]

The hearings on war profits policy started on Wednesday, 13 March, with testimony by Patrick J. Hurley, secretary of war during the Hoover administration and chairman of the War Policies Commission (WPC). He read the WPC report that advocated wartime price controls, presidential authority over the use of national resources, and a 95 percent wartime tax on excess profits. The senators asked about the price controls and wanted to know if Hurley favored fixing prices for the duration of a war at the level they were when the United States declared war. Nye and Clark pointed out that in World War I, significant inflation occurred before the United States declared war. Hurley called for price ceilings instead of fixed prices and said the wartime tax would recapture excess profits. Bone and Clark drew attention to the difficulties of collecting the tax, based on earlier testimony from the shipbuilders. Hurley acknowledged their concerns but provided no specific solutions.[47]

Hurley and Clark provided a harbinger of the munitions committee's eventual demise during an exchange about Woodrow Wilson's decision to enter World War I. In an interesting anomaly, the Republican Hurley defended the Democratic President Wilson from criticism by the Democratic senator. Clark had earlier told reporters that the munitions makers had made necessary the American entry into the war. Hurley mentioned the press story, and, after praising Clark's war record, offered a differing view. "But I would have to go a long ways," the former war secretary said, "before I would tear the last shred of idealism from the name of Woodrow Wilson and from the American people, to say that we committed this mighty Republic to a bloody war for the purpose of making the profits of munitions makers safe. That was not my understanding. I thought that we were committed to that war to make the world safe for democracy, and I believe we succeeded." The inquiry into World War I finance would touch some of the same sensitive nerves and cause southern Democrats to defend Wilson's reputation from attacks by the munitions committee.[48]

The committee sought ideas on war profits legislation from groups outside of government, led by officials of the American Legion and the Veterans of Foreign Wars (VFW). The veteran's organizations favored national service laws that gave the president sweeping wartime powers. One VFW official argued that cutting profits from the "munitions racket" would decrease the number of wars, but the legion spokesman disagreed and suggested that "a large number of stockholders, many of them widows and helpless people" would be hurt if wartime profits were eliminated. The committee also questioned William Hushing, the national legislative representative for the American Federation of Labor. He opposed any universal service law that included "industrial conscription," which he compared to slavery. He spoke against war profiteering, but he offered no specific ideas for legislation.[49]

The war profits debate took on more immediacy in mid-March due to the actions of Adolph Hitler and Franklin Roosevelt. In a blatant challenge to the Versailles Treaty, Hitler on 16 March announced plans to institute a military draft in Nazi Germany and raise a 500,000 man army. Hitler's action showed that if war profits legislation was to be in place before the next war, the committee needed to move quickly. Roosevelt, meanwhile, was dealing with the last war. On 18 March, he announced his intention to veto a cash bonus to World War I veterans. Many veterans, angered by their poverty in contrast with the wealth of the wartime profiteers, continued to seek the bonus after the fiasco of the 1932 march. Some observers thought the veteran's disappointment with the government might be soothed by legislation to eliminate future wartime profiteering, as had been called for by the American Legion and the VFW. FDR linked the two issues and called for tight control of war profits when he vetoed the bonus two months later.[50]

The munitions committee presented its version of war profits legislation on 19 March 1935 when John T. Flynn discussed the plan developed by his staff. He argued that excessive war profits stemmed from wartime inflation, which was in turn caused by large-scale borrowing. The United States would have to control wartime debt creation in order to end profiteering, so he designed a "pay as we fight" plan that collected revenue sufficient to pay wartime expenses without borrowing. He called for a wartime tax on corporations of 50 percent on profits up to 6 percent of capital value and 100 percent on profits over 6 percent of capital value. For individuals, Flynn proposed a maximum income of $10,000 with the government collecting 100 percent of any income above that figure. "That may look very, very drastic to the man who is making $50,000 now, or $75,000 now, and who made $100,000 a year in the last war," Flynn admitted, "but it ought not to be so bad, because, after all, you ought not to be accused of unreasonableness when you ask a man to run a factory for the same sum that you pay a general commanding in the field." He said that a Constitutional amendment to "practically suspend the fifth amendment" during wartime would be necessary to back up the plan. As the hearing concluded, Vandenberg and Barbour congratulated Flynn on his work.[51]

President Roosevelt met with committee members later that day. Ignoring Hull's six points, he instead indicated strong agreement with several aspects of the Flynn plan. Roosevelt's attitude surprised Nye, who thought the plan "so radical that the approval of the Administration could hardly have been expected." The president surprised committee members again by urging them to examine neutrality policy, saying that he agreed with the ideas of former Secretary of State William Jennings Bryan. The senators agreed to study the issue and consult with the president before introducing legislation. Talking to reporters after the meeting, committee members described FDR as being generally in agreement with the Flynn plan. On the following day, Roosevelt seemed to be less supportive when questioned by reporters. "Oh, we have not considered it in detail," he said.[52]

Historians have speculated about Roosevelt's motivations during the 19 March meeting. Wayne S. Cole concluded that FDR was probably not focused on the issues discussed, while John E. Wiltz suggested that FDR acted "on impulse" in directing the committee onto the neutrality question. Robert Dallek depicted a more purposeful Roosevelt, finding that the president put the committee onto neutrality as a means of "taking the issue away from the Senate Foreign Relations Committee." In Dallek's analysis, Roosevelt feared that Key Pittman's committee would demand an impartial and mandatory neutrality bill. Thus, FDR hoped that by working with the munitions committee he could get a bill providing presidential discretion. Robert A. Divine suggested that FDR was losing patience with the slow progress on neutrality and "could well have been using the Nye committee as a way of forcing the State Department to act."[53]

The munitions committee hardly offered a reliable means for Roosevelt to gain speedier action on the neutrality question. A discretionary neutrality bill, allowing the president to determine the extent of trade restrictions with belligerent nations, could expect to find even less favor from the Nye committee than from the Foreign Relations Committee. The president's endorsement of William Jennings Bryan's ideas probably did not encourage the senators to support discretionary neutrality. Roosevelt knew the Foreign Relations Committee had jurisdiction over neutrality legislation and that Pittman could be expected to keep the issue for his committee. Roosevelt's earlier efforts to gain control over the war profits question show that he had given serious consideration to the munitions inquiry, leading away from the suggestion that he acted impulsively and with little forethought in talking to the senators.

Roosevelt's most likely motive was to divert the investigation. With the war profits issue about to be decided in Congress and the investigation of World War I finance causing friction with the British, FDR directed the committee into a dead end. Raushenbush told Joseph Green on 27 March that the committee was "hot on the trail" of neutrality legislation, but by 12 April Nye wanted to drop the issue after Pittman claimed jurisdiction. Noting that the president "laid it on our doorstep," Nye told Joseph Green that he would be happy to turn the neutrality issue over to the Foreign Relations Committee. By the time the committee untangled itself from neutrality, the House of Representatives had already rejected its war profits proposals.[54]

The detour into neutrality did not distract the committee from its plan to examine World War I financial records. Hull wanted to stop the banking inquiry, but when Green discussed the issue with the committee on 20 March he found the senators unwilling to drop the matter. Nye said the finance inquiry formed a critical aspect of the investigation, and Pope offered assurances that he, Bone, and George would protect the administration from embarrassment. On the same day, Ambassador Lindsay underscored his unhappiness in a note to Hull, writing that "to proceed with the investigation of this correspondence of my Government without warning or without attempting to obtain its consent can only be characterized as an act of grave discourtesy." The secretary of state answered on 21 March, expressing surprise at Lindsay's position and describing an agreement with the committee to inform him before any documents involving the British were made public. Hull and Green then met with Nye, Raushenbush, and Hiss on 22 March. After Hiss dismissed the British protests, Nye reaffirmed the agreement on public use of the documents. The committee's fight for access to the World War I banking records, however, was only in the beginning stage.[55]

While the State Department and the munitions committee privately clashed over the banking inquiry, the public hearings into war profits continued. On Wednesday, 20 March, Flynn elaborated on his recommendations for eliminating war profits. He criticized the price-fixing proposals advocated by Bernard Baruch and said that prices would probably be far from normal by the time the United States declared war. From 1914 to 1917, for example, farm prices rose over 75 percent and metals prices went up over 170 percent. During the same period, consumer prices increased by 66 percent and wages rose by 25 percent. Flynn contrasted rises in salaries to the increases in wages. He showed that pay for top company officers sometimes increased dramatically even when reported profits remained flat.[56]

Flynn concluded his testimony with a defense of the maximum income proposal. Flynn saw business leaders as moral men in an immoral society, men who wanted "to do the right thing. Their thinking, however, as to what is the right thing, is largely conditioned by what is going on around them." His plan helped business executives to act ethically and eased labor-management conflict because workers would feel less resentment knowing that the "managers, the bosses, the stockholders, and the profit makers generally are not going to get rich out of war." In the midst of the Great Depression, with class divisions deepened between the "forgotten men" and the "money changers," no senator spoke against the income cap. Even the conservative Vandenberg expressed agreement with Flynn's thinking.[57]

The committee next heard Bernard Baruch's war profits views. Early questioning focused on his World War I experience on the Advisory Committee to the Council on National Defense and later as chairman of the War Industries Board (WIB). Baruch started out with an amiable attitude, noting that "things which this committee has so well brought out are indefensible from the standpoint of economics or business or morals."[58]

Bennett Clark tested Baruch's congeniality, grilling him on the inability of the War Industries Board to hold down prices and showing that the mandated price for copper was over 75 percent above the average cost of production. Baruch agreed that the copper producer's demands were "to say the least, exorbitant" and that the board had been able to do little to moderate the companies. Clark noted that "when the Germans were making their supreme drive, the copper interests of the United States were in a position of holding a club at the head of the Government, to the extent of saying that they would not deliver any more copper unless the price was increased."[59]

After showing the limited success of price-fixing, Clark demonstrated that the other major component of Baruch's plan, excess profits taxes, also failed to work for copper during the war. A 1922 memorandum by Treasury Secretary Andrew Mellon found that ore deposits had been overvalued for invested capital and depletion, meaning that "the copper industry for 1917 and subsequent years has not paid a fair and equitable tax." Mellon decided to let the valuations stand for the war years and attempt to correct the problem from 1919 onward, when the excess-profits tax had expired.[60]

Alger Hiss questioned Baruch about the performance of the steel industry during the war and revealed situations similar to those of the copper producers.

Prices were set high enough to assure a profit for both high- and low-efficiency producers, meaning that high-efficiency companies garnered large returns. By 1917, the WIB had made an industry interest group responsible for setting many of the prices. Hiss entered wartime tax statements of various steel companies into the record and showed that in many cases payments were far less than the amounts stipulated by the excess-profits tax. Raushenbush underlined the difficulties of collecting the taxes, citing a Treasury Department report that it would take twenty-two accountants working for five years to audit the U.S. Steel Corporation.[61]

Nye called the actions of the copper and steel producers a "strike of capital" and stated his support for a constitutional amendment giving the government power to break such a strike. Baruch disagreed and restated his support for excess-profits legislation. "We both admitted we can take it away by taxes," he told the committee, "although you do not think we can determine that taxable amount. That is the difference between us." Baruch reviewed the differences between his proposals, largely embodied in a bill sponsored by South Carolina Congressman John McSwain, and the committee's approach as represented in the Flynn plan. Baruch tried to be conciliatory during the hearings, but two weeks later he publicly attacked the Flynn plan as "a new and wholly experimental system which was never adopted at any time in the world's history in peace or war without an immediate result of collapse and ruin."[62]

On 1 April, the committee issued a preliminary report on its major areas of activity. The report said shipbuilding profits were too high, called private shipyards "expensive luxuries," and concluded that the national interest in a strong defense should not be confused with the shipbuilders' interest in profits. On war profits, the committee opposed the McSwain bill and endorsed the Flynn plan. Regarding neutrality, the committee called for export controls over munitions and contraband during times of war. "This is the only phase of the neutrality problem which the Committee considers to be within its jurisdiction," the report noted in bowing toward the protests of the Foreign Relations Committee.[63]

War profits formed one issue dividing the administration and the munitions committee by the spring of 1935. Differences between the administration and some members of the committee on the question of government ownership were highlighted when Secretary of War George Dern called proposals for nationalization of the munitions industry "suicidal" in a story printed by the *New York Times* in late March. Problems of a more personal nature came up when committee members met with military officials and heard about "White House pressure" related to the activities of Elliott Roosevelt. Raushenbush's memorandum of the meeting left unclear the details of the matter, but he double-underlined Roosevelt's name for emphasis. The committee had evidence of Elliott's involvement in a 1934 scheme to sell at least fifty Fokker airplanes to the Soviet Union.[64]

Policy differences over war profits took center stage when the House of Representatives began to debate the McSwain bill in early April. A few congressmen offered amendments with tax provisions similar to those of the Flynn plan, but their efforts were voted down. The mood of Congress changed on Saturday, 6 April, which was Army Day and the eighteenth anniversary of America's declaration of war on Germany. Crowds packed the sidewalks along Washington's Constitution Avenue to view over 4,000 parading veterans, and House members found themselves disposed to thrash war profiteers. McSwain amended his bill with a 100 percent excess-profits tax, a position he had earlier opposed. House members approved an amendment to conscript "all persons responsible for the management, direction, and control of industry, commerce, and transportation." One congressman wanted all government employees, including members of Congress, to "receive exactly the same pay that the fighting men in the death trenches receive . . . then, indeed, there would be no more war."[65]

The veterans and demonstrators went home after the weekend, and on Tuesday, as the House prepared for its final vote on the McSwain bill, the munitions committee revisited the issue of the hour. Lieutenant Colonel C. T. Harris testified again on the War Department's position that victory was the one essential goal. Flynn followed to provide further argument for his own plan and against the McSwain bill. Over in the House of Representatives, enthusiasm for reigning in profiteers had dissipated and most of the amendments from 6 April were stripped from the bill. Essentially in its original form, the McSwain bill passed the House by a vote of 368 to 15, with forty-seven not voting and one member voting as present. The bill authorized the president to fix prices during wartime and to commandeer essential resources. Stock and commodity exchanges could be closed, and most businesses would need licenses in order to continue operations. The bill did not include Flynn's proposals to bar deficit financing of the war, limit annual individual income to $10,000, and tax heavily business and industry. A few members saw approval of the bill as only a first step, with a Nye committee-type bill coming later.[66]

As events unfolded, neither the McSwain bill nor the Flynn plan emerged from the legislative process. When the McSwain bill reached the Senate, Nye managed to have it sent to the munitions committee where it was rewritten to include many of Flynn's recommendations. The Military Affairs Committee reported favorably on the revised bill, which then went to the Finance Committee and on to a subcommittee chaired by Texas Senator Tom Connally. Not until the spring of 1936 did the subcommittee act, and by then Connally had emerged as a leading critic of the increasingly controversial munitions investigation. The administration offered tepid support for war profits legislation during the subcommittee hearings, and the full Senate never voted on the bill. Nye and others introduced other war profits bills over the years leading up to Pearl Harbor, but none was enacted.[67]

While the House approved the McSwain bill, Nye introduced in the Senate two neutrality resolutions sponsored by himself and Clark. The first, Senate Joint Resolution 99, denied passports to Americans traveling in war zones or on ships of warring countries. The second, Senate Joint Resolution 100, prohibited loans and credits to belligerent nations in a declared war and gave the president discretionary power to invoke the ban for undeclared wars. Raushenbush called Green at the State Department on the next day to explain that the resolutions were the individual efforts of Nye and Clark, and thus did not violate the 19 March understanding that FDR could comment upon any committee-sponsored neutrality legislation before it went to the senate. Key Pittman also contacted the State Department to assert his committee's jurisdiction over all phases of neutrality legislation. He asked the department to not provide information on the issue to the munitions committee.[68]

On 11 April, Secretary of State Hull sent his recommendations on war profits and neutrality to Roosevelt in a memorandum that covered some of the same points, using some of the same language, as the earlier 14 March letter that FDR had largely ignored when he last met with the committee. Hull expected another meeting soon and counseled Roosevelt to pursue a cautious path with the senators. He suggested that FDR not endorse any specific neutrality legislation. He offered to submit drafts of neutrality proposals to the president, but he noted, "I am not prepared to advocate this or any other specific program for legislation on this subject at this time." He likewise recommended that FDR avoid committing himself to any particular version of war profits legislation "until a great deal of further careful study has enabled the Administration to formulate some definite program for dealing with this complicated matter." Hull encouraged FDR to seek support from the senators for a State Department proposal to license arms exporters. Lastly, he suggested that Roosevelt discourage the committee from its investigation of World War I finance. "It can scarcely be maintained with reason that such a study is a necessary preliminary to the study of legislation for taking profits out of war particularly as the Committee has already prepared its Bill on that subject," he concluded.[69]

Roosevelt and Hull met with Nye, Clark, and Bone on 13 April and urged postponement of the inquiry into World War I finance. The senators again refused to retreat, but they renewed their pledge to confer with Hull before making public any documents that involved the British or French governments. Shortly afterward, Hull responded to Ambassador Lindsay's continuing concern and reaffirmed the agreement on publicity. "I realize that the arrangement which I have been able to make with the Committee does not entirely meet the desires of your Government," Hull wrote apologetically, "but I hope that it will at least serve as a practical means of obviating the embarrassments which it was felt might result from the investigation which the Committee is undertaking."[70]

While the administration struggled to gain control over the munitions committee, the 1935 hearings moved to conclusion on 26 April. The senators wanted to know more about a labor conflict at the Colt's Patent Fire Arms Company, particularly because the National Labor Board had found the company in violation of the National Industrial Recovery Act. In such instances the government normally discontinued purchases from the offending business, but Colt turned out to be a special case. Army officers testified that no other company could supply the weapons patented by Colt and that an executive order gave the military departments discretion to continue contracts with non-complying companies if the supplies were vital to national defense. Clark asked if munitions makers were "independent of the Government, so far as the enforcement of penalties of N.R.A. applying to Government contracts are concerned?" Army Captain H. U. Wagner and Lieutenant Colonel Harris believed the answer was probably yes. Soon after Clark exposed this rather large gap in NRA enforcement power, Nye adjourned the hearings for 1935.[71]

Chapter 6

From the Early Thirties to the Later Thirties: Crossing the Divide, April 1935 to January 1936

Over eight months passed before the Nye committee resumed hearings, a time during which far-reaching changes in the United States and in the world served to undermine support for the munitions inquiry. Mussolini's initiation of war against the Ethiopians provided the sharpest example of how the global situation changed from April of 1935 to January of 1936. The 1935 Neutrality Act, which received vital support from members of the munitions committee, marked a decisive step in the American approach to growing world tensions. The Second New Deal formed another facet of a new order, and Roosevelt sought support for it from progressives like Nye and Bone. More subtle intellectual and cultural signs indicated that not only had the world changed, but also the world view of many Americans. Increasing resistance to the munitions inquiry mirrored developments in the history of ideas that saw the idealistic Social Gospel abandoned in favor of Reinhold Niebuhr's realist views.

By the spring of 1935, the balance of power within the committee was firmly established. The core of the investigation consisted of Nye, Clark, and Raushenbush. Vandenberg, Bone, Pope, and Hiss played important roles from time to time, while Barbour and George participated infrequently. The core group all had unusually strong ties to pre–World War I America. Nye's love for rural, agricultural America linked him to the nineteenth century's distrust of huge, centralized sources of power in economics and politics. Clark's strong link to the past came through his father, former House Speaker Champ Clark, who had questioned U.S. entry into World War I. On Army Day in 1935, when thousands of veterans marched in Washington, Clark honored his father at a ceremony in the Capitol building. Raushenbush's world view grew out of the teachings of his father, Walter Rauschenbusch, leader of the Social Gospel movement.[1]

The progressive, Social Gospel vision had been under attack within the liberal Christian community at least since the publication in 1932 of Reinhold Niebuhr's *Moral Man and Immoral Society*. From the Social Gospel perspective, if the munitions makers would mend their ways, the primary cause of war would cease to exist. The political Left, whether Christian or not, generally agreed on this point. But Niebuhr turned such views upside down. Instead of "soulless madmen" corrupting an otherwise pacific society, the immoral society corrupted the men. Niebuhr dismissed the belief that greedy capitalists caused war. The munitions inquiry represented the Social Gospel perspective, still dominant among liberal Protestants in 1934.[2]

While the munitions committee gathered evidence and prepared for hearings during the summer of 1934, Niebuhr worked on his next book, *An Interpretation of Christian Ethics*. He was already drawing the wrath of Social Gospel Protestants, many of whom defended their ideas from the challenge of *Moral Man and Immoral Society*. In July of 1934, *Christian Century* called Niebuhr "the most conspicuous offender among American writers. . . . His use of liberalism as a whipping boy derogates from the effectiveness of his terrific attack upon the insufficiency of our Christian strategy in human society." But in spite of their efforts, Social Gospel leaders watched supporters fade away during the following months. Sherwood Eddy, an influential leader of the Young Men's Christian Association (YMCA), broke from the Social Gospel ranks and sided with Niebuhr. The *World Tomorrow*, an important voice for the pacifistic view, ceased publication in August of 1935.[3]

Niebuhr went straight into the void created by the crumbling Social Gospel with his 1935 publication of *An Interpretation of Christian Ethics*. He again criticized liberal Protestants, finding the optimism of the Social Gospel to be "the fruit of a period of history in which technical achievement and an expanding capitalism gave a momentary plausibility to the hope that human reason could create a universal social harmony in the world." For Niebuhr, the moment of hope for reason had passed. He specifically criticized the ideas of Walter Rauschenbusch and especially attacked the pacifistic approach of the Social Gospel, but he struggled with the question of when to abandon peaceful tactics. Finding that "so many contingent factors arise in any calculation of the best method of achieving equal justice that absolute standards are useless," he concluded that his argument was "tainted with the implied principle that the end justifies the means."[4]

The demise of the *World Tomorrow* opened the way for a new Christian journal, and Niebuhr launched *Radical Religion* in November of 1935. The death of the *World Tomorrow* and the birth of *Radical Religion* symbolized the shift from the old Social Gospel to Niebuhr's new "Christian realism." By the end of 1935, Niebuhr had attracted an audience large enough to claim ascendancy. Historian Richard Wightman Fox wrote that "*Radical Religion* had the power that derived from the renown of its one dominant voice. By the mid-thirties Niebuhr was by far the most formidable man of the Christian left in America. His personal charisma was unmatched; his key ideas set the terms for debate. The journal could not help but lead the way in redefining the agenda for liberal and radical Christians after 1935." Niebuhr's redefinition led away from the

Social Gospel's assumptions about the cause of war. Within the history of ideas, the Social Gospel supported the munitions committee while Niebuhr's realism undermined it. Stephen Raushenbush saw the teachings of his father become increasingly irrelevant as Niebuhr's agenda advanced.[5]

Nye likewise saw his views become increasingly irrelevant as the New Deal advanced. The vision of an American democracy securely anchored by small, independent farmers belonged to the past and had been crushed, if not obliterated, in the 1896 presidential election. Nye still believed in the small farmer and carried on the fight for rural America, an effort that did not necessarily place him at odds with Franklin Roosevelt or the New Deal legislation of 1933. FDR, too, shared a love for the myth of the small farmer. AAA policies, however, sometimes harmed the smallest farmers and made larger farmers less independent. The NRA appeared to serve the interests of larger businesses at the expense of smaller ones. These recovery programs, as well as the variety of relief programs, brought about a centralization of power in Washington.

Roosevelt's legislative agenda for the summer of 1935 called for greater centralization of economic power through the Banking Act and expansion of a centrally directed welfare state through the Social Security Act and Works Progress Administration. The Wagner Act empowered industrial workers. The Second New Deal looked forward to a centralized, industrialized, and interdependent welfare state rather than backward at a decentralized, rural nation of independent farmers and merchants. The Second New Deal aimed to decrease slightly the power of big business and increase the power of government and labor, thereby bringing into a better balance three major elements of modern industrial society. The yeoman farmer was not part of the mix, making Nye's world view increasingly obsolete by 1935.[6]

Clark, too, found his world left behind. He maintained friendships with leaders from his father's era, like Virginia Senator Carter Glass, and with younger southern Democrats like James F. Byrnes and Pat Harrison. Most of the southern Democrats supported Roosevelt's 1933 legislative agenda, but many were reluctant to support him in 1935. As FDR realized, his grip on the southern Democrats was slipping. Clark found himself associated with the old base of the party, while northern Democrats like New York Senator Robert Wagner took on higher profile roles.[7]

During the spring of 1935, in the aftermath of his World Court defeat, Roosevelt held back from publicly pressing an agenda on Congress. When the munitions hearings adjourned on 26 April, bills seemed to be lost in a legislative morass and critics wondered if Roosevelt had lost his touch or simply did not know what to do. FDR had been active behind the scenes, as when he sidetracked the munitions committee into the neutrality issue, but the political landscape presented a difficult path for the president to navigate. He sought the munitions committee's support for administration initiatives, but he came into conflict with Nye and Clark on other issues.[8]

The State Department moved forward with its plan for a national licensing system for munitions importers and exporters, a proposal that Hull had twice asked Roosevelt to recommend to the munitions committee. Joseph Green met with Raushenbush on 6 May to encourage action on the department's draft of a National Munitions Act but learned that FDR had expressed little or no concern about the issue during meetings with the committee in March and April. Raushenbush said the committee would do nothing with the bill unless the president indicated an interest. Two days later, Hull asked Roosevelt to inform the committee of presidential support for the munitions bill, and on 13 May FDR did so in a meeting with Nye, Clark, and Key Pittman. With Roosevelt's position established, Green found committee members ready to discuss the bill on 16 May. Still tender from the neutrality dispute with Pittman, they made jurisdiction the first item for consideration.[9]

While seeking Nye's support for the bill, Roosevelt became embroiled in a serious dispute with him and other progressives in the Senate over the treatment of New Mexico Senator Bronson Cutting. Cutting, a progressive Republican, had supported FDR in 1932, but the president failed to return the favor when Cutting ran for re-election in 1934. Roosevelt endorsed every other progressive Republican who had openly supported him, but he allowed his aides to work against Cutting. When Cutting narrowly won, FDR encouraged the losing Democrat, Dennis Chavez, to contest the election. After going to New Mexico to secure affidavits related to the electoral challenge, Cutting died in a plane crash en route to Washington. The Democratic governor of New Mexico then appointed Chavez to fill the seat, and when he appeared in the Senate on 20 May, Nye and four other progressive Republicans left the chamber in protest. They saw Cutting as a casualty of political assassination, with FDR pulling the trigger.[10]

Roosevelt had already taken steps to mend fences, meeting with several progressive senators on 14 May and promising to support their agenda. Nye, who had not openly endorsed Roosevelt in 1932, did not receive an invitation to the meeting. While Roosevelt worked to restore relations with the progressive Republicans, he came into conflict with Democrat Bennett Clark over the veterans' bonus. During the munitions hearings Clark often contrasted the sufferings of the doughboys against the actions of the profiteers, and his own war record lent credibility to his rhetoric. When the Senate took up the bonus issue in May, Clark led efforts to pass a bill endorsed by the American Legion. Because Roosevelt had already promised to veto a bonus bill, the ability to override formed an important consideration for the senators. The Senate passed an alternative bill with support from senators close to the administration who later voted to uphold Roosevelt's veto. Clark, who believed his bill would have gathered enough support to override the veto, was outfoxed by the president.[11]

Roosevelt delivered his veto with a lion's roar, signalling an end to his low-profile approach to Congress. The veto message came on 22 May, five days before the Supreme Court struck down the NRA in *Schechter v. United States.*

He carefully planned the message, seeking input from Samuel I. Rosenman, who had not been involved in writing FDR's speeches since the 1932 campaign, and arranging for a nationwide radio broadcast in order to make his veto the first ever heard live by millions of Americans. He delivered it in person to a joint session of Congress. It was the first time a president appeared before legislators to veto a bill. Roosevelt told the Congress that all veterans were not entitled to special treatment. Remaining true to his humanitarian feelings, Roosevelt approved of assistance for veterans disabled during the war but argued that the "healthy veteran who is unemployed owes his troubles to the depression." In vetoing the bill, FDR indicated his agreement with those who argued that many Americans had reaped undue wealth from the war. "That is true, bitterly true," he said, "but a recurrence of that type of war profiteering can and must be prevented in any future war." The president offered no specific ideas on war profits legislation, however, and the administration did not encourage congressional action.[12]

The Senate upheld the veto on the next day, but munitions committee Democrats Bone, Clark, and George joined the Republican Nye and voted to override. Pro-bonus forces worked on through the summer to pass another bill crafted to withstand a presidential veto. Roosevelt moved quickly onto new issues and announced his support for the Wagner Act on 24 May, two days after the bonus veto. On 27 May, the Supreme Court struck down the NRA. Felix Frankfurter wrote to Roosevelt on 29 May with his thoughts on the court's decision, suggesting that because of popular reaction against it "the Clarks, the Nyes and all the currents of opinion they represent will be with you in addition to the support you have today." As events turned out, however, Clark and Nye ended up opposing the president as often as not during the summer of 1935.[13]

Roosevelt's efforts to work more closely with the progressives improved his relations with Nye in the wake of the Cutting episode. The president's move toward a progressive agenda came partly because business leaders pushed him. The U.S. Chamber of Commerce took sharply critical positions toward the New Deal during its May annual meeting, actions that bothered the president and led to his meeting with the progressive senators. Faced with business opposition not only from the Du Pont's Liberty League but also from the more broadly based Chamber of Commerce, Roosevelt abandoned his faltering hope of an all-class coalition and embraced the progressive agenda.[14]

In June, Roosevelt blasted the Supreme Court's NRA decision as a "horse and buggy" interpretation of the Constitution. He then held back while Congress debated holding company legislation. The administration's proposal for a "death penalty" to abolish holding companies drew support from progressives like Nye, Pope, and Bone, but southern Democrats, including Clark and George, voted against it in another sign of the divisions between FDR and the conservatives. Conservative Democrats joined with conservative Republicans, including Vandenberg and Barbour, to oppose the death penalty clause. It squeezed through the Senate by a single vote. Shortly afterward, Roosevelt met with congressional leaders and announced a "must list" of legislation that made up the Second New Deal. FDR did not ask for an increase in income tax rates on the wealthy, an omission that led Nye to work with other senators to bring such legislation to a vote. Roosevelt quickly added a tax bill to his list, and Nye became a leader in the effort to pass it. After a rather contentious spring, Nye and Roosevelt found themselves once again standing together.[15]

In the surge of action on progressive legislation, Roosevelt had not forgotten about the munitions makers. The president succeeded in gaining Nye committee support for the licensing of armaments importers and exporters. On 5 June, Senator Pope introduced a bill for a National Munitions Act and a National Munitions Control Board. Nye, Clark, Bone, and George also sponsored the bill, which quickly received approval from the Foreign Relations Committee. Munitions issues received attention in a 14 June cabinet meeting that found administration officials linking the commercial, defense, and foreign policy aspects of the armaments industry. In Attorney General Homer Cummings's summary of the discussion, if the Europeans "stop manufacturing munitions, it would produce an unemployment problem of the first order. If they keep on manufacturing munitions, it is a fair bet that sooner or later they will find a use for them." In this analysis, the employee's need for a job, rather than the employer's greed for profits, led to war.[16]

The Nye committee kept the munitions issue in the spotlight with the publication of its first full report on 24 June. Focusing on the shipbuilding industry, the 389-page document provided few surprises for those who had followed closely the spring hearings. The report found little real competition among bidders and strongly suggested that the shipbuilders colluded in setting their bids. "If there was no collusion, there was a sympathetic understanding among the big companies of each other's desires," it read. "If there were no conversations about bidding among them, there was telepathy." The process of "protective bidding," which had been thoroughly dissected in the hearings, received considerable attention. The report charged that the companies reaped excessive profits from work on navy ships and that the cost of auditing to control the situation would be so high as to call into question the "continuance of private yards as naval contractors. They have the appearance of being expensive luxuries." The committee held back from recommending an end to private-sector construction of naval vessels, however, pending further study on the costs of government shipbuilding.[17]

The "merchants of death" made themselves conspicuous by their absence from the report. The committee went beyond the merchants of death to describe a nascent military-industrial complex of shipbuilders "allied in interest with naval suppliers and subcontractors, including the steel companies, the electrical manufacturing groups, the boiler producers, the instrument people. These spread out over the country. . . . Connections with the biggest banking interests in the Nation, as well as with the smaller ones, are involved." The U.S. Navy formed another important element of the combination, anxious to work with the companies in order to get funding for more ships. The committee saw potential dangers in the activities of a naval-shipbuilding complex that "ultimately have a bearing on our foreign policy," but did not find that shipbuilders fomented wars. The lack of a hard-hitting attack on the death merchants may have been due to Raushenbush's restraint when drafting the document. Nye wanted a tougher report.[18]

Reaction to the report came quickly in the Senate. On the day of its release, Republican L. J. Dickinson charged that Raushenbush harbored socialist views and might not be loyal to the United States. He placed in the record an article titled "In Our Socialist Times," in which Raushenbush urged government workers to use their positions to further social democratic goals. Two days later, Nye, Vandenberg, Clark, and George all spoke in defense of their chief investigator. Each proclaimed satisfaction with Raushenbush's work. His record of service during World War I was cited as evidence of his loyalty. Clark pointed out several similarities between Dickinson's speech and a letter written by William Shearer, suggesting that the shipbuilding lobbyist engineered the episode in order to discredit the committee's first report. Dickinson was not present to hear committee members respond to his attack, which he renewed later in the summer.[19]

Nye seized the opportunity to go on the attack during the 4 July holiday when he spoke to delegates at the National Education Association conference in Denver. Freed from Raushenbush's restraining hand, Nye unleashed himself. The death merchants, missing from the first report, showed up in Nye's speech. "We may expect the next war to 'make the world safe for Du Pontcracy,'" he told the educators. "We need to show in our textbooks the part played by banking and commercial interests in moving countries into war for the personal gain of individuals." Nye had little time to spend speaking in the West, however, because a tough legislative battle over neutrality had erupted to further complicate the situation in Congress. Deeply involved in the tax and neutrality bills, he quickly returned to Washington.[20]

Neutrality legislation began to pick up momentum on 26 June when the Foreign Relations Committee reported out Nye and Clark's resolutions 99 and 100. The first of these, it will be recalled, denied passports to Americans traveling in war zones or on ships of warring countries. The second prohibited loans and credits to belligerents in a declared war. Clark submitted an additional proposal, Senate Joint Resolution 120, that called for a mandatory, non-discretionary embargo on arms exports to belligerents, but the Foreign Relations Committee delayed action on this measure. The three resolutions had much in common with proposals advocated in 1934 by Charles Warren, an international lawyer and former assistant attorney general. The State Department studied Warren's program and accepted many of his recommendations for tight controls on trade with all belligerents, but with one important change. The department's draft of neutrality legislation gave the president power to apply the restrictions, although not in a discriminatory manner. Trade restrictions could be applied to all belligerents or to none. The administration could not form a consensus on neutrality, however, and some of the State Department's own officials objected to the draft. The Navy Department also voiced disagreement.[21]

Unable to devise an acceptable neutrality bill, Hull preferred to do nothing on the issue in 1935. The Foreign Relations Committee's action upset his plans and left him particularly angry because he believed Pittman had promised to stop the Nye and Clark resolutions. The administration launched a campaign against resolutions 99 and 100, and Norman Davis of the State Department met with Pittman on 27 June. At Davis's urging, Pittman agreed to stop the resolutions. Hull believed Pittman to be unreliable, however, so he met with the senator and also brought the president into the controversy. FDR met with Pittman on 29 June and underscored the importance of stopping the resolutions. As the Nye and Clark proposals in many ways represented the neutrality views of William Jennings Bryan during World War I, views supported by Roosevelt in his 19 March meeting with committee members, the president's opposition to the resolutions in late June indicated some fluidity in his attitudes.[22]

Acting as individual senators in sponsoring the resolutions, rather than in the name of the committee, Nye and Clark obscured the connections between the munitions investigation and neutrality legislation. With Raushenbush active behind the scenes, however, the core group of the munitions committee—Nye, Clark, and Raushenbush—formed a nucleus of energy in the neutrality debate. Without their involvement, the neutrality legislation of 1935 would have been different or may not have been enacted. Some historians have speculated that the committee's hearings contributed to a national mood in favor of strong neutrality legislation, but the interaction between public opinion and the munitions investigation cannot be definitively established. It seems fair to assume that headlines from the hearings did little to increase the desire of Americans to involve themselves with the world's problems. With the hearings showing European leaders to be feculent and South American and Asian officials to be corrupt, the world according to the munitions committee failed to merit American sacrifice.[23]

In addition to differences over neutrality policy, the planned investigation into World War I finance continued to create problems between the committee and the administration. Hull and Roosevelt failed to dissuade the committee from the inquiry, and the prospect of hearings continued to concern the British and the French. In late May, Italian officials joined their former Entente partners in expressing concern but said that nothing in the record would embarrass them. Some Americans were not so sure about the investigation's impact on their country. Frank L. Polk, a former State Department official, wrote to Undersecretary of State William Phillips on 1 July that "this investigation is taking a line which will have to lead, if pursued, to attacking the motives of President Wilson." Phillips's response indicated the department's attitude. "This investigation is indeed very strange and, as you know, there have been many problems arising from it," he wrote.[24]

The banking investigation concerned not only the former Allied governments but also American exporters, as Roosevelt learned in a 6 July letter from Thomas J. Watson, president of International Business Machines (IBM). Although FDR had parted ways with most business leaders, he had reason to listen to Watson. A member of the U.S. Chamber of Commerce, Watson immediately wrote to the president after the group's May meeting to pronounce his disagreement with the attacks on the administration. He was one of a few business leaders who supported the New Deal. Writing from Berlin, Watson believed that the banking inquiry would interfere with U.S. export opportunities. Public hearings would remind the Central Powers of how the Americans assisted the Allied Powers, "with the result as I see it of a general loss of confidence and good will."[25]

The banking investigation probably seemed to be too remote for FDR to pay much attention while in the midst of enacting the Second New Deal. War profits legislation formed a more immediate concern, and Roosevelt had promised action on this issue during his dramatic veto of the bonus. By July, a bill reflecting the munitions committee's proposals was under consideration in the Senate. Nye met with the president on 12 July, seeking support to move the bill through the Finance Committee, but received no definite promises. At a 24 July press conference, Roosevelt was asked if war profits legislation would emerge from the current session of Congress. "I don't know," he answered, showing little commitment to the issue. The Nye committee kept war profits on the public agenda with publication of its second report, submitted to the Senate on 20 August, too late in the session to spur action in 1935.[26]

A group of issues largely generated by the committee—war profits, the banking investigation, and neutrality—occupied the administration during the critical months of July and August, as the political battle for the Second New Deal reached a climax. The neutrality issue became the most troublesome for Roosevelt and nearly caused a filibuster that threatened holding company legislation, the progressive tax bill, and reform of the coal mining industry.

The confrontation with the administration over the Nye-Clark neutrality resolutions escalated in July hearings before Pittman's Foreign Relations Committee. Prior to the hearings, Hull and Roosevelt again asked Pittman to stop the resolutions. The chairman refused to commit himself, and instead he invited Hull to speak before the committee. After listening to Hull and Assistant Secretary of State R. Walton Moore on 10 July, the full committee voted to recall the resolutions for further consideration. Nye and Clark presented their arguments in a letter to Pittman on the same day and focused directly on the issue dividing them from the State Department. "These resolutions do not leave it optional with the President to impose those controls, for the reason that the policy must be fixed before a war breaks out," they wrote. "Once a large traffic in munitions has grown up, it is asking a great deal of a President to act in opposition to it." They wanted mandatory legislation.[27]

On the following day, 11 July, the Senate sent the resolutions back to the Foreign Relations Committee. Nye and Clark refused to surrender, however, and quickly organized a campaign to promote their views. Munitions committee member Homer Bone and progressive senators George Norris and Robert La Follette agreed to speak on the floor for at least an hour each day in favor of mandatory neutrality legislation. FDR did not want the neutrality issue to stall action on the New Deal bills, and Pittman tried to help the president by working out a compromise with Nye and Clark. On 17 July, the Foreign Relations Committee established a special subcommittee to work with State Department officials and draft a comprehensive neutrality resolution. In exchange, Nye called off the speaking campaign. He and Clark were not official members of the special subcommittee, but they involved themselves in its activities.[28]

Roosevelt, meanwhile, directed the State Department to seek a discretionary arms embargo, a policy opposed by Nye and Clark as well as several members of the Foreign Relations Committee. FDR told cabinet members that he hoped to trade his support of neutrality legislation for Senate acceptance of executive discretion in its application. The president pursued no fixed course on the issue, however, and behaved like the quarterback he once compared himself with who would not call the next play until he learned the results of the last one. In this case, his play for discretionary neutrality did not come up a winner.[29]

On 30 July, in a meeting attended by Nye and Clark, the special subcommittee heard from Undersecretary of State Phillips, and on the next day Pittman received a State Department draft of proposed legislation. In a covering letter, Phillips noted that three of the eight sections in the draft dealt with issues pertinent to the Nye and Clark resolutions. The essential conflict was with Clark's mandatory arms embargo. The State Department draft called for presidential discretion in applying the embargo. Regarding the other Nye and Clark resolutions, covering travel in war zones and loans to belligerents, the State Department draft was not in substantial disagreement. In order to force the issue, Nye threatened to delay passage of the National Munitions Act favored by the administration and co-sponsored by himself. He said he would try to amend mandatory neutrality measures to the munitions bill. Perhaps spurred to action by Nye's warning, the subcommittee on 7 August voted in favor of a mandatory arms embargo.[30]

During the critical days of early August, Senator Dickinson renewed his attack on the munitions committee and again accused Stephen Raushenbush of holding socialist views subversive to American interests. Speaking to the Senate on 5 August, he also criticized Dorothy Detzer. Senator Vandenberg again defended the investigation, saying that senators should take the committee's work at face value. "If that be treason make the most of it. If it be socialism, make the most of it," he concluded. Senator Clark also spoke and accused Dickinson of trying "to get under the wings of the munitions manufacturers and become a candidate of the American Liberty League for the Presidency of the United States." Detzer thought Vandenberg had taken the right approach, but Clark's counterattack probably better served FDR's purposes. Dickinson formed a chorus of one in his Senate attacks, and as a Republican he carried little weight in the 74th Congress.

Only when Senate Democrats became critical would the investigation be in trouble.[31]

During the remainder of August, a complicated dance involving the administration, the Foreign Relations Committee, and munitions committee members culminated in the Neutrality Act of 1935. On 14 August, the Foreign Relations Committee divided over the mandatory or discretionary question and directed the subcommittee to prepare a compromise bill by 21 August. Joseph Green believed this action killed neutrality legislation for 1935, but internationalist leaders outside of the administration persuaded State Department officials to press for a discretionary arms embargo to last until January of 1936. The temporary embargo could be useful if, as looked likely, Italy commenced war against Ethiopia. Roosevelt approved the idea, but he instructed the department to acquiesce if Pittman demanded that the embargo be made mandatory. The chairman had already decided to prepare his own bill with a mandatory arms embargo, but he did not expect the Senate to act before adjournment. The State Department then turned to the House of Representatives, where Foreign Affairs chairman Samuel McReynolds agreed to introduce a discretionary neutrality bill. He, too, expected no action in 1935.[32]

The approach of war in Ethiopia forced Congress to act. On 19 August, newspapers reported that the Ethiopian crisis had reached a critical stage with the breakup of talks between Italy, Britain, and France. War was imminent. Next to the war stories appeared a statement released by Nye and Clark that called for quick enactment of neutrality legislation. The Foreign Relations Committee met on the same day and voted eleven to three in favor of a mandatory arms embargo to be included in a bill restricting travel in war zones and loans to belligerents. The administration also acted, with Hull asking Pittman for a temporary and discretionary embargo. The Foreign Relations chair did not respond favorably. "I will introduce it on behalf of the administration without comment," he said, "but he will be licked sure as hell." Pittman underscored his opinion in a subsequent letter to Roosevelt's secretary, Stephen Early, and added off the record, "I have been trying to harmonize things and get away from that fool Munitions Committee." Informed of Pittman's opposition, FDR decided not to press for discretionary neutrality legislation in 1935.[33]

Nye and Clark stayed their course and stepped up pressure for a mandatory neutrality law. Garnering support from fellow munitions committee members Bone and Vandenberg, they pulled out their most powerful weapon, the filibuster. Bone initiated the move on 20 August and announced to the Senate that he was ready to stay in session for the rest of the year in order to pass neutrality legislation. He delivered a lengthy speech, which, with occasional interjections by Nye, Clark, and others, filled eighteen pages of the *Congressional Record*. "I do not want my boy to die to further enrich some American millionaire, whose conception of patriotism is the dollar sign," Bone said. Soon after the filibuster started, Pittman brought a neutrality bill to the floor. It included the mandatory arms embargo, a ban on munitions shipments in U.S. vessels, restrictions on travel aboard belligerent nation's ships, and several provisions from the bill for a National Munitions Act. A ban on loans and credits was not included. On 21 August, the Senate passed Pittman's bill by unanimous consent. Four of the seven members of the munitions committee played important roles in the Senate's neutrality denouement. Pope, chief sponsor of the National Munitions Act, was in Europe when the final votes came.[34]

That evening, Hull and McReynolds met with FDR in the White House and discussed the administration's final moves. Although earlier in the day Roosevelt said that he opposed the mandatory provisions, by nightfall he decided to accept them if they were made temporary. FDR instructed McReynolds to amend the bill in the House so that the arms embargo provision lasted for only six months. The House passed McReynolds's amendment on 23 August, and the Senate approved it on the next day. Although displeased, Hull did not recommend a presidential veto. FDR signed the bill on 31 August and used the occasion to criticize the mandatory embargo. "It is conceivable that situations may arise in which the wholly inflexible provisions of Section I [the arms embargo] of this act might have exactly the opposite effect from that which was intended," he said. "In other words, the inflexible provisions might drag us into war instead of keeping us out."[35]

While the administration struggled through August to pass FDR's "must list" of legislation, the munitions committee struggled to gain access to banking records for what several members believed to be the lead item on its "must list" of topics to study. Investigators expected foreign governments, powerful banks, and large companies to resist the inquiry, and the morale of committee personnel suffered when it appeared that some secrets of the armaments industry would never come to light. "These companies all know that our money is low," Donald Wemple wrote to Raushenbush on 10 August, "and I presume they feel that the more trouble and annoyance they can cause us and the longer they can drag this thing out the less possibility there is of much of anything happening." J. P. Morgan and Company put up a spirited defense of its records, retaining former Democratic presidential candidate John W. Davis as legal counsel. Davis argued that information from the bank accounts of foreign governments could not be released without permission from the governments involved. An unsigned munitions committee memorandum from 13 August noted that "it is common talk among the munitions makers that the Committee will never be allowed to see this material."[36]

The committee's effort to get access to the diaries of former Secretary of State Robert Lansing also caused problems. Lansing headed the State Department from 1915 to 1920, crucial years for investigation of World War I finance. His diaries had been placed in the Library of Congress in 1929, with a stipulation that they be closed from public use for twenty years. The committee subpoenaed the diaries over the objections of Library of Congress officials and Lansing's nephews, Allen and John Foster Dulles. In a 12 August meeting, Joseph Green's description of the negative feelings department officials held toward the committee's action surprised Raushenbush.[37]

Later in August, the committee finally secured access to the banking records. The ambassadors of Britain and France informed Hull on 12 August that their governments wanted the records from J. P. Morgan and Company turned over to him. Green explained the offer to the committee on the following day, and the five senators present voted unanimously to accept the procedure. Hull informed the British and French that he would accept custody of the documents, which arrived at the State Department on 19 August. The committee then withdrew a subpoena issued five days before and set its investigators to work. The opposition of Hull, Roosevelt, the British and French governments, a former Democratic candidate for president of the United States, and J. P. Morgan and Company did not stop the committee from winning an eight-month battle to study the World War I financial records.[38]

With access to the banking records secured and mandatory neutrality imminent, Nye forged ahead on war profits and submitted the committee's second report to the Senate on 20 August. It endorsed the Flynn-plan approach to control of war profits and accepted the unanimous recommendation of the committee's staff that three Constitutional amendments would be necessary in order to have a chance for effective legislation. The first allowed Congress, rather than the courts, to determine levels of compensation for property commandeered by the government for use in wartime. The second proposed allowing "Congress to tax for war-profits control on such bases of investment or fixed capital assets as it finds to be fair and just regardless of the possible inequality among taxpayers." A third amendment provided for taxing the interest on tax-exempt bonds during a time of national emergency.[39]

Bernard Baruch, who represented the administration's point of view during the spring hearings, had called for price ceilings and excess-profits taxes rather than the more radical Flynn plan. The report rejected his proposals and depicted Baruch as a tax-evading profiteer, noting that one of his mining companies had cost only $250,000 to buy but had later been allowed a depletion value of nearly $39 million. In another case, a mining company one-quarter owned by Baruch "asserted that all its liquid assets amounted to only $100,000, although in its sworn income-tax return for that same year (1923) the company valued its ores alone at $5,000,000." Like the Du Ponts and others discussed in the report, Baruch found himself criticized as a tax evader. The report showed that Albert Du Pont made $29 million dollars from 1921 through 1926 and paid no federal income taxes.[40]

The 164-page report included several accounts of egregious profiteering from World War I and suggested near extortion on the part of many industrial leaders. The Du Pont's Old Hickory plant received another round of attention, with the report finding that the "Government had no real alternative to accepting the terms of the du Ponts." The steel and copper producers were likewise able to dictate terms for the purchase of their materials. The case of Lukens Iron & Steel

Company merited special attention. Although the company claimed it could barely make money at the government's prices, it actually earned millions in profits and bought $6 million worth of its own stock in 1918. Bethlehem Steel Corporation paid less taxes under the World War I excess profits tax than it had before, even though profits and dividends payments increased.[41]

The report documented what most Americans already knew, that some citizens had profiteered during the war, but the committee found itself unable to provide reassuring remedies. "We must guard against a blind belief that all profiteering can be ended by proposals for war-time taxes and industrial control," the report concluded. Even if the Flynn plan and the Constitutional amendments became law, the committee suspected that war profiteering would persist. They found that "costs are in the last analysis matters of opinion and are not susceptible of scientific determination" and recognized that "profits taxes depend finally upon records kept by the taxpayer and known in their entirety only by him." If only the companies had the information to know, and if even they could not definitively establish a basic item like cost, then the success of war profit laws would depend upon the willingness of the taxpayer to cooperate.[42]

After Congress adjourned on 26 August, Nye set out on a speaking tour to publicize his views on war profits and neutrality. He looked toward 1936, when Congress would reconvene and the six-month arms embargo would lapse. He wanted to build public support for war profits legislation and generate interest in the upcoming banking hearings. On 5 September, Nye tied the munitions makers to the financiers in a radio address carried by National Broadcasting Corporation. Focusing on World War I, he noted that "70 per cent of the business done with the Allies by Du Ponts was negotiated through the Morgan firm. . . . With our economic structure completely broken down by the last such war; with death, despair, debt and destruction our reward for participation in it, how can we consider any problem more important than that of keeping out of another war?" Nye spoke on midwestern university campuses in October, and in December he addressed audiences in New Orleans and Los Angeles. He continually called the Du Ponts "400 per cent patriots," referring to their World War I profits.[43]

Roosevelt also looked toward 1936. He would be a candidate for re-election, and politics never strayed far from his mind. One troublesome element was tragically removed when an assassin killed Huey Long on 8 September. A vocal critic of the New Deal, Long had been viewed as a possible third-party candidate who could mount a serious challenge to the president from the political Left. Some observers, including Roosevelt, imagined Nye in a similar role. The resumption of hearings in January would again put the spotlight on the progressive North Dakotan, increasing his visibility as a possible candidate. The hearings would delve into the workings of the Wilson administration, in which FDR had served as assistant secretary of the navy, and probably criticize the only other Democratic president of the twentieth century. Additionally, Roosevelt would have to fight Nye and Clark if he wanted a discretionary neutrality law.

He might well lose the battle and start the election year with a legislative defeat. While attacks on the Du Ponts served Roosevelt by tarnishing the Liberty League, the negatives of the Nye committee outweighed its merits by 1936.[44]

The key roles played by Nye and others from the munitions committee in passing the Neutrality Act led FDR to more strongly link the arms investigation to isolationism, as revealed in a 17 September letter to Edward House. "You may be interested to know that some of the Congressmen and Senators who are suggesting wild-eyed measures to keep us out of war are now declaring that you and Lansing and Page forced Wilson into the war!" he wrote. Roosevelt surely had Nye in mind, and probably Clark, Bone, and Vandenberg as well. "I had a talk with them," he continued, "explained that I was in Washington myself the whole of that period, that none of them were there and that their historical analysis was wholly inaccurate and that history yet to be written would prove my point. The trouble is that they belong to the very large and perhaps increasing school of thought which holds that we can and should withdraw wholly within ourselves and cut off all but the most perfunctory relationships with other nations. They imagine that if the civilization of Europe is about to destroy itself through internal strife, it might just as well go ahead and do it and that the United States can stand idly by."[45]

Just over two weeks later, Mussolini ordered Italian forces into battle against Ethiopia. Tensions that had been building for months erupted into war, and the 1935 Neutrality Act guided the U.S. response. On 4 October, Roosevelt invoked the arms embargo provision against both belligerents. In its first test, the embargo worked against the aggressor because Ethiopia had no modern military forces and no means to import arms from the United States. Emperor Haile Selassie's mobilization orders underscored the point: "When this order is received all men and all boys able to carry a spear will go to Addis Ababa." Only Italy would suffer from the American ban on arms exports, but a related question that had already been considered in the munitions hearings arose quickly. What about strategic raw materials that fed the war machine? In particular, a U.S. embargo on oil exports could have crippled Italian forces, but FDR did not attempt to legally embargo oil, copper, or other strategic materials. Certainly an oil embargo would have gained little favor with key congressional Democrats from Texas as Roosevelt looked to the 1936 election. Perhaps more importantly, France refused to endorse a League of Nations oil embargo. French leaders wanted to preserve relations with Mussolini, who was not yet allied with Hitler.[46]

After the fighting began in Ethiopia, others joined FDR in finding connections between the munitions inquiry and isolationism. Felix Frankfurter wrote to Henry Stimson in late October and made the point. "And the testimony regarding war profits before the Nye Committee has served as a permeating ferment," he wrote, "of which the over simplified rationale—deeply embedded in the consciousness of the American people—is that at all hazards we must keep out of a European war." Stimson, a vocal advocate of internationalist policies, shared Frankfurter's concerns. The upcoming investigation into World War I finance particularly galled the former secretary of war. He denounced the belief that "the war was a shabby disgraceful act engineered by selfish bankers for the saving of their own investments."[47]

Inside of the administration, discussion of the Italian-Ethiopian War occupied the cabinet during meetings in October, November, and December. The world situation seemed to worsen as winter approached, and on 20 December the cabinet discussed the stockpiling of imported strategic materials. One week later, FDR shared his concerns about the international situation with the cabinet, talking of German and Japanese designs on the Soviet Union and of a possible deal between Great Britain and Nazi Germany. Roosevelt wanted neutrality legislation that would give him the power to decide how much of what materials could be exported to belligerents.[48]

The president met on 31 December with Hull, Pittman, McReynolds, and others to work out the details for administration-backed neutrality legislation. The State Department wanted an exception to the arms embargo for Central and South American countries in the event of war between them and European nations, but it retreated before objections from Pittman. He feared the proposal would raise opposition from the "extreme pacifists" and become an issue with "the Nye political committee, with the attendant annoyances and delays."[49]

Nye also prepared for the next round over neutrality, authorizing Raushenbush on 10 December to draft proposals for the next session of Congress. Raushenbush prepared draft legislation and discussed it with Joseph Green and R. Walton Moore in mid-December. Rather than giving the president discretion over which materials could be exported in what amounts, Raushenbush established quotas to apply evenly to all nations involved in war. He proposed a ban on loans to belligerents, a part of the Nye and Clark package that had not been included in the 1935 Neutrality Act. After Congress reconvened, Nye and Clark introduced the neutrality resolution in the Senate.[50]

The munitions committee also prepared for the banking inquiry, which was planned to build support for the neutrality proposals. Nye's speaking tour generated the headlines, but behind the scenes Raushenbush and the investigators sifted through the evidence and organized for the hearings. The State Department knew what materials the committee planned to use because of the agreements made with Hull concerning the use of documents. Former World Court Justice John Bassett Moore studied the requests made by investigators and concluded in November that the committee "intended to show that the policies of the United States . . . were as a matter of fact unfortunate and led to the entry of the United States in the war." Raushenbush pushed his staff as January approached. He focused on the extensiveness of the military establishment, as he had done in the committee's first report, rather than on the arms merchants who figured more prominently into Nye's public speeches. Raushenbush wanted "to show the terrific influence of the munitions companies when all their ramifications are considered." By mid-month he had hearings set to run from 7 January through

8 February, which he projected to be the final day of munitions committee hearings.[51]

The 1936 hearings would take place in a world far different from that of the earlier hearings. The Second New Deal had decisively put the United States on the road to the welfare state, breaking from the individualistic political philosophies of earlier American history. The rural-oriented ideology of Gerald Nye, based on the independent small farmer, had become an anachronism. With 1936 being an election year, the partisan political landscape looked quite different than it had eight months earlier. Nye loomed as one of Roosevelt's most visible critics from the Left. Vandenberg stood as a possible opponent from the Right. Mussolini's armed aggression in Ethiopia had radically altered the international balance and increased the threat of European war. By October, Roosevelt and others close to him linked isolationism with the activities of the munitions committee, a connection they had earlier not found so noteworthy. In the history of ideas, Reinhold Niebuhr's Christian realism better reflected the new order than did the Social Gospel of Stephen Raushenbush's father. By the end of 1935, Niebuhr was writing and editing his second issue of *Radical Religion*.

Many other events marked a change of the guard between April and December of 1935, hinting at some of the ways in which the world would be different when hearings resumed. In May, Babe Ruth retired from professional baseball after hitting three home runs in his final game. Jane Addams, probably America's best known pacifist and a mentor to Dorothy Detzer, passed away in June. In August, humorist and political commentator Will Rogers died in a plane crash. In September, an assassin murdered Huey Long. In October, the masses of "unskilled" assembly-line workers took a long step toward collective bargaining and broke from the American Federation of Labor to form the Committee (later Congress) of Industrial Organizations. In November and December, Charlie Chaplin edited his final silent feature film. Set to open in February, it carried the title *Modern Times*. When the munitions committee reopened hearings in January of 1936, it operated in an intellectual, cultural, and political context much different from the one which had supported it through its earlier history.[52]

Chapter 7

The Munitions Committee in a New World: Examining World War I Finance, January 1936 to February 1936

"Were I today to deliver an inaugural address to the people of the United States, I could not limit my comments on world affairs to one paragraph," FDR announced in his 1936 State of the Union speech on 3 January. Roosevelt described the new world of the later 1930s to the American people in the first prime-time broadcast of a presidential message to Congress. He noted "trends toward aggression, of increasing armaments, of shortening tempers" that dampened his usual optimism. He outlined the nation's neutrality policy and reassured Americans of his commitment to keeping the United States out of war. He described the administration's effort "to discourage the use by belligerent nations of any and all American products calculated to facilitate the prosecution of a war in quantities over and above our normal exports of them in time of peace." The last issue formed a focal point in the 1936 neutrality debate, and munitions committee members again played a major role.[1]

After speaking for nearly half an hour on world affairs, FDR shifted his focus to the domestic scene and defined the upcoming election. He presented a simple framework of "a people's government" facing the "hatred of entrenched greed." He spoke of an "economic autocracy" that wanted "power for themselves, enslavement for the public." The president did not name the economic autocrats, but he probably included the Du Ponts and the Morgan banking interests among their numbers.[2]

By 1936, the administration and the munitions committee had little in common other than a shared enmity for the Du Ponts. In early January, the administration announced an inquiry into possible tax fraud on financial deals between Pierre Du Pont and John Raskob. Raushenbush subsequently wrote to Nye with information on Du Pont tax evasion and included a report that one person involved had committed suicide. The White House had its own information and took its own actions. In a 24 January cabinet meeting, Roosevelt questioned the patriotism of Du Pont–controlled General Motors after noting that the company was selling dollars short. Three days later, Hull completed a draft speech for possible use by Senator Joseph Robinson, writing that "the Liberty League is to all practical intents and purposes the du Pont League." In 1936, Roosevelt would again see the munitions committee scour his political opponents, but the enemy of his enemies would not necessarily be his friend. From the left-wing edge of the political mainstream, the Nye committee clashed with the administration on the veteran's bonus, nationalization of the munitions industry, and neutrality.[3]

The clash over the bonus issue came first, and most senators on the munitions committee favored it against White House opposition. Public scrutiny of the war's beneficial effects for arms makers and bankers fanned the resentments of veterans and their loved ones against those who stayed home and profited from the war, complicating Roosevelt's position. A new bonus bill passed the House and Senate in mid-January. Of the munitions committee members, only Vandenberg voted against the bonus. The president, perhaps tired of the matter and resigned to defeat, refused to discuss the bonus issue in the cabinet. He issued a perfunctory veto message, after which Congress voted to override and enact the bonus. Roosevelt's meek acquiescence, following his fiery veto of similar legislation a half-year earlier, puzzled some observers. FDR may have wanted the payments to begin in 1936, brightening the spirits of veterans and perhaps stimulating the economy in an election year.[4]

On 7 January, the debate over America's role in the increasingly tense world picked up momentum in the elective branches of the government. In the House of Representatives, the Foreign Affairs Committee opened its hearings on neutrality legislation. In the Senate, J. P. Morgan and Thomas W. Lamont, partners in J. P. Morgan and Company, were sworn in to begin testimony before the munitions committee. Joining them was Frank A. Vanderlip, president of National City Bank during the World War I years. In the executive branch, the pessimism expressed by FDR in his State of the Union address deepened. Secretary of State Hull wrote to Norman Davis, the American representative to naval disarmament talks in London, to express his belief that the negotiations were going nowhere due to Japanese intransigence. Hull had secured Roosevelt's approval of the letter prior to sending it.[5]

In such an atmosphere, the committee started its probe into the wartime actions of Wall Street bankers. Some observers accused the investigation of publicity seeking. *Time* magazine predicted an effort "to dig up enough headline scandals to win committee members headline credit with headline-reading voters." One week later, *Time* found the Morgan hearings designed to "bring the nation's peace passion once more to white heat and whoop Neutrality through Congress." The Roosevelt administration said little in public about the hearings, but the inquiry did not set well with the State Department. Joseph Green wrote on 9 January that Hull and R. Walton Moore were "furious against the Senator and his Committee" and commented that Nye was "having his Roman holiday and the circus proceeds." The president remained quiet, however, and perhaps enjoyed the assault on the economic autocrats whose hatred he believed he had earned.[6]

In the hearing room, the senators quickly moved into their investigation of America's wartime financial ties to England and France. J. P. Morgan freely admitted favoring the Allies before 1917 because "world domination by Germany would bring complete destruction of the liberties of the rest of the world." But it was not the activities of bankers that drew the United States into war. "Germany drove the United States into the war," he concluded in his unrevisionist history, citing submarine warfare and the Zimmermann Note as German actions forcing America to fight. Raushenbush countered, citing Ray Stannard Baker's *The Life and Letters of Woodrow Wilson*, which argued that trade in war supplies drew the United States toward the fight. Thomas W. Lamont cited former German ambassador Johann von Bernstorff, who concluded that submarine warfare forced the United States into the war. Nye mediated the battle of the historians, asking for all to withhold judgment until the exhibits had been introduced and discussed, and "then after that record has been completed, we can all have our say as to what the real cause was."[7]

The committee then examined the power held by Morgan and Company during the period of American neutrality, when the bank acted as a commercial agent for the British and handled almost all munitions orders placed in the United States. The record showed that the bank coveted the agency, "which would serve an excellent purpose and be profitable to us. . . . Great deal of business going on all around us, much of which should be going through us." Morgan and Company became the financial headquarters for a rapidly growing transatlantic war business, using bank credits to facilitate purchases. The Wilson administration made no effort to prevent the use of credits but did oppose loans to belligerent nations.[8]

Allied buying stimulated the American economy, but by the summer of 1915 some newspapers questioned the ability of the Allies to meet their obligations on bank credits. J. P. Morgan wondered whether the reports resulted from "German propaganda or simply by usual idiocy of newspaper men," but either way they complicated his plans to meet British needs by selling bonds to the public. The booming war trade also affected the executive branch. In August, Secretary of the Treasury William Gibbs McAdoo urged Wilson to reverse former Secretary of State Bryan's policy against loans. "To maintain our prosperity, we must finance it," he noted. "Otherwise it may stop and that would be disastrous."[9]

Senator Clark, playing a high-profile role as he had in earlier hearings, argued that Morgan and Company used financial clout to precipitate a foreign exchange crisis and force Wilson's hand in 1915. The bank drew on British government funds to buy sterling notes that accumulated in the United States as a result of the large trade surplus with Britain. This procedure aimed to maintain the value of British currency relative to the dollar, but in mid-August the bank suspended purchases and the value of sterling dropped. Weak sterling made it more expensive for the British to buy American products and threatened U.S. exporters, prompting the governor of the Federal Reserve Board to write to Secretary of State Robert Lansing about the problem on 24 August. Lansing wrote to Wilson the next day, arguing that the "question of exchange and the large debts which result from purchases by belligerent governments require some method of funding these debts in this country." Wilson decided to drop opposition to the loans. Clark saw a "very intriguing coincidence" in the circumstances, noting that "11 days after support had been withdrawn from the exchange market, the President of the United States had approved this change in our neutrality policy."[10]

When J. P. Morgan denied that his bank initiated the drop in sterling value, Clark suggested British responsibility. Morgan and Company had been willing to extend more credit if the British agreed to ship gold to the United States and make collateral available. George Whitney, a Morgan partner, testified that the British had the resources to secure more credit but decided not to use them. From Clark's perspective, it did not matter whether the bank or the British made the decision to suspend sterling purchases. He still saw intriguing coincidences and believed that the British "wanted to use our money instead of using their own, and that this exchange situation was used for that purpose."[11]

After Wilson decided not to object to loans, Morgan and Company organized a $500 million Anglo-French loan in September of 1915. The large undertaking required the bank to find willing investors, and munitions makers led the list of likely candidates. Morgan and Company urged British buyers to contact American munitions companies about the loan. It wanted the buyers to stress that the "Anglo-French external loan is so vital to our American trade that we hope you will join in underwriting and assist in every way possible." American manufacturers underwrote nearly $90 million of the Anglo-French bonds, with over half the amount coming from Du Pont interests. Clark saw Morgan and Company threatening the munitions makers with loss of demand, "bringing pressure on people in this country in filling supplies, to get them to participate in the underwriting of the loan." Morgan and Lamont denied using such tactics.[12]

Underwriters quickly accepted the Anglo-French bonds, but when public interest proved disappointing, Morgan and Company organized a network of distributors to promote the bonds and expand the existing market for securities. Clark asked if the effort "was really the entering wedge of that great development in the distribution of securities of all kinds to the American people." Whitney agreed, saying that "it was the first perhaps large step in opening the markets of this country" and led the United States from being a debtor nation to a creditor nation. Wilson's decision not to oppose the loan opened the way for the middle class to become holders of securities, and widening public investment carried across the twentieth century to the mutual funds of the 1990s.[13]

Some committee members suspected that Morgan and Company used its lending power to coerce the British government as well as the American government. When the British proposed cancelling $55 million in rifle orders because of late delivery, Morgan and Company, which had invested in rifle manufacturing, protested. Bank officials noted that such an action would make other munitions makers pause before taking further orders and, perhaps more ominously, "might go so far as to affect adversely further British financial operations in this country." Morgan officials believed that British needs would place "absolutely unprecedented calls upon the credit institutions of the country—the stupendous requirements not being known to any but ourselves," but Morgan and Lamont denied any misuse of their financial leverage to force Britain to buy unwanted munitions. "If you were the agent for a gentleman and you saw him getting into a position which you thought might increase his difficulties, would you not show him a way out if you could?" Morgan asked.[14]

Some U.S. officials believed that American financial power could prod the British. In late 1916, Edward House, Wilson's personal advisor, and Frank Polk, a State Department official, discussed the possibility of restricting the loans, or threatening to do so, in order to pressure the British to respect American neutral rights. Ultimately, the financiers may even have had the power to stop the war. A November 1916 letter from banker Paul M. Warburg to the Federal Reserve Board suggested that stopping the loans would hasten the end of the war.[15]

Many more loans followed the Anglo-French loan of 1915. The need to sell foreign government bonds overwhelmed the marketing system and pushed the banking system to its limits. J. P. Morgan saw only one way to motivate the financial community to handle the situation. "There is no method of instilling this spirit except by means of profit," he noted in October of 1916. One month later, the Federal Reserve Board greatly complicated his problem by warning member banks to avoid investment in foreign treasury bills. In an effort to counter the board's action, Morgan advised the British to reduce their buying "without rancor but explicitly with possible good effect upon American attitude." Thousands of unemployed Americans would be the means for producing Morgan's "good effect," a connection not missed by the committee.[16]

Before any crisis developed, the Federal Reserve Bank of New York opened an account with the Bank of England in order to get dollars across the Atlantic. Federal Reserve Governor Benjamin Strong believed that the Allies' demands would quickly outstrip their ability to pay and that "the interests of our banks and our exporters may require that the arrangements with the Bank of England be put into operation this fall." Committee members questioned the implications for neutrality of such an account, and at the time the State Department withheld judgment on the proposal until after the election. In December of 1916, the Federal Reserve Bank of New York received authorization to use the account and paid off $52 million of bank credit in exchange for gold.[17]

The government took many other steps to nurture and protect the growing export trade, including bailouts for investors who held foreign securities of suspect value. Federal Reserve regulations were changed in 1915 to allow the Treasury Department to pay for over $100 million in acceptances from the Bank of France, in spite of the fact that the acceptances did not meet normal standards.

Even J. P. Morgan learned from the testimony. "I did not realize that that was undertaken," he said. "I do not agree with that as a good policy." Raushenbush and committee investigator Laurence Brown intimated that information had been withheld from Federal Reserve officials, who only later learned that the acceptances more nearly resembled loans. Raushenbush concluded that "the United States Treasury had to bail out the people who held them," protecting the interests of investors at the risk of American taxpayers.[18]

Raushenbush and Brown also showed that some U.S. government loans to the Allies, made after American entry into the war, paid off previous loans from private banks. The process started quickly, with Britain in April of 1917 using one-half of a $200 million advance from the U.S. Treasury to pay down a demand loan with Morgan and Company. Brown showed that the bank expected the demand loan to be liquidated by "advances to the amount of $400,000,000 to be made to the British Government by the American Government and paid to us for that specific purpose." When the U.S. Treasury balked at using government credit to pay off loans made by private banks prior to U.S. entry into the war, Morgan and Company officials found themselves "greatly distressed" and informed the British that actions would have to be taken for immediate repayment.[19]

In another case, the Italian government could not meet obligations on a $25 million loan made by Lee, Higginson and Company prior to U.S. entry into the war. The Treasury Department, in spite of its stated opposition to such actions, advanced funds for the loan. Albert Rathbone, a former official in the department, viewed the action as part of the war effort. A default on debts owed to Americans by Italy or any ally would have given "the greatest encouragement to the enemy." Raushenbush and Nye saw the Treasury Department routinely rescuing the private bankers, but Rathbone and Russell C. Leffingwell, a Morgan partner and former Treasury Department official, disagreed and suggested that only a few special exceptions were made to the stated policy.[20]

Brown showed that by 1917 the bankers were anxious about their exposed position on some of the British loans. Whitney and Lamont testified to their absolute faith in British promises to repay, but their wartime concerns about collateral surfaced continually in the financial negotiations. Much of the collateral was unsecured, with nearly half pledged from dominions of the British Empire. Brown quite reasonably wondered whether New Zealand, Australia, or South Africa would have turned over unsecured collateral to American bankers if England lost the war. He calculated that the banks held over $850 million in unsecured loans by the war's end, a figure Lamont did not dispute.[21]

The Du Ponts also managed to make the U.S. Treasury responsible for foreign securities. Raushenbush recalled earlier hearings when the Du Ponts "made the point several times very emphatically that all their taking of profit was at the expense of the Allies, and here it develops that some of that was paid directly out of the United States Treasury." Leffingwell protested that the United States did not "pay anybody's bills," but rather "bought obligations" from the Allied governments. Raushenbush agreed with the distinction. He noted that if the French had paid the obligations, there would have been no problems with the procedure. In the end, however, as Raushenbush pointed out, "that high-priced powder was finally paid for by the United States Government."[22]

When the U.S. government purchased Allied obligations from American private banks, it did not necessarily acquire the rights over collateral. Clark asked about British use of $173 million in U.S. government advances to reduce debt owed to Morgan and Company, another instance when the Treasury Department failed to enforce its stated policy. But in this instance, Secretary William McAdoo requested subrogation of collateral from the bank, asking for Morgan's security along with the financial responsibility. The British opposed the idea, leading McAdoo to observe that they treated American bankers more generously than they did the U.S. government. He acquiesced on the subrogation rights in late January of 1918, and U.S. citizens again took responsibility for money loaned by Morgan and Company, but without the rights over collateral that the bank had enjoyed.[23]

The effort to gain subrogation continued, but after the armistice the Treasury dropped the issue. Treasury officials feared that pressing the demand would upset British financial markets and depress the value of sterling, causing a ripple effect that would push other European currencies downward and reduce demand for American exports. In December of 1919, Treasury Secretary Carter Glass ordered the claims to be dropped. The final act did not come until 1923, however, when the United States formally released all claims to subrogation as part of a comprehensive financial agreement. By that time, the securities in question were valued at about $314 million.[24]

The complicated subrogation issue demonstrated the extent to which the committee moved beyond the simple "merchants of death" thesis. During the banking hearings, the committee explored the wide-ranging implications of the World War I military-industrial-financial complex. Subrogation formed one of the implications and it hardly offered a topic designed to draw banner headlines. The wartime military production also had important implications for American neutrality, a point raised by others well before the munitions committee considered the issue. Raushenbush introduced a wartime letter written by John Bassett Moore, a former justice on the World Court, which concluded that "manufacture of arms and ammunition for and under contracts with belligerent governments is an act essentially unneutral; and especially is this at present the case in the United States, where it cannot even be said to be done in the ordinary course of business but is chiefly carried on in plants specially created for the purpose, whose whole output is taken under the contracts for the performance of which they were created."[25]

Committee investigator Robert Wohlforth built on the Moore letter and showed the extent of munitions export growth from 1914 through 1917. He cited examples of companies that entered the munitions field and subcontracted work to all parts of the country. When Lamont countered that Allied demands spurred all kinds of American exports, with munitions making up less than half the overall increase, Nye conceded the point. "It was the commercial activity as a whole," he said, "in which the bankers had a hand, which did finally break down completely our neutrality." Vandenberg agreed and said that investors, munitions workers, farmers, and everyone else involved in the war trade had been "monetized" by their actions. He concluded that "you cannot hope to maintain a neutral state of mind in the country if vast sectors of its people are interested, first, in war trade, and second, in war investments."[26]

Ending such "monetization" would require an embargo on trade with belligerents, and Clark and Lamont debated the nation's earlier attempt to pursue such a policy, Thomas Jefferson's Embargo of 1807–1809. Clark argued that the embargo cost less than the ensuing War of 1812, while Lamont said that it led the United States into the war and on the wrong side. Nye interceded into the historical debate. "We are getting nowhere so fast that I think we had better discontinue this discussion," he said. Actually, though, the committee was getting somewhere. To seal the United States off from a modern total war, an embargo along the lines of that proclaimed by Jefferson would be needed. The nation might have benefitted from a reasonably dispassionate review of that effort. Clark and Lamont, however, were hardly qualified to lead such a discussion and draw lessons from American history.[27]

Clark found himself in disagreement with Lamont and Morgan on many other questions, leading him to conclude that, as with the Du Ponts in earlier hearings, he simply held a different perspective. "If I had been one of a very small group that made $30,000,000 out of buying supplies for the Allies, I would doubtless have a somewhat different viewpoint myself," he commented. Morgan took offense at Clark's remark, but the Missouri senator repeated it several times. Morgan exposed his perspective during a discussion on war profits legislation. "In every war you must interfere with the capital structure in a country," he noted with analytical detachment. Sounding for all the world like an economic autocrat of the type FDR impugned in his State of the Union address, Morgan added that "if the war destroyed the country to such an extent that it destroyed what you might call the leisure class, the people in comfortable positions, that will eventually destroy civilization."[28]

Senator Clark dominated the hearing room in 1936, as he had in 1934 and 1935, and no more so than when he presented his own documentary history of World War I. He subjected Woodrow Wilson to close scrutiny at a time when many members of Wilson's administration, including FDR, held powerful positions in New Deal Washington. Clark first read a four-page chronology of the neutrality period, from August 1914 through May of 1917, and highlighted the interdependence of political, diplomatic, military, and financial events. He took note of various problems that arose, with the issue of England's armed merchant ships receiving particular attention. Secretary of State Lansing advised Wilson in early 1916 that such ships be considered "vessels of war and liable to treatment as such by both belligerents and neutrals." Wilson agreed but did nothing.[29]

Clark introduced letters showing that U.S. war production complicated Wilson's response to British violations of U.S. neutral rights. In July of 1916, the president wrote, "I am, I must admit, about at the end of my patience with Great Britain and the Allies." But Commerce Department officials argued against an embargo on war supplies. Although it could effectively address the problems, it also "might prove in some cases more injurious to American manufacturers than to the countries at war. . . . For success in commerce after the war, we need the friendship of the belligerents if it can be obtained and held without undue sacrifice. Is not their goodwill then likely to be worth more to us than the present temporary restrictions have cost us?" Clark concluded that when President Wilson faced such a choice, he retreated.[30]

Clark also addressed the "secret treaties," by which Britain, France, and Russia in 1916 agreed to create postwar spheres of influence in the Eastern Mediterranean. Wilson denied knowing of the treaties prior to the 1919 Paris Peace Conference, but Clark presented various pieces of evidence that indicated otherwise. He drew on the Lansing diary, the papers of Edward House, communications from American ambassadors, and memoirs by Arthur Balfour and David Lloyd George. After listening to Clark, Nye offered that "the record that has been made and is yet to be made will all clearly reveal that both the President and Secretary Lansing falsified concerning this matter." Neither Nye nor Clark attached exceptional significance to their remarks, but they touched off an explosive reaction. Clark's history attacked the mythical image of the late president as a moral idealist, and it challenged the American memory of World War I as a crusade for freedom and democracy, well-intentioned even if perhaps unsuccessful.[31]

Writing in 1953, historian Ellis N. Livingston found that Clark's exposition "resembled nothing in recent experience so much as some of the 'documented' speeches of Senator McCarthy of Wisconsin." Like Wiltz's *In Search of Peace*, Livingston's judgment reflected the temperament of the 1950s. The documents Clark cited were reputable. Livingston's conclusion that Clark used "carefully selected excerpts from documents which fitted his case" is not without justification. The munitions committee's subpoena powers brought forth new documents to support revisionist views, and Clark assembled these to show that moral outrage over submarine warfare and German atrocities was not the only concern of American policy makers who weighed the critical decision of neutrality or war.[32]

Clark's presentation provoked division within the munitions committee, and the comments about Wilson, Lansing, and the "secret treaties" ricocheted back into the hearing room. Senator Pope, who had been absent when the remarks were made, announced that he and Walter George would boycott the committee because the "purpose of the investigation is being lost sight of and the chance to secure enactment of remedial legislation is rapidly disappearing. Such efforts to disparage Wilson and Lansing, however, do disclose the bias and prejudice with which the investigation is being carried on." Nye defended his statements and, after a brief discussion, Pope exited the hearing room.[33]

The revolt within the committee grew out of earlier debate on the Senate floor, where Tom Connally of Texas and other southern Democrats lashed out at Nye and the munitions investigation. Denouncing Nye's statement that Wilson had been untruthful, Connally described the "ferrets of this committee now—these high-priced expert assistants to the committee, including Mr. Raushenbush or Raushenbottom or some name of that kind—going into the secret files of the State Department, sifting them with microscopes, trying to get something to impeach the record of this country in the World War—something to throw slime over Woodrow Wilson and Secretary Lansing and others who are dead." Senator Kenneth McKellar of Tennessee said the committee could be shut down quickly because it had only $400 to spend. James Byrnes of South Carolina noted that the Works Progress Administration (WPA) had paid the wages of clerical workers serving the committee in New York City, prompting Kentucky Senator Alben Barkley to want more information about the use of relief funds by the munitions investigation.[34]

Clark was the odd man out among the southern Democrats as he defended the committee and himself. "I do not say Wilson lied or falsified. . . . I do say there is an obvious inconsistency," he explained. Clark leveled some personal barbs at Connally, contending that the Texas Senator spent so much time opposing an oil embargo provision to the neutrality act that he could not possibly know what the munitions committee was doing. He suggested that although Connally "always speaks brilliantly and eloquently, frequently with great wit, he would speak much better on any occasion if he knew what he was talking about." Clark said the munitions committee caused neutrality legislation to pass in the first session of Congress.[35]

On the following day, 17 January, Nye spoke on the Senate floor and defended his remarks. He linked the timing of Connally's speech to the inquiry of the Morgan bankers. He made a cutting counterattack against Connally and refused to back down in his statements on Wilson and Lansing. Nye entered several pieces of evidence into the *Congressional Record* to support his contention that Wilson and Lansing had known of the "secret treaties" prior to 1919. He allowed Connally to see a classified document. "Can the Senator read that and feel Lansing did not falsify before the Foreign Relations Committee?" Nye asked. Connally dodged the question and instead criticized the committee's subpoena of the Lansing diaries. Nye cited his wartime support of Wilson to refute any allegations of "malice or political prejudice" against the former president.[36]

Virginia Senator Carter Glass joined the debate with a fist-pounding speech that defended the integrity of Wilson and the Morgan bankers. Glass had served as Wilson's secretary of the treasury from December of 1918 to February of 1920 and had been involved in sorting out some of the postwar questions that arose from the wartime loans to the Allies. The hearings on World War I finance were moving in on the time of his stewardship. He also had close relationships with Morgan and Company partners S. Parker Gilbert and Russell C. Leffingwell. When Glass resigned as treasury secretary, he recommended Leffingwell for the post. After joining the Senate, Glass received a seat on the Banking Committee and in 1933 he argued with investigator Ferdinand Pecora over plans to examine Morgan and Company. Three times in his short attack on the munitions committee, Glass derided the suggestion that Wilson had been pulled toward war by the "House of Morgan."[37]

Tying the investigation to neutrality and isolationism, Glass exposed the growing gap between idealism and realism in international affairs. "Think of it!" he exclaimed. "Some great European nation or nations manufacturing munitions and exporting their products to the belligerents of Europe and Asia, and the United States isolating itself, pretending to be purer and more humane than any other nation, and denying the right of its own nationals to produce and sell!" America was no "shining city on a hill" for Glass, whose view contrasted with that of many who supported the munitions investigation. Pacifistic leaders of the Social Gospel era hoped that the United States could be "purer and more humane than any other nation," but such idealism seemed almost quaint in the world of Mussolini and Hitler. As Reinhold Niebuhr wrote in the winter issue of *Radical Religion*, "the historic situation in western nations does not offer the possibility of breaking through to a new society. It offers only the immediate possibility of defending democratic institutions, however corrupted, against the peril of fascism." Realism was on the rise for politicians and philosophers, with historians soon to follow.[38]

As Senate debate concluded, a quartet of southerners pummeled the munitions investigation. Glass charged that Nye used the committee in a "desperate and constant effort to figure on the front pages of sensational newspapers" but added that "even the sensational newspapers are tired of it." Connally suggested that Nye used the munitions investigation to publicize himself and reap in honoraria from speaking tours. Joseph Robinson, the majority leader from Arkansas, raised the issue of WPA funding for the investigation and called the action a "disgrace" to the U.S. Senate. Byrnes joined cause with Robinson, noting that he was "shocked" when he learned of the WPA funding. "I can think of nothing worse," he announced as the discussion came to a close.[39]

Meanwhile, at the White House, the cabinet met during the Senate debate. Steve Early brought in a report on Glass's speech, which impressed Interior Secretary Harold Ickes as "hot stuff all right." The cabinet officials proceeded to discuss the munitions investigation, with Attorney General Homer Cummings finding Nye's use of State Department files "almost inexplicable on any basis of honorable conduct." The group feared that other sensitive records might be publicized. The use of the Lansing materials also received attention, with Hull noting that the former secretary of state had taken many files upon retirement. Only after Lansing's death were the records returned to the department, a fact that some cabinet members believed could prove embarrassing if made public.

Hull acted quickly to secure the State Department files, and on the following day Joseph Green asked Raushenbush to return all classified documents that the department had not authorized for publication.[40]

The Senate attacks left the committee fractured and vulnerable. Some of the progressive senators who sympathized with the investigation believed that Nye had invited the onslaught with his comments on Wilson. Hiram Johnson wrote on 18 January that Nye had given the Democrats the opportunity to "tear him to tatters." George Norris, who had initially recommended Nye to sponsor the investigation, criticized the North Dakotan's "unfortunate" and "unnecessary" remarks. Dorothy Detzer received messages from peace groups that wanted the committee to press forward, but she was not optimistic. She responded in a 20 January telegram: "Doubt if possible keep munitions investigation alive." On the same day, Secretary of State Hull issued a press release that emphasized his sharp disapproval of the reference to confidential records. He then forwarded a departmental study on the "secret treaties" to Walter George and Key Pittman.[41]

Historian Wayne S. Cole observed that "Nye's statement about Wilson was factually correct, and none of his critics cited any evidence to disprove it." During the committee hearing on 15 January, when Nye made his accusations of falsifying, Clark referred to a 1917 confidential memorandum from British Foreign Secretary Arthur Balfour to Lansing. According to Cordell Hull, the document was a "confidential memorandum given by Arthur J. Balfour, British foreign secretary, to Secretary of State Lansing on 18 May 1917, which referred to Britain's secret agreements with other Allied governments." When Nye showed Connally the Balfour memorandum on the Senate floor and challenged him to vouch for Lansing's veracity, the Texan refused to answer. The senators who rose to defend Wilson's reputation and attack Nye were unwilling to accept a realistic image of the late president.[42]

Southern Democrats, who were moving to the political right by 1936, spearheaded the onslaught against the left-leaning munitions committee. No northern or western Democrats nor any Republicans joined their attack on 16 and 17 January. Many southern Democrats were increasingly uneasy with Roosevelt's New Deal and felt more comfortable with earlier Democratic traditions represented by John W. Davis or Al Smith. In January, Davis and Smith made common cause with the Liberty League and joined the political opposition to Roosevelt's re-election. Smith addressed the first annual Liberty League dinner on 25 January, making a much-anticipated attack on Roosevelt and calling the New Deal a "socialist platform." At least twelve members of the Du Pont family attended. Davis, who represented Morgan and Company before the Nye committee, was also present, as well as some congressional southern Democrats. Dorothy Detzer believed that the event contributed toward a "very depressing interview" she had with Cordell Hull in mid-February, concluding that "the Administration has fallen prey to the fear of business interests which may be due to the attack by the Liberty League." As she had at earlier times in her lobbying career, Detzer saw business leaders frustrating her efforts. She believed, however, that the munitions inquiry had been effective in the face of opposition from the Du Ponts and others. In a letter to historian Merle Curti, she credited neutrality legislation to the committee's efforts and found it "really miraculous that with the very limited amount of money at the disposal of the peace forces, that so much has been accomplished."[43]

On 22 January, several days after the southern attack in the Senate, Raushenbush told Joseph Green that the "internal dissensions in the Committee have been brought to an end" and the investigation would continue. The banking inquiry would not go much further, however, and the controversy over Woodrow Wilson and World War I was the dramatic high point. Afterward, the committee turned to less sensational topics during a final set of eight hearings that produced no confrontational episodes. No prominent businessmen, like the Du Ponts or J. P. Morgan, appeared on the witness stand. The committee questioned more witnesses from companies involved in the armaments industry, revisited issues explored in 1934 and 1935, and examined two "case studies" of the arms traffic that involved Brazil and Cuba. The committee also took a focused look at the question of nationalization in the munitions industry.[44]

Steel formed an essential element in modern warfare, and the committee questioned officials from Carnegie Steel Company, Midvale Company, and Bethlehem Steel Corporation. The testimony offered little flash, with chief investigator Raushenbush probing into how the companies determined cost when billing the government. He showed how the companies charged the government for depreciation of their ship armor production facilities during the 1922–1929 period, even though the government bought no ship armor during the period. Raushenbush saw the practice as a hidden cost of the naval treaties of the 1920s, noting that "naval limitation got paid for later on when we did start building ships." American taxpayers reimbursed the companies for depreciation regardless of whether their government used the facilities or not, another small way in which a fledgling military establishment took care of itself.[45]

Raushenbush moved from depreciation to profits and bidding, topics perhaps more easily grasped by the average American. Committee investigator Donald Wemple demonstrated that Carnegie's armor plate contracts resulted in profits of over 40 percent. Company officials did not dispute Raushenbush's description of "amazingly large percentages of profit" and acknowledged that such margins were typical for the kind of contracts under scrutiny. When Raushenbush asked if Carnegie lowered subsequent bids, R. B. Cooney, the official who prepared the armor plate bids, testified that he did not know how much profit had been earned on the earlier contracts. Raushenbush asked how Carnegie determined bids without knowing how prior work on similar projects had come out, and William Donald, the company's auditor, hardly offered a definitive answer. "I wondered many a time how any man could bid on this kind of contract. That may seem a vague answer to you," he said. Like some of the shipbuilders who had testified a year before, the steel officials were unable to explain certain basic aspects of their business.[46]

In the final days of hearings, the committee questioned officials of the Colt's Patent Fire Arms Manufacturing Company and showed the company's zeal to exploit tensions in South America. In one letter, the company encouraged its agent to avoid delay and talk soon with consulate officials of Colombia, Bolivia, and Peru because "as you know, these opera bouffe revolutions are usually short-lived and we must make the most of the opportunity." Later, when fighting broke out between Bolivia and Paraguay in the Chaco War, Colt seized the opportunity to sell to both sides. Events across the Atlantic received attention in Colt correspondence as well. A company vice-president compared the lack of U.S. munitions work to the surge in orders for European factories after Hitler took power. "Man, it makes my mouth water and here we are, over here, prepared to produce material par excellence, and getting nothing," he noted. Such communications failed to prove that munitions makers fomented war, but they supported contentions that the companies did little to stop conflicts and were always anxious to take advantage.[47]

The committee called in representatives for the Lockheed, Boeing, and Douglas aircraft companies. Their answers reinforced testimony from the 1934 hearings about the overseas activities of the munitions companies. The aircraft companies, too, used commissions that amounted to little more than bribes to foreign officials. They also tried to use sales to one side as a lever to get other sides to buy more. Early in the hearings, Nye, Clark, and Bone might have asked hours, even days, of questions. In 1934, the committee devoted much time to similar issues with officials from Curtiss-Wright and United Aircraft Exports. In the world of the later 1930s, however, the committee's time had passed. The disclosures provided nothing new and the session lasted only two hours.[48]

The committee examined the impact of promotional activities by the Navy League and Army Ordnance Association on behalf of the armed services. Members of the Navy League included steel companies, armaments makers, and chemical producers. The committee studied the use of U.S. Navy produced motion pictures in league promotional campaigns, an issue brought to the committee's attention by Dorothy Detzer. In another case, radio stations owned by navy suppliers General Electric and Westinghouse provided programming and broadcast time to promote the league's Navy Day activities. Letters from various navy officers gave advice and information to league officials on how to influence congressional action. The Navy League saw peace groups as particularly troublesome to their cause, and the "subversive actions of certain teachers in our universities" drew special attention. Ignoring the issues of free speech and academic freedom, the organization's executive committee in late 1933 discussed plans to raise funds for "a movement which might kill the pacifistic movement in the colleges and universities." League officials were not asked if they approved or executed the plan.[49]

Other testimony showed that former Navy Secretary Josephus Daniels barred league members from navy yards and ships. In many ways, Daniels shared the nineteenth-century values of Nye, Clark, and Bone, and his views toward the

Navy League and its corporate sponsors changed little in the years after World War I. In 1938, he wrote to President Roosevelt an informative letter about the congressional campaigns and digressed into the "unholy profits" of the big steel companies during the war. As assistant secretary of the navy during the Wilson administration, FDR served under Daniels but often agreed more with the league's big navy positions than with policies of his superior.[50]

After questioning Navy League officials, the committee turned to the Army Ordnance Association. By this time, the committee included only a few active senators, with no more than three present for any of the final six days of testimony. Nye asked about lobbying efforts and produced a letter in which the association's executive secretary, Leo A. Codd, noted that the "problem narrows down to influence pure and simple. The more direct and personal the better." In another letter, the organization took credit for getting the Roosevelt administration to supply funds to the Picatinny Arsenal in New Jersey. Nye showed that officials from Sperry Gyroscope Company worked closely with the association to get more money for army projects. Codd did not undergo as much scrutiny, however, as the Navy League officials.[51]

The investigation of the promotional groups generated few headlines, and Americans of later decades would be little surprised to learn that such organizations worked hard to promote their own interests. Within the context of the 1930s, however, the issue carried some significance. The domestic munitions industry had grown mightily during World War I and formed a relatively new interest group. The concept of pluralistic politics had only begun to be accepted as FDR established himself in the role of "honest broker" among competing groups. Nye, Clark, and Raushenbush were not ready to accept without question that entrenched interest groups should quietly influence an area so critical as U.S. military policy. Not knowing that Pearl Harbor stood only five years in the future, and that an additional forty-five years of cold war would follow, munitions committee members could not foresee that the interests of the military establishment would come to be closely identified with the interests of the nation.[52]

In its last days, the investigation focused on two case studies of the armaments trade: an attempted revolution in Brazil and a failed filibuster in Cuba. In the Brazilian episode, the committee found evidence of involvement by American concerns, including Guaranty Trust Company and Westinghouse Electric Company. The testimony on efforts to purchase arms and materials for rebels in Brazil generated tales of gunrunning and double-crossing that might have made for an absorbing novel. Frank S. Jonas, a sensational witness in the 1934 hearings, was involved in the transactions that saw the rebels pay $49,000 for equipment bought at surplus for only $350. The rebels financed arms purchases by selling coffee beans. The hearing provided fascinating details, but as far as the American public was concerned, and in terms of front-page news, testimony on coffee beans was not worth a hill of beans.[53]

Having reached a dead end in the Brazilian affair, with the various witnesses contradicting each other on key points, the committee moved on to the Cuban filibuster. Several U.S. companies had been involved in arming the Cuban rebels, and a grand jury had indicted one firm and five individuals for violations of neutrality laws. The planning culminated with a landing in Cuba that achieved about the same level of success as the Bay of Pigs fiasco would a generation later. Cuban troops disarmed the invaders, and some of the captured weapons reached U.S. officials who then identified the dealers. A former Federal Bureau of Investigation agent reviewed suspicious aspects of the arms purchase and said that investigators doubted that the dealers had honestly answered their questions. As with the Brazilian affair, the inquiry into the Cuban filibuster produced a tangled mess of murky intrigue.[54]

With the internationalist Pope and conservative George absent during most of the final hearings, the committee took on a more isolationist and leftist appearance with Nye playing a larger role. At times he was the only senator present. During these last days, the committee considered the radical step of nationalizing the munitions and armaments factories. Representatives from the Interstate Commerce Commission (ICC) testified that a heavy cruiser constructed by a private shipbuilder cost the government about $1 million more than an identical vessel built in a navy yard. They said a $24 million expansion and modernization program would enable the government to meet its naval construction needs and increase per-ship savings, and an additional $23 million would allow the government to produce its own machine guns and airplanes as well as most of its gunpowder.[55]

The committee spent little time with the ICC representatives, though Nye told them that "as time goes on there will be a larger appreciation of the very extensive help that you have afforded." Nye's prediction proved to be wrong, however, and the dry and detailed testimony drew little interest from newspaper and radio reporters who sought more dramatic stories. When historians later wrote on the munitions inquiry, technical issues like expansion of government shipbuilding were buried under the more dramatic "merchants of death." That the committee could seriously ponder nationalization of large parts of the military establishment illustrates one reason its work has been largely dismissed. It would be difficult to imagine any member of the U.S. Senate in the later twentieth century publicly entertaining the thought of nationalizing navy shipbuilding. In the 1930s, a few members of the munitions committee gave the idea a hearing.[56]

As *Fortune* magazine had predicted in its 1934 article "Arms and the Men," the nationalization option would have to include large sections of the modern economy in order to effectively control military production. When the president of the American Manganese Producers Association appeared before the committee, Clark suggested that the ore mines might need to be nationalized. Bone advocated a government take-over of the lumber industry. The committee contemplated nationalizing the means of production for navy ships, gunpowder, machine guns, military aircraft, manganese, and lumber. Once started, the list of vital industries to be nationalized lengthened.[57]

Nye's isolationist views came through clearly during the last hearings, foreshadowing his later image as the personification of isolationism and coloring the history of the munitions investigation. When Nelson Macy, president of the Navy League, asked Nye's opinion on the proper size of the U.S. Navy, the senator pronounced the navy "adequate, and even more than adequate, to repulse any nation that is going to be so foolish as to attack us." He said no other nation would want the Aleutian Islands, so Americans could "abandon from our minds any grave fears about what some other nation is going to do to those islands." During World War II, Americans faced not one nation but the combined force of German wolfpacks and Japanese fleets. Japanese forces occupied some of the Aleutian Islands during the war, and the U.S. Navy, crippled in the Pearl Harbor raid, could not defend the territory. Nye's analysis of future events proved to be faulty on several counts and left him subject to criticism. After Pearl Harbor mocked his preparedness views, realist historians found themselves unable to approach Nye and the munitions investigation from a sympathetic perspective.[58]

Nye's isolationism presented serious problems for the Roosevelt administration during the neutrality debate, for on this issue the munitions committee exerted strong influence. With the temporary arms embargo from the 1935 Neutrality Act due to lapse on 29 February, all sides in the neutrality debate felt an urgent need for quick action. By the time Nye ended the hearings on 20 February, the battle over neutrality had been fought. Administration forces moved first, with House Foreign Affairs Committee chair Samuel McReynolds and Senate Foreign Relations Committee chair Key Pittman introducing bills during brief sessions preceding the State of the Union address. The bills continued the mandatory arms embargo and added a ban on loans to belligerents, although the president had discretion to allow short-term credits. They strengthened the president's power to control exports of materials used in war, as opposed to narrower prohibitions limited to armaments and munitions. The president could designate that exports to belligerents of certain commodities like oil and cotton be limited to prewar levels and that such shipments be made at the risk of the trader. For Roosevelt, however, more important than the details was that a divisive legislative battle be avoided.[59]

Nye and Clark submitted their neutrality resolution on 6 January, one day before the banking hearings began. They proposed to remove executive discretion from the administration's bill. They also called for a cash-and-carry provision, meaning that shipments to belligerents would be carried on foreign ships with title of ownership transferred to the buyer before export. Cash-and-carry went beyond the administration's proposal for presidential authority to proclaim trade with belligerents to be at the seller's risk. The Nye and Clark plan banned short-term credits and automatically established restrictions on raw materials exports to belligerents when a war started.[60]

The House Foreign Affairs Committee endorsed the administration's bill on 28 January, but McReynolds soon concluded that the full body would not pass it. In the Senate, Pittman quickly abandoned the administration's bill and called for an extension of the existing legislation to May of 1937. A tangle of interests, including Italian Americans, oil producers, cotton growers, internationalists, and nationalists could find no common ground, and extension of the 1935 act appeared to be the only feasible option. The administration gave up its fight for executive discretion, and Hull told the cabinet on 7 February that he expected the current law to be continued. During a press conference five days later, he publicly endorsed the extension.[61]

With the administration and congressional leaders in agreement, bills quickly emerged from committees. The Senate Foreign Relations Committee approved the legislation on the day of Hull's press conference. A few changes were made to the 1935 Neutrality Act. A ban on loans to belligerents, which Clark had proposed in the first session of Congress, became part of the 1936 neutrality bill. The revised bill extended the mandatory arms embargo to nations that joined an ongoing war. The House Foreign Affairs Committee endorsed an identical bill on 14 February, and the full body passed the measure three days later.[62]

Nye used the munitions committee as a base and organized a block of fifteen senators to fight for a more restrictive law. Bone, Clark, Pope, and Vandenberg worked with Nye, and among the others involved were George Norris and Robert La Follette. When the full Senate debated the neutrality bill on 18 February, members of the munitions committee, supported by Nye's block, tried to amend it. Clark offered an amendment to limit the bill to ninety days and give Congress time to develop a more comprehensive measure. His amendment attracted only sixteen votes and showed the inability of the block to gain broad support. Bone proposed that trade with belligerents be conducted at the risk of the exporter, but his amendment also failed. Pope asked for an amendment authorizing the president to declare an embargo on "articles or materials" of war. The Senate voted against the amendment and shortly afterward passed the extension bill.[63]

Cordell Hull viewed the neutrality extension as the least objectionable measure the administration was likely to get, and he recommended that FDR sign it. On 29 February, Roosevelt signed and took the opportunity to "renew the appeal made last October to the American people that they so conduct their trade with belligerent nations that it cannot be said that they are seizing new opportunities for profit or that by changing their peacetime trade they give aid to the continuation of war." The administration's "moral embargo" lacked legal means of enforcement, however, and it failed to hold down exports to Italy after the invasion of Ethiopia. Petroleum exports in particular grew quickly. Oil shipments to Italy in November of 1935 rose 300 percent above peacetime levels.[64]

Members of the munitions committee lacked support for mandatory controls over such exports, while the administration could not muster a majority for its proposal of executive discretion. The addition of the ban on loans meant that the 1936 Neutrality Act encompassed the three main points proposed by Nye and

Clark in their resolutions of 1935. Civilian travel on belligerent's ships, arms shipments to belligerents, and loans to belligerents were all strictly regulated. Despite their failed efforts to add amendments, the 1936 act represented a victory for Nye and Clark. What had become clear between passage of the first neutrality act and debate over the second was the critical importance of essential war materials like oil and cotton. With the nation still mired in depression, these sectors desperately needed increasing demand from somewhere. If far-off wars led to orders, struggling businessmen, hungry workers, and desperate farmers were inclined to make the best of it. Candidates for re-election in 1936 did not want to be responsible for putting Americans out of work.

In the wake of the last hearings and the neutrality debate, while the committee prepared its remaining reports, a rapid series of dramatic events sealed for decades the historical assessment of the munitions investigation. On 20 February, the last hearing took place. On 26 February, Japanese military officers who favored expansion in Asia and felt restrained by the civilian government attempted a coup d'état. On 29 February, President Roosevelt signed the 1936 Neutrality Act. On 7 March, Hitler's Nazi forces occupied the Rhineland. The events connected up so easily: the munitions committee strengthened isolationist sentiments and forced through the neutrality legislation that encouraged the aggressors. Looking back through the smoking ruins of World War II, historians saw the Nye committee, rather than the munitions industry, as a villain bearing responsibility for the carnage. In the spring of 1936, however, such connections were yet to be made. The Rhineland occupation did not immediately appear to be a momentous act, and only later did historians understand its crucial importance to strengthening Hitler's position in Nazi Germany. FDR made no mention of it in a 10 March press conference, and less than two weeks later he sailed to the Bahamas for a fishing trip. The upcoming election occupied the president's mind, and in political terms Nye and the munitions investigation could be potential assets much as they had been in 1934.[65]

The munitions investigation found the going harder in 1936 than it had in 1934 and 1935. With the hearings taking place in the beginning of an election year, the inquiry was bound to become politicized. While in 1934 the hearings divided Republicans, with the progressive Nye opposed to the conservative Du Ponts, in 1936 the banking inquiry divided Democrats. Within the committee, Pope and George split from Clark and Bone. Coming in the middle of a neutrality debate, which itself took place during a foreign war to which Americans were exporting war materials, the hearings were bound to touch on sensitive issues. Thousands of Americans were already, in Vandenberg's words, "monetized" in relation to the Italian-Ethiopian War.

Chapter 8

Beyond the Merchants of Death: Recovering the History of the Munitions Committee

The work of the munitions committee and its impact on politics carried past the hearings on through 1936. The final reports of the committee, published during the summer, have received less attention than the rhetoric of Nye's inflammatory stump speeches. Nye's rhetoric supported the usual view of the committee as a group of simpleminded cranks who tried, and failed, to prove that arms makers caused war. This view emerged in the post–World War II era, when realist historians created a "straw man" from the munitions investigation for use as an object of scorn and ridicule, a prime example of the folly that resulted when idealism infected a realistic consideration of world affairs. The committee's reports, however, went beyond the merchants of death and reflected the more sophisticated thinking of Stephen Raushenbush. They realistically grasped the implications of total war for a modern society.

On 20 April 1936, the committee published "Report on Activities and Sales of Munitions Companies." The 282-page document outlined the committee's assessment of its accomplishments and stressed the roles it played in passing the neutrality acts and in promoting war profits legislation. Significantly, in light of the emphasis later placed on the issue, the report noted that "the evidence before this committee does not show that wars have been started solely because of the activities of munitions makers." To the extent that Nye or anyone else on the committee ever held that position, they quickly moved beyond it. A careful reading of the hearings suggests that of the leading figures in the committee, perhaps only Bone ever embraced the idea that the munitions makers alone caused wars.[1]

Instead of an international ring of armament barons, the committee found a large and growing American military establishment. Over 100 companies produced munitions for export as well as for domestic use. Hundreds more contracted with the military branches for various goods and services. For Americans coming of age in the cold war, a thriving military sector formed a central feature of American culture and few questioned its necessity. In the 1930s, however, many Americans, indeed many people in the industrial world, were unaccustomed to the demands of modern total war. A huge, sprawling, and permanent military supply system was a new and, for some, troubling phenomenon. The munitions committee assigned the preeminent role in this system to the Du Ponts. Unlike 1934 and 1935, when Nye's melodramatic speeches portrayed the Du Ponts as soulless death merchants, the 1936 report presented them in the grand manner of a late nineteenth–century trust, with tentacles extended through American society.[2]

The committee summarized its findings about the military system and outlined the links between the military branches, supply companies, and lobbying organizations. The report noted that companies and lobbying groups often hired reserve or retired military personnel, an early version of the "revolving door" between government and special interests. The senators said much less, however, about the role of congressional committees in what would later be called the "legislative triangle" of executive departments, interest groups, and committees. The hearings revealed instances of the triangle in action, but the senators ignored their colleagues when considering "relations of munitions companies with departments and officials of the United States Government." The hope for enactment of the committee's recommendations made it good politics to avoid alienating fellow members of Congress.[3]

While historians later found the munitions committee to blame for German, Japanese, and Italian aggression because it fueled isolationist sentiment and blocked a realistic U.S. response to aggression during the 1930s, the committee instead held culpable American businesses that sold to the aggressors. Many U.S. munitions firms did substantial business in Germany during the 1930s, and some experienced huge increases in orders after Hitler took power. For the munitions committee, it was "apparent that those who stood to profit by the rearming of Germany were *(a)* those who sold her the arms; *(b)* those who would profit by the scare of a rearmed Germany, which would have tremendous repercussions on the armament program of the other continental countries."[4]

The next committee report appeared six weeks later. While Raushenbush and the staff drafted the reports, some leaders in the munitions industry defended themselves and their trade from the committee's criticisms. When Charles M. Schwab, chairman of Bethlehem Steel Corporation, was asked about "the current accusation that munitions makers furnish the wars as well as the munitions," he pronounced the assertion "ridiculous." H. Gerish Smith, president of the National Council of American Shipbuilders, leveled more serious charges when he accused the munitions committee of bias and prejudice. In a public letter to Nye, he described the committee's shipbuilding report as "replete with inaccuracies and conclusions which cannot be justified by the historical facts or by the testimony taken." He pointed to "repeated use of half truths and to the juggling of figures on naval shipbuilding costs" as specific abuses. Smith's letter earned front-page coverage in the *New York Times*.[5]

Smith's letter appeared on 26 April, less than one week after publication of the committee's third report. Coincidentally, action on the committee's war profits proposals inched forward at around the same time. Senator Tom Connally of Texas, chair of the Finance subcommittee handling the legislation, called for a bill less radical than the munitions committee's Flynn plan. Connally wanted lower exemptions during wartime and a "graduated surtax up to 80 per cent on all net income in excess of $1,000 a year." He did not outline which brackets would incur what rates or define what would constitute net income. While a bill to remove the profit from war never became law, the concept sounded good to many. Americans would hear about it again in the fall, when President Roosevelt made it an integral part of one of his most noted campaign speeches.[6]

Although issues raised by the munitions committee drew attention in the United States, events in Europe dominated the newspapers. Early in May, Ethiopian resistance to Italian forces collapsed. Soon thereafter, the administration removed its "moral embargo" on shipments of arms and vital raw materials. For the first time since World War I, a sovereign nation had been overrun by foreign invaders. The League of Nations proved unable to maintain peace among its members. Writing after World War II, Hull remembered that with Mussolini's victory "the major war against which some of us had been warning since 1933 had become all the more probable. Its chilling shadow already lay upon us." For some members of the munitions committee and for leaders of pacifist organizations, the drive for legislation to deter American commercial involvement in the impending conflict became still more urgent.[7]

In this context, the committee issued its fourth, fifth, and sixth reports during the first week of June. The fourth report, which ran a brief seventy-six pages, dealt with War Department mobilization plans and emphasized the need to control profiteering. Not surprisingly, the committee rejected the department's war profits bill and endorsed its own. The committee noted its essential difference with the department, finding the military to be too focused on "smooth functioning of the procurement machine rather than on profit limitation." It also took issue with department proposals to allow wartime restrictions on the rights of labor and opposed "work or fight" laws or a "labor draft." The committee wandered outside consideration of the War Department bills to flash its isolationist leanings and recommend a national referendum on the "military draft of men for service outside continental America."[8]

The committee found that the government had to yield to the demands of industrial leaders during times of war. The report contended that industrial leaders had gone on strike during the Great War and compelled the government to meet profit demands. It cited Du Pont's Old Hickory powder plant as prime evidence. The actions of copper producers and steel companies were also criticized. The committee took credit for bringing such cases to light and publicizing facts "not generally known until the hearings of this committee 16 years later. In such cases it is impossible to use the pressure of public opinion in order to compel cooperation." But the report found little hope for effective pressure from the public or anywhere else to restrain private industry during wartime. The people active in the industry on a day-to-day basis held the keys to productivity, and the government had to rely on their expert opinion. Effective replacement personnel could not be quickly trained during the crisis of war. By emphasizing the barriers to effective government control over the munitions industry, the committee began to establish a case for its own solution. It was revealed in the final report.[9]

In its fifth report, issued on 5 June, the committee examined existing legislation in eighty-seven pages of analysis and 143 pages of exhibits. The committee endorsed the Neutrality Act of 1936 but found previous legislation to be ineffective. For the munitions committee, the national experience in World War I under the pre-1935 laws proved their finding. Sensitive to the outbursts provoked by the earlier criticism of Woodrow Wilson, the committee praised the former president. Wilson held "the highest motives and the most profound convictions as to the justice of the cause of our country and was devoted to peace. He was caught up in a situation created largely by the profit-making interests in the United States, and such interests spread to nearly everybody in the country." With this argument, the committee reinforced its movement beyond the simple belief that a few powerful bankers and munitions makers had driven the United States into war. In his decisions of war and peace, Wilson recognized that a complex of interests involved millions of Americans in a new dynamic.[10]

Invoking the revisionism of Harry Elmer Barnes and Charles Beard, the committee noted the administration's willingness to overlook British violations of neutral rights. A U.S. embargo against Britain was problematic because, as the secretary of commerce told State Department officials in October of 1916, American manufacturers might be harmed more than the British. Letters from Ambassador Walter Hines Page and Secretary of State Robert Lansing made the same essential argument. Wilson did not threaten the British with an embargo, and the munitions committee found American policy to be largely responsible for pushing Germany toward unrestricted submarine warfare. The United States had evolved into an "auxiliary arsenal" for the Allies.[11]

Returning to the controversial "secret treaties," the report included selections from the record and allowed readers to draw their own conclusions. It cited sources that showed that Wilson and Lansing knew of the agreements prior to the 1919 peace conference. It quoted testimony from Wilson and Lansing before the Senate Foreign Relations Committee in which both denied knowing of the treaties before the peace conference. The committee found that Wilson did not inform Congress or the public about the treaties, justifying his actions with the erroneous belief that the United States could control the Allies after the war due to their financial dependency. For the munitions committee, Wilson's actions questioned the wisdom of allowing any one individual so much control over issues of war and peace. The committee raised the specter of an "imperial presidency."[12]

The *Report on Existing Legislation* offered little new or unexpected for those who had followed the hearings closely. The central members of the munitions committee, led by Nye, Clark, and Raushenbush, had set out to find evidence that financial interests played an important part in drawing the United States into World War I. In examining the Wilson administration, they found such evidence, enough to show that financial factors crossed the minds of the major decision makers at critical times. The committee's sixth report, released on 6 June, served as a supplement to the *Report on Existing Legislation* and shifted the focus from the government to the bankers and financiers. The committee pronounced itself ready to "leave to historians the intricate task of analyzing in detail the evidence which it has made available as public record." On the other hand, the committee found that "certain factors stand out clearly enough so that it can lay them with assurance before the Senate of the United States." A 184-page overview of the banking hearings followed.[13]

The committee described "de facto ownership of munitions plants by the British Government" and consequent problems posed by the financial arrangements. Morgan and Company's loans played a crucial role in the committee's analysis, creating an inflationary war boom that tied American prosperity to British war orders. Relations "had become so intimate that it was necessary for the British Government to buy rifles which it did not need in order that the American industrial and financial community should not be angered and refuse to cooperate in British financing in the United States. This refusal would certainly have damaged the British ability to prosecute the war." The committee recommended that the Neutrality Act be made more restrictive in regard to credits, loans, and exports. The conclusions were predictable, based on the testimony given and from the role played in the neutrality debates by a majority of the committee's members.[14]

The remainder of the report, gleaned from the testimony and exhibits of the banking hearings, focused on the role of Morgan and Company. The committee recognized that the issues transcended the profit motives of bankers and that the question of America's role in world affairs formed the ultimate divide. In 1916, banker Paul M. Warburg wrote to Federal Reserve Board Governor Benjamin Strong, Jr. and noted that due to the loan-fed war trade Americans "were now in a fair way of becoming the masters of the world." The report cited Vandenberg's arguments that "the American people enjoyed this abnormal trade and appreciated the profit from it" so much that they wanted to "keep it going." Through all the analysis of efforts to sell rifles, promote the Anglo-French loan, and deal with the 1916 exchange crisis, the report stressed the key role of Morgan and Company and the American banks. Less noticeably, however, the committee recognized that the bankers did not cause the United States to fight in World War I. Instead, the bankers promoted the development of a military, industrial, and financial complex that oriented the United States toward deeper involvement in the war.[15]

In its seventh and final report, issued on 19 June, the committee considered government ownership of the means of munitions production. The 123-page document offered a fine example of an exercise in futility, for there existed virtually no chance that the United States would nationalize the munitions industry. President Roosevelt had demonstrated little desire for government take-overs, and such a bold proposal as nationalization would have had tough going through Congress even during the 100 Days. In 1936, with Roosevelt's congressional support weakening, the depression lifting, and the overseas threat growing, legislation to nationalize powerful shipbuilding concerns and munitions companies stood no chance of enactment. The only person close to the administration who spoke in favor of such action was First Lady Eleanor Roosevelt.[16]

The committee found that the U.S. munitions production system allowed for the "legalized use of a national emergency to obtain high profits" and criticized the government's reliance on the private producers. The question of how many ships, planes, and other armaments the United States needed figured prominently into the discussion of government ownership. The committee's proclivity toward isolationism showed itself in the report's conclusion that "under few, if any, imaginable circumstances will the Nation again be both willing and able to transport millions of troops to nations other than continental America, and that therefore the problem of the desirability of a Government monopoly of certain munitions resolves itself into providing adequate plant for peacetime and wartime supplies for any army of not more than 1,000,000 men."[17]

The committee's foray into the morass of issues involved with limiting war profits led to the conclusion that private munitions companies could not be effectively regulated. In order to do so, the government would need a permanent force of accountants and auditors to oversee munitions production and a bevy of lawyers to handle the resulting litigation. The report cited instances in which Remington Arms Company, Midvale Steel & Ordnance Company, and other munitions makers withheld important information from the government regarding the cost of production. Unable to determine the cost of production, the government could hardly gauge the amount of profits earned.[18]

A leading argument offered against nationalization noted that the government would have to maintain a large and costly production system that would be fully utilized only for the unusual periods of wartime. In peacetime, factories and shipyards operated at a fraction of wartime capacities. The committee attacked this argument and showed that the government paid for the privately owned system in the same way because "the munitions companies charge into their costs to the Government all the overhead of idle plant, with resultant high costs to the Government." The munitions committee made a reasonable point. A munitions production system sufficient to meet wartime needs, whether privately or publicly owned, would almost have to be underutilized during times of peace. Someone would have to pay for peacetime maintenance of the system, and one way or another American citizens would get the bill. With government ownership, the costs would be paid through higher taxes, while with private ownership they would be paid through higher prices during times of greater demand.[19]

Regarding government ownership of the munitions industry, Nye, Clark, Bone, and Pope endorsed the idea. They recommended that the government own "facilities adequate for the construction of all warships by the United States Navy Department, also all gun forgings, projectiles, and armor plate, and of facilities adequate for the production of powder, rifles, pistols, and machine guns necessary for the United States War Department." They exempted the aircraft industry "because airplane and engine construction are still rapidly developing arts and in that way different from the somewhat more standard articles" for which nationalization seemed to be appropriate. The only surprise among the majority recommendations came with Pope's agreement. Generally supportive of the New Deal and loyal to the administration, the Idaho senator endorsed a course of action strenuously opposed by Roosevelt's top military officials.[20]

The more conservative members of the committee opposed government ownership. They accepted the basic argument offered during the hearings by the Du Ponts and predicted "inevitable local, political pressure to maintain these plants at full capacity production regardless of actual defense needs, and the result will be to encourage armament rather than disarmament." Late in the twentieth century, as the nation reduced the size of its military establishment, events upheld the arguments offered by Senators Vandenberg, Barbour, and George. When a military facility headed for closure, affected localities mobilized political support to keep open what were often the linchpins of their economic livelihoods. The minority supported all other committee findings but believed that "rigid and conclusive munitions control" would serve the country better than nationalization. The record of military procurement in the later twentieth century, with frequent cost overruns on ships and aircraft, showed "rigid and conclusive munitions control" to be an elusive goal.[21]

The majority recommendation was dead at birth. The impetus to investigate the munitions industry peaked in the middle of 1934 and resulted in the creation of the Nye committee. By 1936, the world and America had changed. The nineteenth-century values and progressive views held by the committee's majority had been eclipsed by the more modern values represented in the Second New Deal's politics and Reinhold Niebuhr's realism. The forces creating the committee had barely succeeded in getting started in 1934, when the resolution to form the munitions investigation passed almost by accident. There had never been a powerful surge of congressional support for the munitions investigation, and even at the height of public interest in the "merchants of death," a bill for nationalizing munitions companies would not have passed through Congress. By 1936, with the public's interest diminished, the majority recommendation for government ownership meant absolutely nothing.

One week after the committee issued its final report, the Democratic party nominated Franklin Roosevelt for a second term as president. FDR delivered a ringing acceptance speech and called Americans to their "rendezvous with destiny." He attacked the "economic royalists" who opposed the New Deal. He did not find it necessary to name the Du Ponts as economic royalists, though they remained his chief critics and made generous campaign contributions to his opponent, Republican Alf Landon.[22]

Aside from the economic royalists, Roosevelt campaigned for the support of every voting constituency. As a means of appealing to peace-minded voters, Interior Secretary Harold Ickes initiated efforts to bring Senator Nye into the Roosevelt camp. Ickes believed that peace would be an important campaign issue on which "Nye can help as well as, or better than, any other man in the country." On 6 August, he met with the North Dakota senator and outlined a scenario in which FDR would make a strong peace statement and Nye would endorse the president's stand. Nye listened but made no commitment. Four days later, Ickes discussed the plan with a receptive Roosevelt, who then made the peace statement during a 14 August speech in Chautauqua, New York. After the speech, Ickes phoned Nye and encouraged him to issue the endorsement. Nye refused but said he would be happy to meet with the president if asked to do so.[23]

Roosevelt's Chautauqua speech offered a strong plea for peace and stressed the horrors of modern war. In one of his most quoted speeches, FDR described the effects of war. "I have seen war on land and sea," he said, perhaps with a little exaggeration. "I have seen blood running from the wounded. I have seen men coughing out their gassed lungs. I have seen the dead in the mud. I have seen cities destroyed. I have seen two hundred limping, exhausted men come out of line—the survivors of a regiment of 1,000 that went forward forty-eight hours before. I have seen children starving. I have seen the agony of mothers and wives. I hate war."[24]

The president did not blame the bankers and munitions makers but instead found many causes of war. Of all the causes, however, governments could effectively legislate against only one: the "economic source" of war could be controlled by neutrality and war profits laws. Warming to this theme, Roosevelt embraced much of the thinking of the munitions committee. "Industrial and agricultural production for a war market may give immense fortunes to a few men," FDR said, without having to name J. P. Morgan or the Du Ponts, but "for the nation as a whole it produces disaster." Calling war profits "fool's gold," the president ridiculed the arguments offered for shipping supplies and extending credit to belligerent nations. "If we face the choice of profits or peace, the nation will answer—must answer—'we choose peace,'" he concluded.[25]

The speech said much of what the peace movement wanted to hear, and it also endorsed some of the findings from the munitions investigation. Afterward, Ickes pursued his plan and asked the White House to invite Nye to Roosevelt's home in Hyde Park, New York. Ickes wanted Nye's statement to "show very clearly that those elements in this country who would profit from a war, namely, the international bankers and munitions makers, are all on the side of Landon." On 22 August, Ickes phoned Roosevelt and talked with him shortly before the president met with Nye. Despite the efforts of Ickes, which continued into October, the North Dakota senator never issued the endorsement.[26]

In October, the munitions committee flashed across the headlines one more time when Nye released an affidavit concerning Elliott Roosevelt's efforts to profit from airplane sales to the Soviet Union. Publicity about one of the president's sons, coming in the final weeks of the campaign, hardly seemed coincidental. Nye released the information in response to criticism that the committee had covered up the episode, but other committee members were not understanding. Democrats Walter George and Bennett Clark let Nye know of their displeasure, but the incident had little impact on Roosevelt's campaign. Just three weeks later, FDR closed off his re-election bid with a thrilling speech in which he welcomed the hatred of the economic royalists and expressed his desire "to have it said of my second Administration that in it these forces met their master." Voters responded by giving Roosevelt their overwhelming support. He received over 60 percent of the popular vote and carried the Electoral College by a margin of 523 to eight.[27]

The president found his relation to the Du Ponts quickly altered after his re-election. Less than two weeks after the voting, one of his sons, Franklin D. Roosevelt, Jr., announced plans to marry Ethel Du Pont, a niece of Irénée, Lammot and Pierre Du Pont. Ethel's father, Eugene Du Pont, was an active member of the Liberty League. In June of 1937, the president traveled to Delaware and attended the "wedding-of-the-year" that had become a *Time* magazine cover story. Presiding over the ceremony was Endicott Peabody, rector of the Groton School that FDR had attended as a young man. The wedding marked the beginning of the end of Roosevelt's feud with the Du Ponts.[28]

The story of the second Roosevelt administration lies outside the scope of this study, but a few points merit attention. Presidential speechwriter Samuel I. Rosenman saw the Chautauqua speech as Roosevelt's first effort to "warn the people of the United States and the world of the dangers which lurked in all dictatorships." Rosenman found Roosevelt returning to the same theme in October of 1937 with the "Quarantine the Aggressor" speech. Coming fourteen months after the Chautauqua speech and during a year without any national elections, "Quarantine the Aggressor" again emphasized the horrors of modern warfare and stressed Roosevelt's desire to follow a peaceful policy. In the earlier speech, FDR had said "I hate war." In the later address, he said "America hates war." There existed an important difference between the two addresses, however, with the latter making no mention of war profiteers as impediments to peace. After the Chautauqua speech, the president occasionally expressed concern about the role of munitions in fostering warfare and he received reports critical of the Du Pont's role in the arming of Nazi Germany. Yet he kept his thoughts private, saying little about the "merchants of engines of destruction" he had attacked in 1934 or about the evils of war profiteering he had castigated in 1936. Unlike the fall of 1934 or the fall of 1936, issues raised by the munitions investigation were of no political value to the president by 1937.[29]

Issues raised by the munitions committee were likewise of little value to realist historians of the post–World War II period. Their history so tightly wrapped together the munitions investigation, Gerald P. Nye, isolationism, appeasement, and the "merchants of death," that untangling them presents a daunting task. One textbook of the 1990s told the story in this typical and generally accepted way: "Nye's committee concluded that profiteers, whom it called 'merchants of death,' had maneuvered the United States into the war for financial gain. Most of the Nye Committee's charges were dubious or simplistic, but they added momentum to the growing isolationist movement." Such a view misrepresents the work of the munitions committee.[30]

First, the investigation did not belong to Senator Nye. Nye did not seek out the role of chief critic of the munitions makers. Only after three visits from Dorothy Detzer did he agree to sponsor a resolution calling for the investigation. Detzer and Nye then drafted a resolution directing the Foreign Relations Committee, of which he was not a member, to conduct the inquiry. Once the committee formed, others, most notably Stephen Raushenbush and Bennett Clark, made contributions equally important to those of Nye. Raushenbush and Clark took the lead in much of the questioning during the hearings, and Raushenbush also directed the preparation of the seven reports. A continuing emphasis of Nye's role has been convenient for writers of history, allowing the investigation to be more easily linked with his isolationism. Calling the munitions committee the "Nye committee" emphasizes his part, but calling it "Nye's committee" places undue emphasis on his role.

Second, the committee did not call arms dealers "merchants of death." The term appeared in some of Nye's comments made outside of the hearing room, but the committee rarely used it during the hearings. In its final reports, the committee specifically noted that it had not shown that munitions makers caused wars. In retrospect, it was unfortunate that Engelbrecht and Cleary's *Merchants of Death* appeared in the spring of 1934, just as the Senate formed the investigation. The powerful image conveyed by the book's title became cemented to the committee. Political analyst Samuel Lubell, for example, reduced the munitions inquiry to "the 'Merchants of Death' investigation headed by Senator Gerald Nye." In March of 1934, *Fortune* magazine presented a less dramatic and accusatorial critique of the munitions industry in "Arms and the Men." The committee studying links between arms and the men reads with less impact than a story about chasing evil death merchants. The former is, however, a more accurate description of what happened.[31]

Third, the assertion that the committee found profiteers taking the United States into World War I for financial gain explains only part of the story. By the end of the hearings, the committee's definition of profiteers included millions of Americans. As Vandenberg noted, farmers, factory workers, miners, and nearly all occupations had been, to some extent, "monetized" by the war's booming economy. The committee saw the Wilson administration responding to the needs of the U.S. economy, and not just to the demands of J. P. Morgan and the Du

Ponts. Certainly the committee found Morgan and the Du Ponts profiteering more than others, and it did view some of the banker's actions as steering the country toward war. But in the end, the committee realized that total war involved the entire nation and most elements of a modern industrial economy, just as "Arms and the Men" had suggested.

Fourth, the charge that the committee held simpleminded and suspect views about the armaments industry in particular and world affairs in general has been an enduring one. Only a handful of historians defended the munitions inquiry from this criticism, and several of those, led by Charles A. Beard and Merle Curti, did so before Pearl Harbor. Wayne S. Cole, Walter LaFeber, and Paul A. C. Koistinen led the small minority of post–World War II historians who allowed that the committee might have approached the investigation with some degree of sophistication. Wiltz disparaged the committee from the beginning of *In Search of Peace*, describing how Americans rallied to support a "curious investigation" that came at a time when they were "willing to hear such odd gospel." He concluded, however, that even though the committee promoted a "national distraction during a critical period," its positive contributions exceeded its negative effects.[32]

Published in 1963, *In Search of Peace* appeared in between the Cuban Missile Crisis of 1962 and the Tonkin Gulf Resolution of 1964. President John F. Kennedy had called for the nation to "pay any price and bear any burden" in the global confrontation with communism. The spirit of the times showed through in Wiltz's analysis, as when he criticized John T. Flynn's war profits tax that received the committee's backing. "If taxation made war as uninviting as Flynn anticipated, might not Americans become reluctant to defend rights much worth defending?" he asked. For Wiltz and many other realist historians, the American people were, like Senator Nye, too shallow and undisciplined to correctly decide whether a war was worth the price. From the perspective of Americans at the end of the twentieth century, burdened with a huge national debt after fighting and winning a forty-five year cold war, a public debate on which prices were worth paying and which burdens worth bearing might have been useful.[33]

This study has examined the munitions committee and questioned the traditional assumptions found in history textbooks and casual generalizations. Senator Nye's role has been balanced against those of Clark, Raushenbush, and others in order to separate the image of Nye from the work of the committee. The "merchants of death" theme has been reduced to a level more attuned to what the committee, in its hearings and reports, actually dedicated to it. The committee has been viewed within its proper chronological home, as part of the first Roosevelt administration, rather than only as an introduction to the appeasement of the later 1930s. Finally, the committee has been connected to the political, intellectual, cultural, and social currents of the middle 1930s, instead of being reduced and confined within the debate between internationalism and isolationism. In this way, an attempt has been made to meet the call for greater synthesis in American history. The Du Pont's Liberty League, Reinhold

Niebuhr's realism, and Roosevelt's Chautauqua speech were among the many parts that formed the whole history of the munitions investigation.[34]

Working from these starting points, the munitions inquiry becomes an integral part of American history instead of an odd distraction. Wiltz's study of the munitions investigation has gone largely unchallenged, with no other published book-length works available, and historians have relied on it for over thirty years. Robert David Johnson, in his 1995 study *The Peace Progressives and American Foreign Relations*, used *In Search of Peace* to support his analysis of the munitions investigation. Johnson wrote that the "Nye hearings boiled down the 1920s beliefs and singled out arms manufacturers as the sole problem." He mentioned Senator Nye over fifteen times in discussing the inquiry, without once naming Clark, Raushenbush, or Vandenberg. The image of Nye's committee chasing evil arms merchants survives into the 1990s, not only in survey text-books but also in scholarly monographs.[35]

In order to more fully understand, the munitions committee must be placed within its proper context of the first Roosevelt administration. Most historians have passed over the committee while discussing the New Deal, instead considering it as part of the road to war. From the perspective of the cold war, the committee folded comfortably into isolationism and appeasement, both anathema to the internationalist and containment doctrines of the 1950s and early 1960s. But the entire official history of the munitions committee took place during Roosevelt's first term, all prior to "Quarantine the Aggressor" and the Munich Conference. Different facets of the investigation are highlighted when it is moved from the area of isolationism and appeasement into the realm of domestic policy. Most importantly, a new and clear explanation of FDR's actions becomes apparent. Historians have variously viewed FDR as enthusiastically behind the investigation, halfheartedly in support, resigned to its existence, and warily suspicious of it. Roosevelt took all of those positions, but he did so for reasons that went well beyond isolationism and internationalism. Roosevelt's flexibility allowed him to support the committee when it suited his political goals and clash with it when it did not. Thus, FDR warmed to the investigation and the interests it represented when elections neared in 1934 and 1936, while he challenged or ignored its actions and ideas in 1935 and 1937.

Roosevelt did not initially view the investigation as an isolationist vehicle. He first made that connection after the World Court vote in January of 1935, and he more fully linked the committee to isolationism after passage of the 1935 Neutrality Act in August. The more connected the munitions committee and isolationism became in FDR's mind, the less support he gave to the investigation. His record challenges arguments that he supported the committee because he was an isolationist or because he wanted to appeal to or appease isolationists. Immersed in the fierce fight for the Securities and Exchange Commission Act in March of 1934, when the road to war did not yet have a look of inevitability, the president initially saw the munitions investigation in political terms. Veteran's groups and pacifist organizations would be pleased. With the Pecora investigation coming to a close, a munitions inquiry offered another opportunity to discredit the big businessmen and financiers who opposed the New Deal. That the Du Ponts would be leading targets of any such investigation suited FDR, for they were the leading critics of his administration. Roosevelt probably expected a committee led by senators more loyal to the Democratic party and the New Deal, but in this case John Nance Garner accepted the list of applicants supplied by Nye and Vandenberg. After the selection of Nye as chairperson, FDR went out of his way to back the committee. This Republican-led investigation of big business well served the president's political needs, and he showed much more than halfhearted support when he appeared with Nye in front of 35,000 people in August of 1934.

After the 1934 election, Roosevelt quickly moved to gain control over the investigation through his appointment in December of the Baruch-Johnson committee on war profits. In the spring of 1935, after the World Court defeat and as the shipbuilding hearings threatened to upset his naval rearmament plans, Roosevelt found himself troubled by the committee. When he wrote to Cordell Hull in February and attached a memorandum on how the committee intended to embarrass the administration, the president had evolved from enthusiastic supporter to halfhearted opponent. In his 19 March 1935 meeting with the committee members, Roosevelt resorted to one of his favorite devices, deception, in an attempt to divert the investigation. He said he supported their war profits proposals when the record shows that he did not. He steered the senators into the neutrality cul-de-sac and the investigation wasted weeks of time and much energy on an issue outside of its jurisdiction. After the 1935 Neutrality Act passed, FDR strongly connected Nye and the committee to building isolationist sentiments, as his September letter to Edward House made clear. By the end of 1935, FDR directly opposed the committee's planned investigation into World War I.[36]

While the investigation created problems for the Roosevelt administration, it made life miserable for conservative leaders of big business and finance. When the axe fell on the munitions committee, it was wielded not by Roosevelt but by conservative southern Democrats in the Senate. Carter Glass, who rarely supported New Deal bills, had earlier defended the Morgan bankers during the Pecora inquiry. In 1936, he rose to defend the "House of Morgan" from the munitions committee. Southern Democrats like Glass, often unhappy with the liberal direction of New Deal policies, shut down the radical munitions committee. The investigation had driven a wedge between itself and the administration, and when the attack came from the right the committee received no support from Roosevelt. If FDR wanted to campaign from the left, the pesky Nye committee, with its leading spokesman as a potential opponent, may have looked like an obstacle ripe for removal.

President Roosevelt initially endorsed the munitions investigation with enthusiasm, then opposed it halfheartedly, and finally viewed the hearings with wary suspicion. His approach was often shaped by the political uses he could make of the munitions committee and its hearings. FDR at first used the hearings to unbalance his opponents in the 1934 elections but then retreated when the investigation threatened to jeopardize his own re-armament plans and challenge the administration positions on war profits and neutrality. After the hearings ended and the reports were issued, the committee no longer posed a threat to the administration and FDR again embraced the thinking of the committee in time for the 1936 election. He stood on the platform in North Dakota with Gerald Nye in August of 1934 and met with him at Hyde Park in August of 1936.

In addition to providing a better understanding of Roosevelt's actions, extracting the investigation from the "road to war" historiographic context also allows a wider consideration of what it accomplished. As its foremost achievement, the committee created a documented analysis of the nation's modern armaments industry that enabled Americans to focus attention on this important new sector of the economy and society. The armed services already understood the complexity of modern warfare, as demonstrated in their detailed plans to use 12,000 plants for war production. Congress and the public, however, had not yet come to terms with the implications of modern total war. As the hearings established the breadth and scope of the armaments industry, the focus widened beyond the Du Ponts, Morgan banks, and corporate elites to include the hundreds of thousands of Americans who had their livelihoods tied to the defense sector. The committee did not argue that economics alone determined one's view of war, but rather that an individual might not truly know the ways in which economics affected their attitudes. The Du Ponts and J. P. Morgan argued that the incredible riches they garnered from World War I had no impact on their opinions toward the war. Is it really "odd gospel" to suspect that such may not have been the case?

Of possible interest to Americans in the post–cold war era is the glimpse provided of problems that occur during a time of retrenchment in the defense industry. While many sectors of the American economy boomed during the Roaring Twenties, producers of military supplies faced shrinking demand after orders stopped with the end of World War I. From the later 1930s through the 1980s, the defense industry generally experienced growth. In the 1990s, after the Soviet Union collapsed and the threat from communism diminished, the defense industry found itself again dealing with contraction. Witnesses before the munitions committee testified on affairs during the interwar period and produced a record of how companies responded to a similar situation. The arms makers pushed hard, sometimes desperately, to secure business in foreign markets and resorted to bribery to get orders. They lobbied intensely for government appropriations. They tried to transform their facilities from military to civilian production, with, for example, the shipbuilders lobbying for government spending on the merchant marine. Some members of the munitions committee wondered if such activities were in the national interest. In the 1990s, the armament makers pursued similar tactics and raised similar concerns for many Americans.[37]

The munitions committee played a leading role in a critical debate on the lessons of twentieth-century U.S. history. Both sides in the debate believed that the United States made a great mistake during the Wilson presidency. Isolationists saw the great mistake in 1917, while internationalists found it in 1919. After World War II, internationalists seized a "second chance" for the United States to take its proper place in the global community. For internationalist-minded historians of the cold war, the munitions investigation became the prime exhibit against isolationism. They drew from the experience of World War II, much as the munitions committee drew on the lessons of World War I. The committee erred in thinking the lessons of the earlier war would apply to the next one, but internationalist leaders did little better in applying the lessons of World War II to other conflicts.

The committee's examination of the complicated World War I issues of depreciation, international exchange policy, and subrogation of collateral showed that the financiers and munitions makers had, in fact, involved the United States in the war. Wilson administration officials spent considerable time and energy dealing with exceedingly complex questions that arose from Morgan's loans and Du Pont's sales to the Allies. This is not to say that at any point the bankers or munitions makers wanted Americans to fight and die to increase their profits. They just wanted to increase their profits. The munitions committee's history of World War I supported Charles Beard's argument that America's vision had been clouded by commercial interests that were not necessarily in the national interest.

For Nye and Clark, entry into the war clearly appeared as a mistake and an aberration from more normal American policy. In this way, they represented the tradition of nineteenth-century Americans who viewed the British with suspicion and found little to fear from German actions. Not until the end of the nineteenth century did America reorient its policy in the face of German expansionary moves toward Samoa in the Pacific. During the Boer War of the 1890s, many Americans favored the Boers against imperialistic Britain. American officials backed the British, however, and a divide opened between the foreign policy experts and the common citizens. During the twentieth century, the experts, usually eastern elites working through organizations like the Council of Foreign Relations, took the lead in making foreign policy. In this context, the munitions investigation represented an effort to re-establish nineteenth-century foreign policy patterns, to return to normalcy. In the munitions committee, elected representatives rather than elites framed the debate. Every senator on the committee had attended public schools, unlike the leaders of the foreign policy establishment.[38]

The munitions investigation, then, appears as a final crusade of nineteenth-century America. It represented not only an earlier foreign policy orientation, but also exhibited strong ties to the previous century's cultural and social values. Though the election of 1896 is often considered to be the transition point from an older agricultural America to a modern industrial nation, the evident failure of modernism in World War I and the Great Depression allowed the earlier vision to re-assert itself in the form of the Nye committee. Even in a time of intense dissatisfaction with the modern industrial order, however, the committee could not turn America back. Instead, the nation groped its way down newer and untried paths, toward the Second New Deal's welfare state and Reinhold Niebuhr's ironic "realist" world view. The committee's strong symbolic links to America's past placed it in contrast to the Pecora investigation, which also took place during FDR's first term and also served Roosevelt's interests by attacking the "economic royalists" who opposed the New Deal. But Ferdinand Pecora, an Italian-born immigrant and resident of New York City, hardly symbolized nineteenth-century American values in the manner of Nye, Clark, or Raushenbush.

The egalitarianism of some committee members also represented a pre-industrial American ideal, a noble call for fairness that many did not see as "odd gospel." Their call for equal sharing of war's burdens was idealistic, seemingly out of place in the world of Hitler, Mussolini, and Stalin. Within the larger context of American history, however, animosity toward the "rich man's war and the poor man's fight" existed in other times, most notably during the Civil War. Whatever role, if any, munitions makers had in fomenting war, the result did not have to be a lottery that sent some, like Bennett Clark, to the trenches while others, like Irénée Du Pont, reaped incredible wealth. Wars were, after all, human creations and humans determined their form. Similar questions of fairness have been raised in contemporary times. In 1995, Secretary of Health and Human Services Donna Shalala remarked that "the best and the brightest sons" of America were able to avoid the agony of the Vietnam War.[39]

Perhaps the burdens of war will never be equalized. Munitions committee members certainly thought it unlikely. But calling their ideals "odd gospel" amounts to an arrogant dismissal of goals pursued by countless Americans over the years. Characterizing Senator Nye as intellectually shallow, narrow, and undisciplined provides another example of arrogant dismissal. Other individuals who played important roles in the committee's history defied such simple constructions. Could Clark, a combat veteran, or Raushenbush, a graduate cum laude of Amherst College, or Dorothy Detzer, who had lived in the Soviet Union and worked in Geneva, be considered shallow and narrow? All of them shared at least parts of Nye's understanding of how the world was and how it might be.

The munitions investigation stretched across an intellectual watershed of the middle 1930s. When the balance weighed on the side of the earlier nineteenth-century and progressive values, the committee earned respect and praise. After the balance shifted in 1935, the committee found its thinking out of place. In January of 1936, Carter Glass displayed the new realism in his speech attacking the committee and the neutrality views of Nye and Clark. Glass derided the thought of Americans acting morally superior and forsaking commercial rights. Americans like Raushenbush and Detzer wanted the nation and the world to be morally superior. Such hopes were idealistic, as Glass realized, and failed to meet the needs of the day, as Reinhold Niebuhr understood. Much as Walter

Rauschenbusch's optimistic Social Gospel succumbed to Niebuhr's foreign policy of realism, the munitions committee's idealism lost out to the realities of modern total war. It became part of America's lost soul and remained in limbo during the cold war.[40]

But that does not make its ideas odd nor does it make those who endorsed such thinking simple and shallow. Speaking in the 1940s, Nye reviewed his twenty-year career in the Senate and took the most pride from his work with the munitions committee. In her 1948 autobiography, *Appointment on the Hill*, Dorothy Detzer wrote that "no Senate committee ever rendered to the American people a more intelligent or important service. It was the nation's loss that it did not comprehend it." Pearl Harbor and World War II had not daunted Nye and Detzer, but very few outside observers shared their views. Only with the Vietnam War, when the foreign policy experts appeared to be so completely wrong and the question of war's fairness again emerged, did some of the issues raised by the munitions committee find an interested public. The committee itself, however, buried under the epitaph "merchants of death," remained an object of ridicule in most accounts of the American past.[41]

As for the individual members of the munitions committee, most lived out their years after the investigation in historical obscurity. Nye earned re-election to the Senate in 1938 and became a frequent critic of Roosevelt's efforts to aid Britain and France. After France surrendered to Germany in June of 1940, Nye charged the president with pursuing a reckless foreign policy designed to take the United States into the war. He called for Roosevelt to resign and by the end of the year was active in America First. Interventionist groups vigorously attacked America First and Nye, linking the organization and the Senator with fascism and anti-Semitism. By 1944, Nye's foreign policy views became the focus of controversy. In his re-election campaign, he placed second in a three-way contest. Two years later, he tried to regain his Senate seat but finished last in a three-way contest. His political career over, Nye went into the information management business and later served the Federal Housing Administration. The radicalism of his earlier years calmed, and he supported efforts to combat communism abroad and expose it at home. In the 1960s, he practiced law in Washington, D.C., and served on the Senate Committee on Aging. He died in 1971, having lived to see one of his sons wounded in Vietnam and another son fly missions in Southeast Asia. Nye may have wistfully remembered the prediction, made in the munitions committee's final report, that Americans would never again send their sons to fight on distant continents.[42]

Bennett Clark, in many ways the most spirited senator on the committee, lived in Washington for the rest of his life. He served on the board of regents for the Smithsonian Institution while holding his Senate seat from 1940 through 1944. He was defeated in the Missouri Democratic primary of 1944, and in the following year President Truman appointed him to the United States Court of Appeals for the District of Colombia. He served in that position until his death in 1954. He was sixty-four years old. Despite the prominent role he played in the hearings, he never became as strongly associated with isolationism as Nye.[43]

James Pope, the committee's most consistent New Dealer and an internationalist, lost his bid for re-nomination in the 1938 Idaho primary. Roosevelt took care of the former senator, appointing him as a director of the Tennessee Valley Authority in 1939. Pope held the position for twelve years, leaving Idaho behind and establishing himself in eastern Tennessee. During the 1950s, he worked in the private sector as an attorney and also served as director of the Federal Savings & Loan Association of Knoxville. He moved to Alexandria, Virginia, in 1963, and lived out his final years in suburban Washington. He died in 1966 at the age of eighty-one.[44]

Homer Bone, probably the most idealistic member of the committee, realized that his foreign policy views might prove to be detrimental in his campaign for re-election in 1944. In that year he accepted an offer from Roosevelt for appointment to the U.S. Circuit Court of Appeals, a position he held until 1956. He practiced law in San Francisco after leaving the bench and retired in 1968. Two years later, he died in Tacoma, Washington, at the age of eighty-seven. The legacy of the munitions investigation followed Bone more closely than any other member of the committee except Nye, perhaps because Bone took increasingly isolationist positions in the later 1930s.[45]

Arthur Vandenberg, who like Clark played a leading role in the hearings, and like Nye and Bone embraced isolationist positions in the 1930s, redeemed himself with the internationalists after World War II. Moving away from his earlier views, Vandenberg by the war's end believed that "oceans have ceased to be moats which automatically protect our ramparts," and he spoke favorably of collective security. He served as a delegate to the first United Nations Conference in San Francisco in 1945 and also as a delegate to U.N. General Assembly sessions in 1946. He represented the United States at the 1947 Pan American Conference in Rio de Janeiro. Republicans took control of the U.S. Senate in the elections of 1946 and named Vandenberg to chair the Foreign Relations Committee. He had only four years, however, to exercise leadership in the position. He died in office in 1951. His later internationalism washed away memories of his earlier work on the munitions committee, even though Nye and Vandenberg were closely tied together in news reports on the investigation during the 1930s.[46]

The two remaining senators on the committee, Democrat Walter George and Republican W. Warren Barbour, had been little involved with the investigation. George remained in the Senate longer than any other member of the munitions committee. During the Eisenhower administration he embraced the internationalism of the times and served as special ambassador to the North Atlantic Treaty Organization. He retired from the Senate in 1957 and died eight months later. Barbour did not live to see the end of World War II. He was defeated in a bid for re-election in the Roosevelt landslide of 1936, but he ran again and won when a New Jersey Senate seat became vacant due to a resignation. He died in office in 1943.[47]

Stephen Raushenbush enjoyed a long and productive life. During World War II, he served on the technical staff of the U.S. naval attaché in London, where he helped devise battle plans used against German submarines. He was a consultant to the United Nations from 1947 to 1950 and directed economic research for the Public Affairs Institute in Washington during the 1960s. He retired in 1969 at age seventy-three. The legacy of the munitions investigation perhaps affected Raushenbush's personal life as much as his public one. He remarried later in his life to Josephine Joan Burns, who had served as the committee's investigator of State Department files. He died on the Fourth of July, 1991, at the age of ninety-five.[48]

Dorothy Detzer also lived a long and productive life, passing away in 1981 as Ronald Reagan entered the White House committed to spending billions of dollars on the armaments that she had worked so hard and so long to curtail. Detzer resigned from the Women's International League for Peace and Freedom at the end of World War II and published her memoirs, *Appointment on the Hill*, in 1948. She showed a keen perception of how history would treat her life's avocation, noting that many commentators would make "the peace movement a convenient whipping boy for the world's desperate state." She accepted this and took a philosophical view of the failed efforts to achieve peace, writing that the organized peace movement "was less than fifty years old; the war system—in one form or another—was as old as recorded history." Detzer worked as a free-lance foreign correspondent in the 1950s and 1960s. During the 1970s, history student Rosemary Rainbolt interviewed Detzer for research on a master's thesis that led to a presentation at the 1976 American Historical Association conference. Rainbolt concluded that Detzer had been "neglected by historians and students of women's history."[49]

Detzer has been largely overlooked and deserves greater recognition for her achievements in what was an almost exclusively male world of foreign policy makers, but the reasons that she has been relegated to a small role may be difficult to change. From the perspective of diplomatic history, Detzer's accomplishments will receive little attention if the munitions committee, her greatest achievement as a peace lobbyist, is viewed as an odd distraction. From the point of view of women's history, Detzer's attitudes toward gender relations may hold little appeal for feminist historians. Her values closely matched the structure that historian Donald K. Pickens called domestic feminism, while many contemporary writers of women's history hold views shaped by the autonomous feminist movement of the 1960s and 1970s. Detzer's middle-class and midwestern background may also dampen interest from historians who seem to focus more on women with connections to the private colleges of the East Coast. Finally, she worked in the area of international affairs while the women's movement has been more focused on domestic issues such as reproductive rights and workplace equality. Detzer's efforts marked a path that led to a woman serving as U.S. secretary of state in the 1990s.[50]

The questions that Detzer and the munitions committee raised in pre–cold war times may be asked again in the post–cold war world, for it seems that whenever humans use weapons against each other, the role of those who supply the arms becomes subject to scrutiny. In 1993 and 1994, *The Christian Science Monitor* questioned the ethics and morals of those who sold land mines for use in the conflicts of the developing world. In 1995 and 1996, American soldiers took up positions in Bosnia amid thousands of land mines. The Lockheed Corporation, questioned by the munitions committee in 1936 about bribery in foreign countries, was in 1995 implicated in sales tainted by the same tactics. As military spending dropped in the 1990s, communities fought to keep jobs provided by bases and defense contracts, their citizens "monetized" just as Vandenberg had predicted. World War II cut off a discussion started by the munitions committee. The cold war continued the interruption, and with its end the voices of Nye, Clark, Raushenbush, and Detzer deserve to be heard again. The leaders of the munitions investigation made their share of mistakes, but in the end their work provided the first critical examination of America's modern military establishment. For this, they deserve acknowledgment.

Notes

CHAPTER 1

1. John E. Wiltz, *In Search of Peace: The Senate Munitions Inquiry, 1934–1936* (Baton Rouge: Louisiana State University Press, 1963), 3, 232.

2. Richard D. Burns, Introduction to *Merchants of Death: A Study of the International Armament Industry*, by Helmuth Carol Engelbrecht and Frank Cleary Hanighen (1934; reprint, New York: Garland Publishing, 1972), 10; Edward Pessen, *Losing Our Souls: The American Experience in the Cold War* (1993; reprint, Chicago: Ivan R. Dee, 1995), 11–27.

3. Ellis D. Slater, *The Ike I Knew* (Ellis Slater Trust, 1980), 240–41; *New York Times*, 18 January 1961, 22; Oliver Stone, director, *JFK* (Los Angeles, California: Warner Brothers, 1991), feature film.

4. "One Blast After Another," *The Christian Science Monitor*, 3 March 1994, 18; Robert A. Seiple, "A Sower of Land Mines Pleads to End Them," *The Christian Science Monitor*, 2 October 1996, 19.

5. Charles A. Beard and Mary R. Beard, *America in Midpassage* (New York: Macmillan, 1939), 421; Merle Eugene Curti, *Peace or War: The American Struggle, 1636–1936* (Boston: J. S. Canner and Company, 1959), 285.

6. Robert A. Divine, *Second Chance: The Triumph of Internationalism in America During World War II* (New York: Atheneum, 1967), 35, 48; Patrick J. Maney, *The Roosevelt Presence: A Biography of Franklin Delano Roosevelt* (New York: Twayne, 1992), 200–201.

7. *Congressional Record*, 77th Cong., 2nd sess., 2928; Allen Weinstein, *Perjury: The Hiss-Chambers Case* (New York: Alfred A. Knopf, 1978), 144; Harry S. Truman, *Memoirs by Harry S. Truman* (Garden City, New York: Doubleday and Company, 1955), 1: 153, 189–90.

8. Ellis N. Livingston, "Senate Investigating Committees, 1900–1938" (Ph.D. diss., University of Minnesota, 1953), 153, 167; Dexter Perkins, *The New Age of Franklin D. Roosevelt, 1932–1945* (Chicago: University of Chicago Press, 1957), 96; Selig Adler, review of *Senator Gerald P. Nye and American Foreign Relations* by Wayne S. Cole,

American Historical Review 68 (April 1963): 774; James J. Martin, *American Liberalism and World Politics, 1931–1941: Liberalism's Press and Spokesmen on the Road Back to War Between Mukden and Pearl Harbor* (New York: Devin-Adair Company, 1964), 1: 468–69, 2: 1312; Robert A. Divine, *The Reluctant Belligerent: American Entry Into World War II* (New York: John Wiley and Sons, 1965), 10; Manfred Jonas, *Isolationism in America, 1935–1941* (Ithaca, New York: Cornell University Press, 1966), 26, 61.

9. Paul Birdsall, "Neutrality and Economic Pressures, 1914–1917" in *The Shaping of American Diplomacy*, edited by William Appleman Williams (Chicago: Rand McNally and Company, 1956), 561; Wayne S. Cole, *Senator Gerald P. Nye and American Foreign Relations* (Minneapolis: University of Minnesota Press, 1963), 96; Paul A. C. Koistinen, "The 'Industrial-Military Complex' in Historical Perspective: The Interwar Years," *Journal of American History* 56 (March 1970): 831–39; Walter LaFeber, *The American Age: United States Foreign Policy at Home and Abroad Since 1750* (New York: W. W. Norton and Company, 1989), 364.

10. Wiltz, *In Search of Peace*, 3–4, 232, 22–27; Robert E. Burke, review of *In Search of Peace* by John E. Wiltz, *Journal of American History* 51 (June 1964): 131.

11. W. C. Carpenter to Wiltz, 24 December 1958, in *Congress Investigates: A Documented History, 1792–1974*, edited by Arthur M. Schlesinger, Jr. and Roger Bruns (New York: Chelsea House, 1975), 4: 2912–15.

12. Wiltz, "The Nye Munitions Committee, 1934," in *Congress Investigates*, edited by Schlesinger and Bruns, 4: 2767, 2744.

13. Wiltz, *In Search of Peace*, 98, 232.

14. Richard D. Burns, Introduction to *Merchants of Death*, 10; Burke, review of *In Search of Peace*, 131.

15. Selig Adler, *The Isolationist Impulse: Its Twentieth Century Reaction* (New York: Abelard-Schuman, 1957), 257; Robert A. Divine, *The Illusion of Neutrality* (Chicago: University of Chicago Press, 1962), 67; Wiltz, "The Nye Munitions Committee, 1934," in *Congress Investigates*, edited by Schlesinger and Bruns, 4: 2767; Wayne S. Cole, *Roosevelt and the Isolationists, 1932–1945* (Lincoln: University of Nebraska Press, 1983), 141; LaFeber, *American Age*, 363–64; Michael E. Parrish, *Anxious Decades: America in Prosperity and Depression, 1920–1941* (New York: W. W. Norton and Company, 1992), 443–44; Maney, *Roosevelt Presence*, 113; Robert David Johnson, *The Peace Progressives and American Foreign Relations* (Cambridge, Massachusetts: Harvard University Press, 1995), 292–93.

16. James MacGregor Burns, *Roosevelt: The Lion and the Fox* (New York: Harcourt Brace and Company, 1956), 254; Selig Adler, *The Uncertain Giant, 1921–1941: American Foreign Policy Between the Wars* (New York: Macmillan Company, 1965), 161; Robert Dallek, *Franklin D. Roosevelt and American Foreign Policy, 1932–1945* (New York: Oxford University Press, 1979), 86; James MacGregor Burns, *The Crosswinds of Freedom* (New York: Alfred A. Knopf, 1989), 155; Kenneth S. Davis, *FDR: The New Deal Years, 1933–1937* (New York: Random House, 1986), 553–54; Maney, *Roosevelt Presence*, 113.

17. L. Ethan Ellis, *Frank B. Kellogg and American Foreign Relations, 1925–1929* (New Brunswick, New Jersey: Rutgers University Press, 1961), 239; Jonas, *Isolationism in America*, 259; Warren F. Kuehl, "Midwestern Newspapers and Isolationist Sentiment," *Diplomatic History* 3 (Summer 1979): 306; Warren F. Kuehl, "Webs of Common Interests Revisited: Nationalism, Internationalism, and Historians of American Foreign Relations," *Diplomatic History* 10 (Spring 1986): 108.

18. *Congressional Record*, 65th Cong., 1st sess., 213.

19. Walter Rauschenbusch, *Christianity and the Social Crisis* (New York: Macmillan, 1907), 270, 350; Walter Rauschenbusch, *Christianizing the Social Order* (New York: Macmillan, 1912), 279.

20. Howard K. Beale, *Theodore Roosevelt and the Rise of America to World Power* (Baltimore: Johns Hopkins University Press, 1956), 341; Arthur S. Link, *Woodrow Wilson: Revolution, War, and Peace* (Arlington Heights, Illinois: Harlan Davidson, 1979), 97.

21. Paul M. Minus, *Walter Rauschenbusch: American Reformer* (New York: Macmillan, 1988), 177–94.

22. Warren I. Cohen, *The American Revisionists: The Lessons of Intervention in World War I* (Chicago: University of Chicago Press, 1967), 6–18; Peter Novick, *That Noble Dream: The "Objectivity Question" and the American Historical Profession* (Cambridge: Cambridge University Press, 1988), 207; Harry Elmer Barnes, "Woodrow Wilson," *American Mercury* 1 (April 1924): 484.

23. Cohen, *American Revisionists*, 64–85; Novick, *Noble Dream*, 206–15; Charles A. Beard, *The Open Door at Home* (New York: Macmillan, 1934), 173.

24. John D. Hicks, *Republican Ascendancy, 1921–1933* (New York: Harper and Brothers, 1960), 279; Parrish, *Anxious Decades*, 36–37; William E. Leuchtenburg, *The Perils of Prosperity, 1914–1932* (Chicago: University of Chicago Press, 1958), 117–18, 186–88.

25. Richard Wightman Fox, *Reinhold Niebuhr: A Biography* (New York: Pantheon Books, 1985), 115–41; Reinhold Niebuhr, *Moral Man and Immoral Society: A Study in Ethics and Politics* (1932; reprint, New York: Charles Scribner's Sons, 1949), xii, 116, 16.

26. Charles DeBenedetti, *The Peace Reform in American History* (Bloomington: Indiana University Press, 1980), 33–78.

27. Eleanor M. Barr, ed., "Records of the Women's International League for Peace and Freedom, United States Section, 1919–1959: Guide to the Scholarly Resources," (Wilmington, Delaware: Scholarly Resources), 4–8.

28. Cole, *Senator Gerald P. Nye*, 67; Dorothy Detzer, *Appointment on the Hill* (New York: Henry Holt and Company, 1948), 7–35, 104–5.

29. Dorothy Detzer, "Memorandum on the History of the Munitions Campaign of the Women's International League for Peace and Freedom," June 1934, Dorothy Detzer Papers, Swarthmore College Peace Collection, Swarthmore, Pennsylvania.

30. Arthur S. Link, "Whatever Happened to the Progressive Movement in the 1920s?" *American Historical Review* 64 (July 1959): 833–51; Ellis W. Hawley, *The Great War and the Search for Modern Order: A History of the American People and Their Institutions, 1917–1933* (New York: St. Martin's Press, 1979), 60–61; Clarke A. Chambers, *Seedtime of Reform: American Social Service and Social Action, 1918–1933* (Minneapolis: University of Minnesota Press, 1963), 253.

31. Leuchtenburg, *Perils of Prosperity*, 225–40; David Burner, *The Politics of Provincialism: The Democratic Party in Transition, 1918–1932* (1967; reprint, New York: Alfred A. Knopf, 1968), 217–43; Samuel Lubell, "The Revolt of the City," in *The New Deal: The Critical Issues*, edited by Otis L. Graham, Jr. (Boston: Little, Brown and Company, 1971), 3–11.

32. Cole, *Senator Gerald P. Nye*, 22–26.

33. Ibid., 25–40; Divine, *Illusion of Neutrality*, 64; Francis E. Brown, "The Crusading Mr. Nye," *Current History and Forum* (February 1935): 521–27.

34. Cole, *Senator Gerald P. Nye*, 10–12, 22–23.

35. Ibid., 43–47; Wiltz, *In Search of Peace*, 29–31.

36. Cole, *Senator Gerald P. Nye*, 49–51; Wiltz, *In Search of Peace*, 30–31; Burner, *Politics of Provincialism*, 210–16; Nye to Smith, 23 March 1928, and Smith to Nye, 26 March 1928, Gerald P. Nye Papers, Herbert Hoover Library, West Branch, Iowa.

37. Harvey Green, *The Uncertainty of Everyday Life, 1915–1945* (New York: HarperCollins Publishers, 1992), 87, 233; Frederick Lewis Allen, *Since Yesterday: The 1930s in America* (New York: Harper and Row, 1939), 33–34; Carl L. Becker, "Everyman His Own Historian," *American Historical Review* 37 (1932): 228–31.

38. Allen, *Since Yesterday*, 202–6; Fox, *Reinhold Niebuhr*, 157.

39. Donald A. Ritchie, "The Pecora Wall Street Exposé, 1934," in *Congress Investigates*, edited by Schlesinger and Bruns, 4: 2562–63; Cole, *Senator Gerald P. Nye*, 55; Allen, *Since Yesterday*, 100–101.

40. Parrish, *Anxious Decades*, 261–62; Allen, *Since Yesterday*, 6.

41. Parrish, *Anxious Decades*, 258–61; Allen, *Since Yesterday*, 83–86.

42. Koistinen, "The 'Industrial-Military Complex' in Historical Perspective," 829–30; Wiltz, *In Search of Peace*, 33; Cole, *Senator Gerald P. Nye*, 69; "Report of the War Policies Commission," cited in *Congress Investigates*, edited by Schlesinger and Bruns, 4: 2834–36; C. David Tompkins, *Senator Arthur H. Vandenberg: The Evolution of a Modern Republican, 1884–1945* (East Lansing: Michigan State University Press, 1970), 124–25.

43. Allen, *Since Yesterday*, 102–6; Arthur M. Schlesinger, Jr., *The Coming of the New Deal* (Boston: Houghton Mifflin, 1958), 46, 103; Cole, *Roosevelt and the Isolationists*, 129–32.

44. Cole, *Senator Gerald P. Nye*, 54–56; Frank Freidel, *Franklin D. Roosevelt: A Rendezvous with Destiny* (Boston: Little, Brown and Company, 1990), 136–45; Schlesinger, *Coming of the New Deal*, 77–79; Edward L. Schapsmeier and Frederick H. Schapsmeier, *Henry A. Wallace of Iowa: The Agrarian Years, 1910–1940* (Ames: Iowa State University Press, 1968), 201–4.

45. Freidel, *Rendezvous with Destiny*, 133–43; William E. Leuchtenburg, *Franklin D. Roosevelt and the New Deal, 1932–1940* (New York: Harper and Row, 1963), 78–80.

46. Harold L. Ickes, *The Secret Diary of Harold L. Ickes* (New York: Simon and Schuster, 1953), 108–9; Elliott Roosevelt, ed., *FDR: His Personal Letters, 1928–1945* (New York: Duell, Sloan, and Pearce, 1950), 1: 369; House to Roosevelt, 12 November 1933, Franklin D. Roosevelt Papers, President's Personal File, Franklin D. Roosevelt Library, Hyde Park, New York.

47. Gerard Colby, *Du Pont Dynasty* (Secaucus, New Jersey: Lyle Stuart, 1984), 308–9; *New York Times*, 31 January 1934, 25, and 3 March 1934, 6; *Decisions of the National Labor Board, August 1933–March 1934* (Washington, D.C.: Government Printing Office, 1934), 65.

48. Detzer, *Appointment on the Hill*, 151–58.

CHAPTER 2

1. Dorothy Detzer, *Appointment on the Hill* (New York: Henry Holt and Company, 1948), 151–58; Memorandum by Detzer, 11 April 1934, Dorothy Detzer Papers, Swarthmore College Peace Collection, Swarthmore, Pennsylvania; Detzer to Beard, 28 August 1934, Records of the Women's International League for Peace and Freedom, United States Section, 1919–1959, Swarthmore College Peace Collection, Swarthmore, Pennsylvania (henceforth cited as WILPF-U.S. Records).

2. Detzer to Undersecretary of State William Phillips, 7 November 1933, and Detzer to Senator Royal Copeland, 9 November 1933, WILPF-U.S. Records; Detzer, *Appointment on the Hill*, 153–54.

3. Detzer, *Appointment on the Hill*, 151–58; Wayne S. Cole, *Senator Gerald P. Nye and American Foreign Relations* (Minneapolis: University of Minnesota Press, 1963), 68.

4. Nye memorandum, 8 January 1935, WILPF-U.S. Records; Detzer, *Appointment on the Hill*, 158, 169; Cole, *Senator Gerald P. Nye*, 43–44; Drew Pearson and Robert S. Allen, "Washington Merry-Go-Round," 1 January 1936, Detzer Papers; *Congressional Record*, 74th Cong., 1st sess., 12902–20, and 77th Cong., 2nd sess., 2928; Detzer to Huldah Randall, 20 August 1935, WILPF-U.S. Records.

5. Detzer, *Appointment on the Hill*, 157–58; Green memorandum, 18 January 1934, Record Group 59, Department of State Decimal File, 1930–1939, 811.113/Senate Investigation/1, National Archives (henceforth cited as R.G. 59).

6. Detzer, *Appointment on the Hill*, 157–59.

7. J. Pierrepont Moffat to William Phillips, 14 February 1934, and Hull press conference, 20 February 1934, R.G. 59, 811.113/Senate Investigation/3 and 4; Casey memorandum, 23 February 1934, Munitions Committee Exhibit 1032, cited in Special Committee Investigating the Munitions Industry, Hearings, Part 12, 2725. Committee exhibits generally appear in the appendices to the published hearings. Henceforth, exhibits are cited by their number, followed by hearing part and pages. For the current example, Exhibit 1032, 12: 2725.

8. Detzer, *Appointment on the Hill*, 159–69; Cole, *Senator Gerald P. Nye*, 69; *Congressional Record*, 73rd Cong., 2nd sess., 4228–29, 4758, 5829; Detzer memorandum, 11 April 1934, Detzer Papers.

9. "Arms and the Men," *Fortune* 9 (March 1934): 125.

10. Helmuth Carol Engelbrecht and Frank Cleary Hanighen, *Merchants of Death: A Study of the International Armament Industry* (1934; reprint, New York: Garland Publishing, 1972), 22–37.

11. *Congressional Record*, 73rd Cong., 2nd sess., 3688–92; *New York Times*, 6 March 1934, 12, and 8 March 1934, 9; William Taylor of Du Pont to L.W.B. Smith of Imperial Chemical Industries, 25 May 1934, Exhibit 1090, 12: 2880.

12. Detzer, *Appointment on the Hill*, 161; Green memorandum, 23 February 1934, R.G. 59, 811.113/386.

13. Frank Freidel, *Franklin D. Roosevelt: The Apprenticeship* (Boston: Little, Brown and Company, 1952), 209–19; Carroll Kilpatrick, ed., *Roosevelt and Daniels: A Friendship in Politics* (Chapel Hill: University of North Carolina Press, 1952), 4, 35, 21–22.

14. Ted Morgan, *FDR: A Biography* (New York: Simon and Schuster, 1985), 369; Michael E. Parrish, *Anxious Decades: America in Prosperity and Depression, 1920–1941* (New York: W. W. Norton and Company, 1992), 287; Frank Freidel, *Franklin D. Roosevelt: Launching the New Deal* (Boston: Little, Brown and Company, 1973), 169–71; Paul A. C. Koistinen, "The 'Industrial-Military Complex' in Historical Perspective: The Interwar Years," *Journal of American History* 56 (March 1970): 828–29.

15. Roger Biles, *A New Deal for the American People* (DeKalb: Northern Illinois University Press, 1991), 40; Arthur M. Schlesinger, Jr., *The Coming of the New Deal* (Boston: Houghton Mifflin, 1958), 463–67.

16. Robert Carpenter to John Raskob, 16 March 1934, and Raskob to Carpenter, 20 March 1934, Exhibits 1384 and 1385, 17: 4425–26; George Wolfskill, *The Revolt of the Conservatives: A History of the American Liberty League, 1934–1949* (Boston: Houghton Mifflin, 1962), 25.

17. *New York Times*, 17 October 1920, 3.

18. *Congressional Record*, 73rd Cong., 2nd sess., 6478–79; Cordell Hull, *The Memoirs of Cordell Hull* (New York: Macmillan, 1948), 1: 398–400; Hugh Wilson to Hull, 21 March 1934, Cordell Hull Papers, Library of Congress, Washington, D.C.; Detzer, *Appointment on the Hill*, 161.

19. Hull to the American consulate in Dublin, 26 March 1934, R.G. 59, 811.113/398; Detzer to Roosevelt, 26 March 1934, WILPF-U.S. Records.

20. "The Profits of War and Preparedness," Nye radio address, 10 April 1934, Record Group 46, United States Senate, Special Committee Investigating the Munitions Industry, National Archives, Washington, D.C. (henceforth cited as R.G. 46); *Congressional Record*, 73rd Cong., 2nd sess., 6472–85; Detzer, *Appointment on the Hill*, 161–63.

21. Roosevelt to Hugh S. Johnson, 27 March 1934, Hugh S. Johnson Papers, Franklin D. Roosevelt Library, Hyde Park, New York; U.S. Department of State, *Foreign Relations of the United States, 1934* (Washington, D.C.: Government Printing Office, 1951), 1: 75; Gerard Colby, *Du Pont Dynasty* (Secaucus, New Jersey: Lyle Stuart, 1984), 342; Hull, *Memoirs*, 1: 398, 388.

22. *Congressional Record*, 73rd Cong., 2nd sess., 6485; Wayne S. Cole, *Roosevelt and the Isolationists, 1932–1945* (Lincoln: University of Nebraska Press, 1983), 146; John E. Wiltz, *In Search of Peace: The Senate Munitions Inquiry, 1934–1936* (Baton Rouge: Louisiana State University Press, 1963), 42; Detzer, "Memorandum on the History of the Munitions Campaign of the Women's International League for Peace and Freedom," June 1934, Detzer Papers.

23. Lionel V. Patenaude, *Texans, Politics, and the New Deal* (New York: Garland Publishing, 1983), 40; James T. Patterson, *Congressional Conservatism and the New Deal* (1967; reprint, Westport, Connecticut: Greenwood Press, 1981), 268; *Biographical Dictionary of the United States Congress, 1774–1989* (Washington, D.C.: Government Printing Office, 1989), 166; Pope to J. J. Handsaker, 15 November 1932, Records of the National Council for Prevention of War, Swarthmore College Peace Collection, Swarthmore, Pennsylvania; Wiltz, *In Search of Peace*, 45.

24. Wiltz, *In Search of Peace*, 44–45; Schlesinger, *The Politics of Upheaval* (Boston: Houghton Mifflin, 1960), 119–23, 135; Cole, *Roosevelt and the Isolationists*, 50.

25. Frank Freidel, *Apprenticeship*, 141–43; *New York Times*, 4 February 1933, 2; Patterson, *Congressional Conservatism*, 18–20, 113.

26. Patterson, *Congressional Conservatism*, 44–45; Frank Freidel, *Franklin D. Roosevelt: A Rendezvous with Destiny* (Boston: Little, Brown and Company, 1990), 282–87.

27. Cole, *Senator Gerald P. Nye*, 53–54; Cole, *Roosevelt and the Isolationists*, 25–50.

28. Patterson, *Congressional Conservatism*, 101–3; Wiltz, *In Search of Peace*, 43–44; C. David Tompkins, *Senator Arthur H. Vandenberg: The Evolution of a Modern Republican, 1884–1945* (East Lansing: Michigan State University Press, 1970), 125; Cole, *Roosevelt and the Isolationists*, 550–51.

29. Wiltz, *In Search of Peace*, 45–46; Cole, *Senator Gerald P. Nye*, 71; Barbour to Roosevelt, 1 July 1933 and 17 October 1933, Franklin D. Roosevelt Papers, Official File, Franklin D. Roosevelt Library, Hyde Park, New York; Cole, *Roosevelt and the Isolationists*, 266.

30. *Congressional Record*, 73rd Cong., 1st sess., 43–45.

31. Cole, *Senator Gerald P. Nye*, 71–72; Wiltz, *In Search of Peace*, 46; Nye speech, 30 March 1971, Gerald P. Nye Papers, Herbert Hoover Library, West Branch, Iowa.

32. Hull, *Memoirs*, 1: 398–400; Hull to Nye, 27 April 1934, R.G. 59, 811.113/Senate Investigation/7.

33. Detzer, *Appointment on the Hill*, 164–66. Stephen Raushenbush Americanized, or de-Germanized, his name after World War I. His birth name had been Hilmar Rauschenbusch.

34. Ibid., 166–68.

35. Wiltz, *In Search of Peace*, 51–52; Detzer to Robert La Follette, Jr., 22 May 1936, WILPF-U.S. Records; Robert Wohlforth, "Armaments Profiteers: 1934," *Nation*, 14 March 1934, 299–301; Raushenbush to Nye, 11 July 1934, R.G. 46.

36. Allen Weinstein, *Perjury: The Hiss-Chambers Case* (New York: Alfred A. Knopf, 1978), 143; J. P. Wenchel to Nye, 21 August 1934, R.G. 46.

37. Weinstein, *Perjury*, 5, 141–44, 124, 184–85.

38. Wiltz, *In Search of Peace*, 52–53.

39. Weinstein, *Perjury*, 75–76, 124–35.

40. Edward L. Schapsmeier and Frederick H. Schapsmeier, *Henry A. Wallace of Iowa: The Agrarian Years, 1910–1940* (Ames: Iowa State University Press, 1968), 203–4; Weinstein, *Perjury*, 153–55; Schlesinger, *Coming of the New Deal*, 78–80.

41. Memorandum of meeting, 5 June 1934, R.G. 46; "Revised Outline of the Committee's Work," 6 June 1934, Nye Papers.

42. *New York Times*, 18 May 1934, 9; *Congressional Record*, 73rd Cong., 2nd sess., 9095; "Arms Manufacturers and the Public," *Foreign Affairs* 12 (July 1934): 639.

43. *New York Times*, 30 May 1934, 10, and 12 June 1934, 17; Kellogg to Nye, 29 May 1934, R.G. 46.

44. Moffat diary cited in Cole, *Roosevelt and the Isolationists*, 149; Edgar B. Nixon, ed., *Franklin D. Roosevelt and Foreign Affairs* (Cambridge, Massachusetts: Harvard University Press, Belknap Press, 1969), 2: 159; *New York Times*, 14 June 1934, 6; Patenaude, *Texans, Politics, and the New Deal*, 40.

45. *New York Times*, 7 July 1934, 15, 8 July 1934, 21, 11 July 1934, 4, and 26 July 1934, 11; Wohlforth to Nye, 27 June 1934, R.G. 46.

46. Schlesinger, *Coming of the New Deal*, 505; Cole, *Senator Gerald P. Nye*, 58–59; Roosevelt's speech, 7 August 1934, Nye Papers.

CHAPTER 3

1. MacArthur to Nye, 8 August 1934, and MacArthur to Raushenbush, 4 August 1934, Record Group 46, United States Senate, Special Committee Investigating the Munitions Industry, National Archives, Washington, D.C. (henceforth cited as R.G. 46); Memorandum on State Department agreement, 8 August 1934, Gerald P. Nye Papers, Herbert Hoover Library, West Branch, Iowa.

2. MacArthur to Lammot Du Pont, 8 August 1934, in Special Committee Investigating the Munitions Industry, Hearings, Part 5, 1074–75 (henceforth cited as Hearings, followed by part and page. For the current example, Hearings, 5: 1074–75); Rexford Tugwell, *The Democratic Roosevelt* (Garden City, New York: Doubleday and Company, 1957), 349–50; *Time*, 3 December 1934, 13–15.

3. Robert Comerford, "The American Liberty League," Ph.D. diss., St. John's University, 1967, 129–30; George Wolfskill, *The Revolt of the Conservatives: A History of the American Liberty League, 1934–1949* (Boston: Houghton Mifflin, 1962), 58–63, 27–28; Frederick Rudolph, "The American Liberty League, 1934–1940," *American Historical Review* 56 (October 1950): 20–21; Arthur M. Schlesinger, Jr., *The Coming of the New Deal* (Boston: Houghton Mifflin, 1958), 486.

4. Donald Day, ed., *Franklin D. Roosevelt's Own Story: Told in His Own Words from His Private and Public Papers* (Boston: Little, Brown and Company, 1951), 221–22; Roosevelt to James Gerard, 5 October 1934, and Roosevelt to William E. Dodd, 25 August 1934, Franklin D. Roosevelt Papers, President's Personal File, Franklin D. Roosevelt Library, Hyde Park, New York.

5. *New York Times*, 18 August 1934, 26, and 28 August 1934, 15.

6. Ibid., 2 September 1934, 12, and 30 August 1934, 1.

7. Green memorandum on meeting with Simons, 28 August 1934, and Green memorandum on meeting with Raushenbush, 25 August 1934, Record Group 59, Department of State Decimal File, 1930–1939, 811.113/Senate Investigation/38 and 15, National Archives, Washington, D.C. (henceforth cited as R.G. 59).

8. Daniel Yergin, *The Prize: The Epic Quest for Oil, Money, and Power* (New York: Simon and Schuster, 1991), 308; *New York Times*, 29 August 1934, 11; Cordell Hull, *The Memoirs of Cordell Hull* (New York: Macmillan, 1958), 1: 288; Henry L. Stimson diary entry on meeting with Norman Davis, 8 October 1934, Henry Lewis Stimson Diaries, Manuscripts and Archives, Yale University Library, New Haven, Connecticut.

9. Hearings, 1: 36–38, 21–22, 82–83; Green to Stimson, 1 June 1934, Henry Lewis Stimson Papers, Manuscripts and Archives, Yale University Library, New Haven, Connecticut.

10. Hearings, 1: 117; Henry Carse to Lawrence Spear, 15 January 1934, Munitions Committee Exhibit 84, cited in Special Committee Investigating the Munitions Industry, Hearings, Part 1, 375 (henceforth, exhibits are cited by their number, followed by hearing part and pages. For the current example, Exhibit 84, 1: 375); Spear to C. W. Craven of Vickers-Armstrong, Ltd., 6 August 1928, Exhibit 127, 1: 407.

11. Hearings, 1: 90, 159–60; Commander Luis Aubry, U.S. naval attaché, Brazil, to Spear, 27 October 1924, Exhibit 65, 1: 355.

12. Joyner to Carse, 18 December 1928, Exhibit 181, 1: 287; Joyner to Carse, 11 March 1929, Exhibit 183, 1: 289; Hearings, 1: 297–98.

13. Hubert Allen, Driggs agent in Turkey, to Louis Driggs, 22 January 1929, Exhibit 219, 2: 538–39; unsigned telegram to Driggs Ordinance, 20 January 1932, Exhibit 223, 2: 544; *New York Times*, 8 September 1934, 1.

14. Hearings, 2: 463–64, 517.

15. Hearings, 3: 554–55; John Ball, director, Soley Armament Company, Ltd., to the American Armament Corporation, 6 February 1934, Exhibit 258, 3: 674–75; Miranda to Ball, 22 February 1934, Exhibit 262, 3: 682–85; Miranda to Joaquim Samper, American Armament agent in Colombia, 4 December 1933, Exhibit 240, 3: 658.

16. Hearings, 4: 693–94, 702, 731; Webster to Lawrence Leon, Curtiss-Wright Export Corporation agent in Argentina, 10 February 1933, Exhibit 360, 4: 939; Clifton Travis of the Compania de Aviacion Faucett, Peru, to Owen Shannon of Curtiss-Wright, 17 May 1933, Exhibit 361, 4: 939–40.

17. Webster to Clifton Travis, 8 February 1933, Exhibit 348, 4: 930–31; Jonas to Owen Shannon, 27 December 1933, Exhibit 338, 4: 918–19.

18. Hearings, 4: 818–22; Rear Admiral E. J. King, U.S. Navy, to Burdette Wright, chief of Curtiss-Wright's Bureau of Aeronautics, 28 June 1933, Exhibit 438, 4: 844–45; Burdette Wright to Curtiss-Wright Export, 1 July 1929, Exhibit 412, 4: 828; W. F. Goulding, vice-president of Curtiss-Wright Export, to F. C. Nichols of Colt's Patent Firearms, 12 October 1932, Exhibit 414, 4: 983.

19. Hearings, 5: 1081; Kellogg to Hull, 7 September 1934, R.G. 59, 811.113/Senate Investigation/41; Welles to Hull, 5 September 1934 and 7 September 1934, Cordell Hull Papers, Library of Congress, Washington, D.C.; Hull, *Memoirs*, 1: 400.

20. Moore to Hull, 7 September 1934, Cordell Hull Papers; Hull, *Memoirs*, 1: 401; *Foreign Relations of the United States, 1934* (Washington, D.C.: Government Printing Office, 1951), 1: 437–38.

21. Telegram, 13 September 1934, and Alvin T. Rowe memorandum, 27 October 1934, R.G. 59, 811.113/Senate Investigation/33 and 160; Bardo to Ray Berdean, 28 September 1934, Nye Papers.

22. Hackworth to Hull, 13 September 1934, R.G. 59, 811.113/Senate Investigation/30; Welles to Hull, 5 September 1934, Cordell Hull Papers.

23. R. Walton Moore to Hull, 7 September 1934, Cordell Hull Papers; Charles Brown to Roosevelt, 15 September 1934, Roosevelt to MacIntyre, 24 September 1934, and J. Edgar Hoover memorandum, 10 October 1934, all in R.G. 60, Department of Justice, File 235644, National Archives, Washington, D.C.

24. Hearings, 5: 1028–29, 1042.

25. Ibid., 5: 1044–48.

26. Ibid., 5: 1055, 1073–75, 1137–38.

27. Ibid., 5: 1121, 1138–41.

28. Ibid., 5: 1149–52.

29. Aiken Simons to John Young, president of Federal Laboratories, 28 December 1932, Exhibit 482, 5: 1134.

30. Hearings, 5: 1171, 1244–60.

31. Ibid., 5: 1266–67.

32. Phillips memorandum, 13 September 1934, R.G. 59, 811.113/Senate Investigation; J. Pierrepont Moffat, *The Moffat Papers: Selections from the Diplomatic Journals of Jay Pierrepont Moffat, 1919–1943* (Cambridge, Massachusetts: Harvard University Press,

1956), 113–15; Hull remarks at press conference, 20 September 1934, R.G. 59, 811.113/Senate Investigation/99.

33. Hearings, 6: 1420, 1498–1501; A. B. Butterfield, Pratt & Whitney installation engineer, to Thomas Hamilton, Pratt & Whitney representative in Europe, 9 May 1933, Exhibit 589, 6: 1582–83.

34. Jonas to Kendrick Van Pelt, Federal Laboratories agent in Brazil, 15 October 1932, Exhibit 665, 7: 1866–67; Jonas to Rauol Leon, Federal Laboratories agent in Argentina, 11 August 1932, Exhibit 671, 7: 1870–71; Jonas to Van Pelt, 12 July 1932, Exhibit 729, 7: 1908; Hearings, 7: 1828.

35. Hearings, 8: 1990, 2001–10.

36. Ibid., 8: 2017–34.

37. Ibid., 8: 2035–36.

38. Carter Tiffany to Anthony H. G. Fokker, 9 May 1934, and Fokker to Tiffany, 16 May 1934, Nye Papers.

39. Moore to Roosevelt, 27 August 1934, and Roosevelt to Hull, 25 September 1934, Roosevelt Papers, Official File; Hull, Memoirs, 1: 388–89, 405; New York Times, 1 October 1934, 3.

40. Stimson diary entry, 30 October 1934, Stimson Diaries; Senator Royal Copeland to Nye, 9 November 1934, R.G. 46; Washington Post, 9 December 1934, 5.

41. New York Times, 30 September 1934, 24, and 4 October 1934, 5; Raushenbush to Nye, 19 October 1934, R.G. 46; Mabel Vernon, WILPF-U.S. campaign director, undated memorandum, "Congressional Election Campaign—Women's International League, 1934," Hannah Clothier Hull Papers, Swarthmore College Peace Collection, Swarthmore, Pennsylvania.

42. Raushenbush to Nye, 3 November 1934, R.G. 46.

43. Roosevelt to Michael Francis Doyle, 6 September 1934, Garner to Roosevelt, 9 November 1934, and Roosevelt to Garner, 13 November 1934, all in Roosevelt Papers, President's Personal File; Frank Freidel, Franklin D. Roosevelt: A Rendezvous with Destiny (Boston: Little, Brown and Company, 1990), 141; New York Times, 7 November 1934, 1.

44. Hull, Memoirs, 1: 232–33; New York Times, 14 November 1934, 12; Green memorandum, 1 December 1934, R.G. 59, 811.113/Senate Investigation/164.

45. Dern to Nye, 20 November 1934, R.G. 46; Green memorandum, 21 November 1934, R.G. 59, 811.113/Senate Investigation/159; Complete Presidential Press Conferences of Franklin D. Roosevelt (New York: DaCapo Press, 1972), 4: 247–48; Department of Justice, File 235644, R.G. 60.

46. Lammot Du Pont to Nye, Nye to Du Pont, and Green memorandum, all dated 3 December 1934, R.G. 59, 811.113/Senate Investigation/169 and 170.

47. Green memorandum, 1 December 1934, R.G. 59, 811.113/527; Time, 3 December 1934, 13–15.

48. Johnson to Roosevelt, 4 December 1934, Roosevelt Papers, President's Personal File.

CHAPTER 4

1. Special Committee Investigating the Munitions Industry, Hearings, Part 10, 2281, 2340 (henceforth cited as Hearings, followed by part and page. For the current example, Hearings, 10: 2281, 2340); Casey to Steffen & Heymann (German import and export company), 14 February 1924, Munitions Committee Exhibit 868, cited in Special Committee Investigating the Munitions Industry, Hearings, Part 10, 2285–86 (henceforth, exhibits are cited by their number, followed by hearing part and page. For the current example, Exhibit 868, 10: 2285–86).

2. Hearings, 10: 2320–44.

3. Ibid., 16: 3931–33.

4. Ibid., 15: 3674–75.

5. Ibid., 11: 2458–67.

6. Casey to Colonel William Taylor, Du Pont representative in Europe, 5 November 1926, and Aiken Simons to the Du Pont Company, 15 October 1925, cited in Hearings, 9: 2185–2200.

7. Hearings, 13: 3193; Pierre Du Pont to E. G. Buckner, vice-president of Du Pont, 1 November 1917, Exhibit 1132, 13: 3144; Pierre Du Pont to General William Crozier, U.S. Army chief of ordinance, 2 November 1917, Exhibit 1135, 13: 3147.

8. Robert S. Brookings, of the War Industries Board, to Secretary of War Newton Baker, 7 November 1917, Exhibit 1139, 14: 3264; Hearings, 14: 3174–76; Pierre Du Pont to the board of directors, 28 November 1917, Exhibit 1149, 14: 3275.

9. Hearings, 14: 3222–25.

10. Ibid., 14: 3257 and 15: 3592–93.

11. Ibid., 14: 3227–28; *New York Times*, 15 December 1934, 1.

12. Hearings, 14: 3222–25; John E. Wiltz, *In Search of Peace: The Senate Munitions Inquiry, 1934–1936* (Baton Rouge: Louisiana State University Press, 1963), 124.

13. Hearings, 15: 3611, 3636–41.

14. Ibid., 15: 3638–41.

15. Ibid., 17: 4280–81.

16. Ibid., 16: 3931–33.

17. Ibid., 17: 4282.

18. Ibid., 17: 4216–18; "Reports of the House Select Committee on Expenditures in the War Department, 1919–1921," Exhibit 1366, 17: 4388–4408.

19. "Reports of the House Select Committee," Exhibit 1366, 17: 4406.

20. Simons memorandum, undated, Exhibit 837, 9: 2255; Casey to Colonel William Taylor, 17 August 1925, Exhibit 849, 9: 2259.

21. Aiken Simons to K.K.V. Casey, 7 April 1932, cited in Hearings, 12: 2724; C.I.B. Henning, Du Pont technical director of military sales, memorandum, 17 November 1924, Exhibit 998, 12: 2661–62; Henning memorandum, 17 November 1925, cited in Hearings, 16: 3959.

22. Casey to F. W. Pickard, vice-president of Du Pont, 25 November 1919, Exhibit 991, 12: 2821; Du Pont Company memorandum, unsigned, 27 July 1923, Exhibit 1026, 12: 2707; "Chemistry's Tremendous Tomorrow," *Literary Digest* (3 November 1923): 23.

23. Charles Weston, Du Pont publicity manager, to Carpenter, 4 December 1919, Exhibit 1059, 12: 2767; Carpenter to Irénée Du Pont, undated, Exhibit 1377, 17: 4241; Hearings, 17: 4235–42.

24. Hearings, 15: 3681–88; Frank Kahrs, assistant advertising manager, *Army and Navy Journal*, to Saunders Norvell, president, Remington Arms Company, Inc., 27 April 1929, Exhibit 1264, 15: 3877; Hearings, 16: 3941; Brigadier General C.L.H. Ruggles, U.S. Army assistant chief of ordinance, to Colonel L. J. Herman, works manager, Remington Arms, 24 April 1928, Exhibit 1287, 16: 4037; Minutes of Remington Arms Company staff meeting, 7 September 1933, cited in Hearings, 16: 3695–97.

25. Report by E. G. Hadley, 14 August 1928, Exhibit 1294, 16: 4041–46; Hearings, 16: 3963–67.

26. Hearings, 17: 4198–4200; Carpenter to Raskob, 16 March 1934, and Raskob to Carpenter, 20 March 1934, Exhibits 1384 and 1385, 17: 4426; *New York Times*, 21 December 1934, 1.

27. Hearings, 17: 4334; War Department report, "The Production of Munitions," unsigned and undated, cited in Hearings, 17: 4337.

28. Gerard Colby, *Du Pont Dynasty* (Secaucus, New Jersey: Lyle Stuart, 1984), 345.

29. Raushenbush to Nye, 18 December 1934, Record Group 46, United States Senate, Special Committee Investigating the Munitions Industry, National Archives, Washington, D.C. (henceforth cited as R.G. 46); Green memorandum, 10 January 1935, Record Group 59, Department of State Decimal File, 1930–1939, 811.113/Senate Investigation/198, National Archives, Washington, D.C. (henceforth cited as R.G. 59).

30. Norman Davis to Roosevelt, 6 November 1934, Cordell Hull Papers, Library of Congress, Washington, D.C.; Robert Dallek, *Franklin D. Roosevelt and American Foreign Policy, 1932–1945* (New York: Oxford University Press, 1979), 88–89.

31. *New York Times*, 13 December 1934, 1–2. Wiltz offered seven possible motivations for Roosevelt's handling of the Baruch-Johnson committee, including that FDR acted "just to see what would happen." See *In Search of Peace*, 121–22. Roosevelt did not need to undercut or shut off the investigation, but rather to assert an executive branch presence where it had been lacking. He acted at the time that he did due to factors considered in the text.

32. *New York Times*, 13 December 1934, 1–2, and 16 December 1934, 2; Detzer telegram, 13 December 1934, and Detzer to Roosevelt, 13 December 1934, Records of the Women's International League for Peace and Freedom, United States Section, 1919–1959, Swarthmore College Peace Collection, Swarthmore, Pennsylvania.

33. "War Profits," *Business Week*, 22 December 1934, 22; Wiltz, *In Search of Peace*, 120–21.

34. Green memorandum, 26 December 1934, R.G. 59, 811.113/Senate Investigation/185; John Kennedy Ohl, *Hugh S. Johnson and the New Deal* (DeKalb: Northern Illinois University Press, 1985), 256; *Congressional Record*, 74th Cong., 1st sess., 42; Minutes of munitions committee meeting, 3 January 1935, and Raushenbush to Flynn, 16 January 1935, R.G. 46.

35. *New York Times*, 18 January 1935, 3; Hull memorandum, 17 January 1935, R.G. 59, 811.113/Senate Investigation/201; Donald Wemple to Raushenbush, 18 January 1935, R.G. 46.

36. Memorandum, "Brief—Shipbuilding Industry," 8 January 1935, R.G. 46; Brent Dow Allison, "Senator Nye Sums Up," *Christian Century*, 16 January 1935, 80–81; *Congressional Record*, 74th Cong., 1st sess., 460; Wayne S. Cole, *Roosevelt and the Isolationists, 1932–1945* (Lincoln: University of Nebraska Press, 1983), 153.

37. Cordell Hull, *The Memoirs of Cordell Hull* (New York: Macmillan, 1948), 1: 388–89; Dallek, *Franklin D. Roosevelt and American Foreign Policy*, 93; *Foreign Relations of the United States, 1935* (Washington, D.C.: Government Printing Office, 1953), 1: 384–85; *New York Times*, 6 January 1935, 1; Cole, *Roosevelt and the Isolationists*, 120–24.

38. Dallek, *Franklin D. Roosevelt and American Foreign Policy*, 96; Elliott Roosevelt, ed., *FDR: His Personal Letters, 1928–1945* (New York: Duell, Sloan, and Pearce, 1950), 1: 449–51; Harold L. Ickes, *The Secret Diary of Harold L. Ickes* (New York: Simon and Schuster, 1953), 1: 287; Roosevelt to Stimson, 6 February 1935, Henry Lewis Stimson Papers, Manuscripts and Archives, Yale University Library, New Haven, Connecticut.

39. Dallek, *Franklin D. Roosevelt and American Foreign Policy*, 91–97; Roosevelt to Stimson, 6 February 1935, Stimson Papers; Cole, *Roosevelt and the Isolationists*, 125–27.

40. Memorandum of meeting, 13 December 1934, R.G. 46.

41. Hull, *Memoirs*, 1: 401; Green memorandums, 6 February 1935 and 7 February 1935, R.G. 59, 811.113/Senate Investigation/209 and 210.

42. *New York Times*, 3 January 1935, 17, and 29 January 1935, 2.

43. Aiken Simons memorandum, 13 January 1933, cited in Hearings, 11: 2466–67.

44. Elliott Roosevelt, ed., *FDR: His Personal Letters*, 1: 452–53; Roosevelt to Hull, 23 February 1935, R.G. 59, 811.113/582.

CHAPTER 5

1. Norman Parker, treasurer of New York Shipbuilding, to Chester Cuthell of the U.S. Shipping Board, 15 February 1918, Munitions Committee Exhibit 1415, cited in Special Committee Investigating the Munitions Industry, Hearings, Part 18, 4847 (henceforth exhibits are cited by their number, followed by hearing part and page. For the current example, Exhibit 1415, 18: 4847); Special Committee Investigating the Munitions Industry, Hearings, Part 18, 4532–35 (henceforth cited as Hearings, followed by part and page. For the current example, Hearings, 18: 4532–35).

2. Hearings, 18: 4545–58; Office of the Resident Auditor, Emergency Fleet Corporation, "Report on Determination of Amortization Claim New York Shipbuilding Corporation," 12 July 1927, Exhibit 1422, 18: 4855–56.

3. "Supplemental Agreement Supplementing Contracts Nos. 151, 151 Supplement 418, 420, 419, and 453, and Relating to 'Requisitioned Ships' Between New York Shipbuilding and the U.S. Shipping Board," 27 July 1920, Exhibit 1431, 18: 4862–65; Hearings, 18: 4599–4602.

4. Confidential report by Internal Revenue Service agent Frank Horton, 30 March 1927, Exhibit 1557, 20: 5603–5; Hearings, 20: 5287–90 and 21: 5818.

5. Hearings, 21: 5758–66.

6. Ibid., 21: 5765–66, 5777–79, 5798–99.

7. Hearings, 18: 4627; *Camden Courier-Post*, 6 June 1934, 12; Bardo to Ray Berdean, 28 September 1934, and Bardo's resignation, Gerald P. Nye Papers, Herbert Hoover Library, West Branch, Iowa.

8. Hearings, 18: 4635.

9. Bardo to Governor Moore, 28 June 1933, Exhibit 1497, 18: 5225; Roosevelt to Moore, 15 July 1933, Exhibit 1517, 18: 5051; Hearings, 19: 5043–52; John Kincaid, "Frank Hague and Franklin Roosevelt: The Hudson Dictator and the Country Democrat," in *Franklin D. Roosevelt: The Man, the Myth, the Era, 1882–1945*, edited by Herbert D. Rosenbaum and Elizabeth Bartelme (New York: Greenwood Press, 1987), 17, 24–27.

10. Bardo to F. P. Palen of Newport News Shipbuilding, 5 September 1928, cited in Hearings, 20: 5458–59.

11. Hearings, 23: 6813–17; Powell to H.T.E. Beardsley, insurance broker for United Dry Docks, 20 September 1933, cited in Hearings, 23: 6816.

12. Charles Bates, vice-president of United Dry Docks, to James Nelson, plant manager, 27 April 1934, cited in Hearings, 23: 6811; U.S. Navy Commander Fred Crisp to Powell, 24 June 1933, Exhibit 1859, 23: 7002; Hearings, 23: 6840–43.

13. Newell to Gannett, 28 January 1932, and Gannett to Newell, 29 January 1932, Exhibits 1802 and 1803, 23: 6961–62; Hearings, 23: 6719–22.

14. John E. Wiltz, *In Search of Peace: The Senate Munitions Inquiry, 1934–1936* (Baton Rouge: Louisiana State University Press, 1963), 11–13; F. P. Palen to F. H. Skinner, attorney for Newport News Shipbuilding, 1 August 1929, cited in Hearings, 20: 5535–37; Shearer to S. W. Wakeman, general manager of Bethlehem Shipbuilding Company, 30 January 1928, cited in Hearings, 20: 5547–48.

15. Hearings, 21: 5969; Shearer to Homer L. Ferguson, 27 March 1929, cited in Hearings, 21: 6083–88; Shearer to Nye, 14 March 1935, Exhibit 1676, 21: 6150.

16. Hearings, 21: 5980–85.

17. Bardo to Mellon, undated telegram, cited in Hearings, 18: 4667; Hearings, 18: 4664–68.

18. Hearings, 19: 5149 and 20: 5528–31.

19. Ibid., 20: 5352–64.

20. Ibid., 21: 5872–76.

21. Ibid., 18: 4691–93.

22. Ibid., 18: 4735–40.

23. Ibid., 18: 4748–58.

24. E. A. Eldred, Mayflower Hotel credit manager, to the munitions committee, 29 January 1935, Exhibit 1488, 19: 5194; Hearings, 19: 4988–93.

25. Hearings, 19: 5003–5.

26. Ibid., 19: 5007–11.

27. Swanson to Senator Park Trammel, chair of the Senate Naval Affairs Committee, 9 August 1933, cited in Hearings, 18: 4763–64.

28. Hearings, 18: 4783–84.

29. Hearings, 20: 5493–99; Memorandum, Newport News Shipbuilding, 21 July 1933, cited in Hearings, 20: 5499.

30. Bardo to Flook, 22 June 1933, Exhibit 1554, 19: 5181; Hearings, 19: 5181–83.

31. Hearings, 23: 6922–23.

32. Ibid., 24: 7114, 7167–75.

33. Ibid., 21: 5900–5902, 5932–33.

34. Ibid., 18: 4799–4800, 4814, 4745.

35. Ibid., 23: 6662, 6725–56.

36. Homer to Eugene Grace, president of Bethlehem Shipbuilding Company, 17 October 1932, cited in Hearings, 19: 4963–64; Hearings, 18: 4829; Homer memorandum, undated, Exhibit 1484, 18: 4921–23; Franklin D. Roosevelt Papers, Assistant Secretary of the Navy File, Franklin D. Roosevelt Library, Hyde Park, New York; *New York Times*, 1 February 1935, 8.

37. Hearings, 20: 5410–11, 5383; Homer memorandum, undated, Exhibit 1484, 18: 4921–23.

38. Hearings, 20: 5581–96.

39. Ibid., 21: 5714, 5726.

40. Ibid., 21: 5783–84.

41. Ibid., 21: 5786; "Arms and the Men," *Fortune* 9 (March 1934): 125–26.

42. Hearings, 18: 4671–80.

43. *Complete Presidential Press Conferences of Franklin D. Roosevelt* (New York: DaCapo Press, 1972), 5: 88; *New York Times*, 2 February 1935, 2.

44. Roosevelt to Hull, 23 February 1935, Record Group 59, Department of State Decimal File, 1930–1939, 811.113/582, National Archives, Washington, D.C. (henceforth cited as R.G. 59); text of Pope's speech, 3 March 1935, Records of the National Council for the Prevention of War, Swarthmore College Peace Collection, Swarthmore, Pennsylvania.

45. Green memorandum, 13 March 1935, *Foreign Relations of the United States, 1935* (Washington, D.C.: Government Printing Office, 1953), 1: 317–18 (henceforth cited as *FRUS*); William Potter, board chairman of Guaranty Trust Company, to Hull, 5 March 1935, and Hull memorandum, 14 March 1935, R.G. 59, 811.113/Senate Investigation/214 and 216.

46. *FRUS 1935*, 1: 318–21; Hull memorandum, 15 March 1935, R.G. 59, 811.113/ Senate Investigation/217.

47. "Report of the Commission Created by Public Resolution No. 98, Seventy-First Congress, Approved June 27, 1930," report dated 5 March 1935, cited in Hearings, 21: 5990–91; Hearings, 21: 5998–6003.

48. Hearings, 21: 6003–5.

49. Ibid., 21: 6019–21, 6032–33, 6058–62.

50. Cordell Hull, *The Memoirs of Cordell Hull* (New York: Macmillan, 1948), 1: 243; *New York Times*, 19 March 1935, 1.

51. Hearings, 22: 6183–86, 6196, 6205.

52. *FRUS 1935*, 1: 363–64; *New York Times*, 19 March 1935, 1; *Complete Presidential Press Conferences of Franklin D. Roosevelt*, 5: 169–70.

53. Wayne S. Cole, *Roosevelt and the Isolationists, 1932–1945* (Lincoln: University of Nebraska Press, 1983), 154; Wiltz, *In Search of Peace*, 175; Robert Dallek, *Franklin D. Roosevelt and American Foreign Policy, 1932–1945* (New York: Oxford University Press, 1979), 102; Robert A. Divine, *Illusion of Neutrality* (Chicago: University of Chicago Press, 1962), 87–88.

54. Green memorandums, 18 March 1935, 27 March 1935, and 11 April 1935, R.G. 59, 811.113/Senate Investigation/228, 237A, and 242; Hull, *Memoirs*, 1: 405; *FRUS 1935*, 1: 339–40, 362–63.

55. Hull, *Memoirs*, 1: 402; *FRUS 1935*, 1: 364–66; Green memorandums, 20 March 1935 and 22 March 1935, R.G. 59, 811.113/Senate Investigation/226 and 230.

56. Hearings, 22: 6210–12, 6232; Charts of prices and wages, 1913–1921, Exhibits 1684–87, 22: 6429–30.

57. Hearings, 22: 6243–45.

58. Ibid., 22: 6262–73.

59. Federal Trade Commission memorandum, undated, "The Cost of Producing Copper During the Year of 1917," Exhibit 1712, 22: 6470–84; Minutes of War Industries Board meeting, 21 September 1917, Exhibit 1703, 22: 6464; Hearings, 22: 6300–6304, 6322.

60. Mellon to C. F. Kelley, president, Anaconda Copper Mining Company, 16 December 1922, Exhibit 1713, 22: 6485.

61. Hearings, 22: 6390–98; T. J. Coolidge, acting secretary of the treasury, to Nye, undated, Exhibit 1740, 22: 6555.

62. Hearings, 22: 6417–22; Baruch to Nye, 12 April 1935, cited in Hearings, 22: 6635.

63. *Congressional Record*, 74th Cong., 1st sess., 4726–27.

64. *New York Times*, 27 March 1935, 8; Raushenbush memorandum, 1 April 1935, Record Group 46, United States Senate, Special Committee Investigating the Munitions Industry, National Archives, Washington, D.C. The Elliott Roosevelt affair is discussed in Chapter 3.

65. *Washington Post*, 7 April 1935, 1; *Congressional Record*, 74th Cong., 1st sess., 5184–97.

66. Hearings, 24: 7078–92; *Congressional Record*, 74th Cong., 1st sess., 5325–26, 5191, 5198.

67. Wayne S. Cole, *Senator Gerald P. Nye and American Foreign Relations* (Minneapolis: University of Minnesota Press, 1963), 85–86; Wiltz, *In Search of Peace*, 143–44.

68. *Congressional Record*, 74th Cong., 1st sess., 8338–41; *FRUS 1935*, 1: 329–30.

69. *FRUS 1935*, 1: 331–39.

70. Hull, *Memoirs*, 1: 403; *FRUS 1935*, 1: 372–73.

71. "Decision of the National Labor Relations Board, 21 February 1935," Exhibit 2009, 24: 7428–32; Hearings, 24: 7377–84.

CHAPTER 6

1. *Washington Post*, 6 March 1935, 5. For more discussion on the backgrounds of Nye, Clark, and Raushenbush, see Chapters 1 and 2.

2. Walter Rauschenbush, *Christianity and the Social Crisis* (New York: Macmillan, 1907), 270; Reinhold Niebuhr, *Moral Man and Immoral Society: A Study in Ethics and Politics* (1932; reprint, New York: Charles Scribner's Sons, 1949), 16.

3. *Christian Century*, 4 July 1934, 887–90; Richard Wightman Fox, *Reinhold Niebuhr: A Biography* (New York: Pantheon Books, 1985), 158.

4. Reinhold Niebuhr, *An Interpretation of Christian Ethics* (New York: Harper and Brothers, 1935), 121–22, 194–96.

5. Fox, *Reinhold Niebuhr*, 168.

6. Carl N. Degler, "The Third American Revolution," in *The New Deal: The Critical Issues*, edited by Otis L. Graham, Jr. (Boston: Little, Brown and Company, 1971), 103; Richard S. Kirkendall, "The Great Depression: Another Watershed in American History?"

in *Change and Continuity in Twentieth-Century America*, edited by John Bracman, Robert H. Bremner and Everett Walters (New York: Harper Colophon Books, 1964), 145–89.

7. Max Freedman, ed., *Roosevelt and Frankfurter: Their Correspondence, 1928–1945* (Boston: Little, Brown and Company, 1967), 282–83.

8. For accounts of Roosevelt's political lethargy in the spring of 1935, see William E. Leuchtenburg, *Franklin D. Roosevelt and the New Deal, 1932–1940* (New York: Harper and Row, 1963), 146; James MacGregor Burns, *Roosevelt: The Lion and the Fox* (Harcourt Brace and Company, 1956), 215; and Frank Freidel, *Franklin D. Roosevelt: A Rendezvous with Destiny* (Boston: Little, Brown and Company, 1990), 152–55.

9. Green memorandums, 7 May 1935 and 25 May 1935, Record Group 59, Department of State Decimal File, 1930–1939, 811.113/608 and 616, National Archives, Washington, D.C. (henceforth cited as R.G. 59); *Foreign Relations of the United States, 1935* (Washington, D.C.: Government Printing Office, 1953), 1: 341 (henceforth cited as *FRUS*).

10. *Washington Post*, 2 December 1934, section 3, 2; *New York Times*, 7 May 1935, 1, and 21 May 1935, 13; Harold L. Ickes, *The Secret Diary of Harold L. Ickes* (New York: Simon and Schuster, 1953), 359.

11. *New York Times*, 6 May 1935, 1.

12. *Congressional Record*, 74th Cong., 1st sess., 7980–83.

13. Ibid., 8066–67; Freedman, ed., *Roosevelt and Frankfurter: Their Correspondence*, 272–73.

14. *New York Times*, 3 May 1935, 1; Leuchtenburg, *Franklin D. Roosevelt and the New Deal*, 147–48.

15. *Congressional Record*, 74th Cong., 1st sess., 9053; Wayne S. Cole, *Roosevelt and the Isolationists, 1932–1945* (Lincoln: University of Nebraska Press, 1983), 138–39, 190; James T. Patterson, *Congressional Conservatism and the New Deal* (1967; reprint, Westport, Connecticut: Greenwood Press, 1981), 41–45.

16. *Congressional Record*, 74th Cong., 1st sess., 8666, 9743; Homer Cummings diary entry, 14 June 1935, Homer Cummings Diaries, microfilm, Franklin D. Roosevelt Library, Hyde Park, New York.

17. Senate Special Committee on Investigation of the Munitions Industry, *Preliminary Report on Naval Shipbuilding*, 74th Cong., 1st sess., 1935, Senate Report 944, 4–9.

18. Ibid., 1, 220–53; *Congressional Record*, 74th Cong., 1st sess., 10132–33.

19. *Congressional Record*, 74th Cong., 1st sess., 9954–56, 10142–43.

20. *New York Times*, 5 July 1935, 5.

21. *Congressional Record*, 74th Cong., 1st sess., 10132; Charles Warren, "Memorandum on Some Problems in the Maintenance and Enforcement of the Neutrality of the United States," August 1934, R.G. 59, 811.04418/28; Secretary of the Navy Claude Swanson to Hull, 15 December 1934, R.G. 59, 811.04418/9.

22. Cordell Hull, *The Memoirs of Cordell Hull* (New York: Macmillan, 1948), 1: 410; Memorandum by William Phillips, 29 June 1935, R.G. 59, 811.04418/55.

23. Raushenbush's involvement in the neutrality issue is evident from the records of the munitions committee. For examples, see his letters to William T. Stone, 10 July 1935, 11 July 1935, and 16 July 1935, Record Group 46, United States Senate, Special Committee Investigating the Munitions Industry, National Archives, Washington, D.C. (henceforth cited as R.G. 46). For further consideration of the relationship between the munitions investigation and neutrality legislation, see Robert A. Divine, *The Illusion of*

Neutrality (Chicago: University of Chicago Press, 1962), 120–21; Cole, *Roosevelt and the Isolationists*, 169–70; and John E. Wiltz, *From Isolation to War, 1931–1941* (Arlington Heights, Illinois: Harlan Davidson, 1968), 49–51.

24. Moffat memorandum, 31 May 1935, Green memorandum, 3 June 1935, Polk to Phillips, 1 July 1935, and Phillips to Polk, 3 July 1935, all in R.G. 59, 811.113/Senate Investigation/265, 266, 269 1/2.

25. Watson to Roosevelt, 3 May 1935 and 6 July 1935, Franklin D. Roosevelt Papers, President's Personal File, Franklin D. Roosevelt Library, Hyde Park, New York.

26. *Complete Presidential Press Conferences of Franklin D. Roosevelt* (New York: DaCapo Press, 1972), 6: 28–29, 53–54; *New York Times*, 21 August 1935, 11.

27. Hull, *Memoirs*, 1: 410; Nye and Clark to Pittman, 10 July 1935, R. Walton Moore Papers, Franklin D. Roosevelt Library, Hyde Park, New York.

28. Raushenbush to William Stone, 11 July 1935 and 16 July 1935, R.G. 46; William Phillips to Hull, 17 July 1935, Cordell Hull Papers, Library of Congress, Washington, D.C.; Norman Davis to William Phillips, 18 July 1935, Moore Papers.

29. Hull, *Memoirs*, 1: 411; Robert Dallek, *Franklin D. Roosevelt and American Foreign Policy, 1932–1945* (New York: Oxford University Press, 1979), 106; Patrick J. Maney, *The Roosevelt Presence: A Biography of Franklin Delano Roosevelt* (New York: Twayne, 1992), 57.

30. Raushenbush memorandums, 30 July 1935 and 9 August 1935, and Raushenbush to William Stone, 9 August 1935, R.G. 46; *FRUS 1935*, 1: 343–50.

31. *Congressional Record*, 74th Cong., 1st sess., 12902–20; Detzer to Huldah Randall, 20 August 1935, Records of the Women's International League for Peace and Freedom, United States Section, 1919–1959, Swarthmore College Peace Collection, Swarthmore, Pennsylvania.

32. Divine, *Illusion of Neutrality*, 107–8; Green memorandum, 16 August 1935, R.G. 59, 811.04418/80; *New York Times*, 18 August 1935, 7.

33. *New York Times*, 19 August 1935, 1; Divine, *Illusion of Neutrality*, 109; Hull, *Memoirs*, 1: 411–12; Pittman letter to the White House, 19 August 1935, Roosevelt Papers, President's Personal File.

34. *New York Times*, 21 August 1935, 1, and 14 August 1935, 6; *Congressional Record*, 74th Cong., 1st sess., 13775–97; John D. Donovan, "Congressional Isolationists and the Roosevelt Foreign Policy," *World Politics* 3 (April 1951): 299–316.

35. Hull, *Memoirs*, 1: 412–15; *FRUS 1935*, 1: 350–52; Hull to Stimson, 22 August 1935, Cordell Hull Papers; *Congressional Record*, 74th Cong., 1st sess., 14434; *New York Times*, 1 September 1935, 1.

36. Lawrence Brown to Raushenbush, 27 July 1935, Wemple to Raushenbush, 10 August 1935, and "Statement on Morgan Subpoenas," 13 August 1935, all in R.G. 46.

37. John E. Wiltz, *In Search of Peace: The Senate Munitions Inquiry, 1934–1936* (Baton Rouge: Louisiana State University Press, 1963), 66; Green memorandum, 13 August 1935, R.G. 59, 811.113/Senate Investigation/290.

38. British Ambassador Ronald Lindsay and French Ambassador Andre de Laboulaye to Hull, 12 August 1935, and Hull's responses, 17 August 1935, R.G. 59, 811.113/Senate Investigation/295–98; Green memorandums, 14 August 1935 and 19 August 1935, R.G. 59, 811.113/Senate Investigation/288 and 305.

39. Raushenbush to Nye, 8 July 1935, R.G. 46; Special Committee on Investigation of the Munitions Industry, *Preliminary Report on Wartime Taxation and Price Control*, Senate Report 944, part 2, 20 August 1935, 3–4. Henceforth the report will be cited as *Report on Wartime Taxation*.

40. *Report on Wartime Taxation*, 28, 42, 47–48.

41. Ibid., 88, 101–9, 65.

42. Ibid., 6, 52.

43. Nye radio address, 5 September 1935, R.G. 46; Nye's college campus speeches, Gerald P. Nye Papers, Herbert Hoover Library, West Branch, Iowa.

44. Elliott Roosevelt, ed., *FDR: His Personal Letters, 1928–1945* (New York: Duell, Sloan, and Pearce, 1950), 1: 452–53.

45. Ibid., 1: 506–7.

46. Dallek, *Franklin D. Roosevelt and American Foreign Policy*, 110–16; Hull, *Memoirs*, 1: 442. Texans chaired nine House and Senate committees during the New Deal years, and Vice-President John Nance Garner was also from the state.

47. Frankfurter to Stimson, 26 October 1935, and Stimson to James Rogers, 6 December 1935, Henry Lewis Stimson Papers, Manuscripts and Archives, Yale University Library, New Haven, Connecticut.

48. Cummings diary entries for 25 October 1935, 15 November 1935, 13 December 1935, and 20 December 1935, Cummings Diaries; Ickes, *Secret Diary*, 483–94; R. Walton Moore to Marvin MacIntyre, 30 December 1935, Moore Papers.

49. Hull, *Memoirs*, 1: 462; Pittman to Hull, 2 January 1936, Cordell Hull Papers.

50. Nye to Raushenbush, 10 December 1935, R.G. 46; R. Walton Moore to Hull, 23 December 1935, Moore Papers; Hull, *Memoirs*, 1: 464.

51. John Bassett Moore to Green H. Hackworth, 5 November 1935, R.G. 59, 811.113/Senate Investigation/323; Raushenbush to Lawrence Brown, 4 December 1935, R.G. 46; Raushenbush to Donald Wemple, 18 December 1935, cited in Special Committee Investigating the Munitions Industry, Hearings, Part 38, 12792; Memorandum, unsigned, "Unfinished Committee Business," 26 December 1935, R.G. 46.

52. *Time*, 3 June 1935, 45; *New York Times*, 17 August 1935, 1; Leuchtenburg, *Franklin D. Roosevelt and the New Deal*, 110–11; David Robinson, *Chaplin* (New York: McGraw-Hill, 1989), 468–73.

CHAPTER 7

1. *Congressional Record*, 74th Cong., 2nd sess., 27–28; *Time*, 13 January 1936, 9.

2. *Congressional Record*, 74th Cong., 2nd sess., 28–29.

3. Raushenbush to Nye, 28 January 1936, Record Group 46, United States Senate, Special Committee Investigating the Munitions Industry, National Archives, Washington, D.C.; Memorandum, unsigned, 22 January 1936, Franklin D. Roosevelt Papers, Official File, Franklin D. Roosevelt Library, Hyde Park, New York; Harold L. Ickes, *The Secret Diary of Harold L. Ickes* (New York: Simon and Schuster, 1953), 523; Hull to Roosevelt, 27 January 1936, Roosevelt Papers, President's Personal File.

4. *Congressional Record*, 74th Cong., 2nd sess., 292, 703; Ickes, *Secret Diary*, 525; Roger Daniels, *The Bonus March: An Episode of the Great Depression* (Westport, Connecticut: Greenwood Press, 1971), 240–41.

5. Special Committee Investigating the Munitions Industry, Hearings, Part 25, 7478 (henceforth cited as Hearings, followed by part and page. For the current example, Hearings, 25: 7478); *Foreign Relations of the United States, 1936* (Washington, D.C.: Government Printing Office, 1953), 1: 22–23; Cordell Hull, *The Memoirs of Cordell Hull* (New York: Macmillan, 1948), 1: 449.

6. *Time*, 6 January 1936, 11, and 13 January 1936, 11; Green to Moffat, 9 January 1936, cited in Wayne S. Cole, *Roosevelt and the Isolationists, 1932–1945* (Lincoln: University of Nebraska Press, 1983), 156.

7. Hearings, 25: 7483–85, 7566–68.

8. H. P. Davison of Morgan, Grenfell & Company, London, to E. C. Grenfell, 16 November 1914, Munitions Committee Exhibit 2162, cited in Special Committee Investigating the Munitions Industry, Hearings, Part 26, 7796–97 (henceforth exhibits are cited by their number, followed by hearing part and pages. For the current example, Exhibit 2162, 26: 7796–97); Hearings, 26: 7517–19.

9. Hearings, 26: 7839; McAdoo to Wilson, 21 August 1915, Exhibit 2219, 26: 8123–25.

10. Hearings, 26: 7853–66; Lansing to Wilson, 25 August 1915, Exhibit 2223, 26: 7865.

11. Hearings, 26: 7886–87.

12. Ibid., 26: 7913–15, 8138.

13. Ibid., 27: 8156–67.

14. Telegram, drafted but not sent, Morgan & Company Export Department to H. P. Davison, 18 September 1916, Exhibit 2098, 25: 7732–33; Thomas W. Lamont to Davison, 14 October 1916, Exhibit 2108, 25: 7742; Hearings, 25: 7601–15.

15. Hearings, 26: 7815–17; Warburg to the Federal Reserve Board, 13 November 1916, Exhibit 2183, 26: 7817.

16. Morgan to Davison, 20 October 1916, Exhibit 2577, 28: 8712; Morgan to E. C. Grenfell, 28 November 1916, Exhibit 2609, 28: 8738–39.

17. Strong to Morgan, 31 August 1916, Exhibit 2477, 27: 8446; Hearings, 27: 8245–51.

18. Hearings, 27: 8235–36.

19. Hearings, 29: 9016–21; J. P. Morgan to Morgan, Grenfell & Company, London, 2 July 1917, Exhibit 2801, 29: 9238.

20. Hearings, 29: 9041–48.

21. Ibid., 28: 8625–33.

22. Ibid., 29: 9083–84.

23. Ibid., 29: 9156–72; McAdoo to Oscar Crosby, acting secretary of the treasury, 26 January 1918, Exhibit 3039, 29: 9454–55.

24. Hearings, 29: 9196–9204; Glass to Albert Rathbone, assistant secretary of the treasury, 15 December 1919, Exhibit 3106, 29: 9483–84.

25. John Bassett Moore to Benjamin Strong of the Federal Reserve Board, 26 August 1915, Exhibit 2141, 25: 7775–78.

26. Hearings, 26: 7810–15, 7893, 7921–25.

27. Ibid., 26: 7921–25.

28. Ibid., 29: 9059–62.

29. Ibid., 27: 8252–56, 8272–77; Lansing to Wilson, 2 January 1916, Exhibit 2518, 27: 8474–75.

30. Wilson to Edward House, 23 July 1916, Exhibit 2536, 28: 8658–59; William Redfield of the Department of Commerce to Lansing, 23 October 1916, Exhibit 2540, 28: 8669; Hearings, 28: 8495–98.

31. Hearings, 28: 8509–14.

32. Ellis N. Livingston, "Senate Investigating Committees, 1900–1938" (Ph.D. diss., University of Minnesota, 1953), 153.

33. Hearings, 28: 8633–37.

34. *Congressional Record*, 74th Cong., 2nd sess., 504–12.

35. Ibid., 504–9.

36. Ibid., 564–69.

37. Rixley Smith and Norman Beasley, *Carter Glass: A Biography* (New York: Longmans, Green and Company, 1939), 160, 198; Carroll Kilpatrick, ed., *Roosevelt and Daniels: A Friendship in Politics* (Chapel Hill: University of North Carolina Press, 1952), 140–41; Donald A. Ritchie, "The Pecora Wall Street Exposé, 1934," in *Congress Investigates*, edited by Arthur M. Schlesinger, Jr. and Roger Bruns (New York: Chelsea House, 1975), 4: 2567; *Congressional Record*, 74th Cong., 2nd sess., 572–73.

38. *Congressional Record*, 74th Cong., 2nd sess., 573; *Radical Religion* (Winter, 1935–1936): 8.

39. *Congressional Record*, 74th Cong., 2nd sess., 573–77.

40. Ickes, *Secret Diary*, 514–15; Cummings diary entry, 17 January 1936, Homer Cummings Diaries, microfilm, Franklin D. Roosevelt Library, Hyde Park, New York; Green memorandum, 18 January 1936, Record Group 59, Department of State Decimal File, 1930–1939, 811.113/Senate Investigation/384, National Archives, Washington, D.C. (henceforth cited as R.G. 59).

41. Hiram Johnson, *Diary Letters of Hiram Johnson, 1917–1945* (New York: Garland Publishing, 1983), volume 5, letter dated 18 January 1936; Norris letter, 20 January 1936, cited in Cole, *Roosevelt and the Isolationists*, 158; Detzer to Harold Fey, 20 January 1936, Records of the Women's International League for Peace and Freedom, United States Section, 1919–1959, Swarthmore College Peace Collection, Swarthmore, Pennsylvania (henceforth cited as WILPF-U.S. Records); Hull, *Memoirs*, 1: 403–4; Hull to George, 28 January 1936, and Hull to Pittman, 29 January 1936, Cordell Hull Papers, Library of Congress, Washington, D.C.

42. Cole, *Roosevelt and the Isolationists*, 159; Hull, *Memoirs*, 1: 403.

43. *New York Times*, 26 January 1936, 1, 36–37; Detzer memorandum, 12 February 1936, and Detzer to Merle Curti, December 1935, WILPF-U.S. Records.

44. Green memorandum, 23 January 1936, R.G. 59, 811.113/Senate Investigation/388.

45. Hearings, 36: 11881, 11903.

46. "Results of three typical armour contracts," Carnegie-Illinois Steel Corporation, Office of the Auditor, undated, Exhibit 4469, 36: 12172; Hearings, 36: 11920–22, 11958–59.

47. Colt's Patent Fire Arms Manufacturing Company to Albert Foster, 5 October 1932, Exhibit 4663, 37: 12467; F. C. Nichols, Colt vice-president, to L. Becker, 31 March 1933, Exhibit 4698, 37: 12550; Hearings, 37: 12488.

48. Hearings, 39: 13324–31.

49. Hearings, 36: 11979–83, 12023–25; Detzer to the munitions committee, 31 May 1934, WILPF-U.S. Records; "Excerpts from Minutes of the Meeting of the Executive

Committee of the Navy League of the United States," 9 November 1933, Exhibit 4577, 36: 12327–28.

50. Hearings, 36: 12018–20; Daniels to Roosevelt, 5 November 1938, Roosevelt Papers, President's Personal File; Frank Freidel, *Franklin D. Roosevelt: The Apprenticeship* (Boston: Little, Brown and Company, 1952), 208, 290–91.

51. Hearings, 37: 12399; Codd to Colonel William Coleman, 13 July 1933, Exhibit 4614, 37: 25505–6; Codd to A. H. Dill, Picatinny Arsenal, Dover, New Jersey, 19 July 1933, Exhibit 4613, 37: 25504–5.

52. Of the seven senators on the committee, only Nye and Clark were present for questioning of Navy League officials. Nye was the only senator present to hear testimony from leaders of the Army Ordinance Association. Hearings, 36: 11971 and 37: 12399.

53. Hearings, 38: 12803–11, 12887, 12955–71.

54. Ibid., 39: 13278, 13305–10.

55. "Cost of Providing Sufficient Government Shipbuilding Facilities to Allow for a Normal Naval Building and Repair Program," report prepared by the Interstate Commerce Commission for the munitions committee, undated, Exhibit 4402, 36: 12054–81; Hearings, 36: 11862–63, 11876–77.

56. Hearings, 36: 11878.

57. "Arms and the Men," *Fortune* 9 (March 1934): 125; Hearings, 36: 11924–31, 11951.

58. Hearings, 36: 12033.

59. Hull, *Memoirs*, 1: 462–63; *Congressional Record*, 74th Cong., 2nd sess., 5.

60. *Congressional Record*, 74th Cong., 2nd sess., 47.

61. Robert Dallek, *Franklin D. Roosevelt and American Foreign Policy, 1932–1945* (New York: Oxford University Press, 1979), 119–20; *Congressional Record*, 74th Cong., 2nd sess., 1143; Cummings diary entry, 7 February 1936, Cummings Diaries; Hull, *Memoirs*, 1: 466.

62. *Congressional Record*, 74th Cong., 2nd sess., 1860, 2123, 2253; Hull, *Memoirs*, 1: 465–66; Cole, *Roosevelt and the Isolationists*, 185.

63. *New York Times*, 14 February 1936, 7; *Congressional Record*, 74th Cong., 2nd sess., 2291–2306.

64. Hull, *Memoirs*, 1: 466–67; Robert A. Divine, *The Illusion of Neutrality* (Chicago: University of Chicago Press, 1962), 130.

65. Mikiso Hane, *Modern Japan: A Historical Survey* (Boulder, Colorado: Westview Press, 1986), 264–65; William L. Shirer, *The Rise and Fall of the Third Reich: A History of Nazi Germany* (New York: Simon and Schuster, 1960), 294–95; *Complete Presidential Press Conferences of Franklin D. Roosevelt* (New York: DaCapo Press, 1972), 7: 179–85; Ickes, *Secret Diary*, 543–48.

CHAPTER 8

1. Special Committee on Investigation of the Munitions Industry, *Report on Activities and Sales of Munitions Companies* (Washington, D.C.: Government Printing Office, 1936), 1–8.

2. Ibid., 59–66, 161–72.

3. Ibid., 159–61.

4. Ibid., 250–60.

5. *New York Times*, 19 February 1936, 21, and 26 April 1936, 1.

6. *New York Times*, 26 April 1936, 31.

7. Cordell Hull, *The Memoirs of Cordell Hull* (New York: Macmillan, 1948), 1: 468–71.

8. Special Committee on Investigation of the Munitions Industry, *Report on War Department Bills* (Washington, D.C.: Government Printing Office, 1936), 1–5.

9. Ibid., 35–40.

10. Special Committee on Investigation of the Munitions Industry, *Report on Existing Legislation* (Washington, D.C.: Government Printing Office, 1936), 4–9.

11. Charles Cheney Hyde to Lansing, 11 January 1916, and William Redfield to Lansing, 23 October 1916, cited in *Report on Existing Legislation*, 31–32, 54; *Report on Existing Legislation*, 75–82.

12. *Report on Existing Legislation*, 82–87.

13. Special Committee on Investigation of the Munitions Industry, *Supplemental Report on the Adequacy of Existing Legislation* (Washington, D.C.: Government Printing Office, 1936), 1.

14. Ibid., 3–7.

15. Warburg to Strong, 23 November 1916, cited in *Supplemental Report on the Adequacy of Existing Legislation*, 129–31; *Supplemental Report on the Adequacy of Existing Legislation*, 134–35, 3.

16. Special Committee on Investigation of the Munitions Industry, *Report on Government Manufacture of Munitions* (Washington, D.C.: Government Printing Office, 1936); *New York Times*, 2 November 1935, 7.

17. *Report on Government Manufacture of Munitions*, 5–7, 66.

18. Ibid., 97–99, 110.

19. Ibid., 122.

20. Ibid., 121–22; *New York Times*, 27 March 1935, 8.

21. *Report on Government Manufacture of Munitions*, 123.

22. Frank Freidel, *Franklin D. Roosevelt: A Rendezvous with Destiny* (Boston: Little, Brown and Company, 1990), 202–3.

23. Harold L. Ickes, *The Secret Diary of Harold L. Ickes* (New York: Simon and Schuster, 1953), 655–63.

24. *New York Times*, 15 August 1936, 4.

25. Ibid.

26. Ickes, *Secret Diary*, 663–65, 698.

27. *New York Times*, 7 October 1936, 3, and 1 November 1936, 1; Ickes, *Secret Diary*, 692; Clark to Nye, 8 October 1936, and George to Nye, 9 October 1936, Record Group 46, United States Senate, Special Committee Investigating the Munitions Industry, National Archives, Washington, D.C. The Elliott Roosevelt affair is discussed in Chapter 3.

28. *Time*, 23 November 1936, 38, and 28 June 1937, 24–28; Freidel, *Rendezvous with Destiny*, 8–10; Gerard Colby, *Du Pont Dynasty* (Secaucus, New Jersey: Lyle Stuart, 1984), 368–80.

29. Samuel I. Rosenman, *Working With Roosevelt* (New York: Harper and Brothers, 1952), 108; *New York Times*, 6 October 1937, 1; William E. Dodd to Roosevelt, 21 September 1936 and 19 October 1936, Franklin D. Roosevelt Papers, President's

Secretary's File, Franklin D. Roosevelt Library, Hyde Park, New York; Roosevelt to Sir Arthur Willert, 16 June 1937, Roosevelt Papers, President's Personal File.

30. James A. Henretta, et al., *America's History*, 2nd ed. (New York: Worth Publishers, 1993), 818.

31. Samuel Lubell, *The Future of American Politics* (Garden City, New York: Doubleday and Company, 1956), 141.

32. Wiltz, *In Search of Peace*, 3, 232.

33. Ibid., 134, 87. Realist historians of the cold war era often faulted the ignorance of the American people for U.S. foreign policy failures of the interwar years. For examples, see Selig Adler, review of *The Illusion of Neutrality* by Robert A. Divine, *American Historical Review* 68 (October 1962): 163, and Robert H. Ferrell, *Peace in Their Time: The Origins of the Kellogg-Briand Pact* (New Haven, Connecticut: Yale University Press, 1952), 264–65.

34. Thomas Bender, "Wholes and Parts: The Need for Synthesis in American History," *Journal of American History* 73 (1986): 120–36.

35. Robert David Johnson, *The Peace Progressives and American Foreign Relations* (Cambridge, Massachusetts: Harvard University Press, 1995), 291–94.

36. Patrick J. Maney, *The Roosevelt Presence: A Biography of Franklin Delano Roosevelt* (New York: Twayne, 1992), 79.

37. Jonathon S. Landay, "Americans Get Creative in Opening Arms Markets," *The Christian Science Monitor*, 17 April 1997, 1, 6–7.

38. Walter LaFeber, *The American Age: United States Foreign Policy at Home and Abroad Since 1750* (New York: W. W. Norton and Company, 1989), 170–71, 225, 364; Wayne S. Cole, *Roosevelt and the Isolationists, 1932–1945* (Lincoln: University of Nebraska Press, 1983), 165. The educational backgrounds of the senators on the munitions committee are given in the *Biographical Dictionary of the United States Congress, 1774–1989* (Washington, D.C.: Government Printing Office, 1989).

39. *Dallas Morning News*, 19 April 1995, Section D, 12.

40. *Congressional Record*, 74th Cong., 2nd sess., 573; Edward Pessen, *Losing Our Souls: The American Experience in the Cold War* (1993; reprint, Chicago: Ivan R. Dee, 1995), 209–11.

41. *Congressional Record*, 78th Cong., 2nd sess., 9686; Dorothy Detzer, *Appointment on the Hill* (New York: Henry Holt and Company, 1948), 171.

42. Wayne S. Cole, *Senator Gerald P. Nye and American Foreign Relations* (Minneapolis: University of Minnesota Press, 1963), 173–93, 215–23; Cole, *Roosevelt and the Isolationists*, 552; *Biographical Dictionary of the United States Congress*, 1579.

43. *Biographical Dictionary of the United States Congress*, 783.

44. Ibid., 166.

45. Ibid., 641.

46. Ibid., 1974; Cole, *Roosevelt and the Isolationists*, 550–53.

47. *Biographical Dictionary of the United States Congress*, 1052–53, 575.

48. *New York Times*, 5 July 1991, 8.

49. Dorothy Detzer Papers, Swarthmore College Peace Collection, Swarthmore, Pennsylvania; Detzer, *Appointment on the Hill*, 253–55; Rosemary Rainbolt, "Women and War in the U.S.: The Case of Dorothy Detzer, National Secretary, W.I.L.P.F.," presented at the American Historical Association Conference, 28 December 1976, Washington, D.C.

50. Detzer, *Appointment on the Hill*, 33, 107; Donald K. Pickens, "Domestic Feminism and the Structure of American History," *Contemporary Philosophy* 12 (November/December 1989): 14–22. Detzer is mentioned once in Susan Ware's *Holding Their Own: American Women in the 1930s* (Boston: Twayne, 1982). She receives no consideration in such documentary collections as Ware's *Modern American Women* (Chicago: Dorsey Press, 1989), Alice S. Rossi's *The Feminist Papers* (1973; reprint, Boston: Northeastern University Press, 1988), or Nancy F. Cott's *Roots of Bitterness* (Boston: Northeastern University Press, 1986).

Selected Bibliography

GOVERNMENT DOCUMENTS

Congressional Record.

Decisions of the National Labor Board, August 1933–March 1934. Washington, D.C.: Government Printing Office, 1934.

U.S. Congress. Senate. Special Committee on Investigation of the Munitions Industry. Hearings. Available on microfiche, this large collection includes transcripts of the ninety-three days of hearings and the exhibits the committee put in the record.

——. Special Committee on Investigation of the Munitions Industry. *Preliminary Report on Naval Shipbuilding.* 74th Congress, 1st sess., 1935. S. Rept. 944, Part 1.

——. Special Committee on Investigation of the Munitions Industry. *Preliminary Report on Wartime Taxation and Price Control.* 74th Congress, 1st sess., 1935. S. Rept. 944, Part 2.

——. Special Committee on Investigation of the Munitions Industry. Records. Record Group 46. National Archives, Washington, D.C. Includes hundreds of letters, memoranda, and policy papers.

——. Special Committee on Investigation of the Munitions Industry. *Report on Activities and Sales of Munitions Companies.* Washington, D.C.: Government Printing Office, 1936.

——. Special Committee on Investigation of the Munitions Industry. *Report on Existing Legislation.* Washington, D.C.: Government Printing Office, 1936.

——. Special Committee on Investigation of the Munitions Industry. *Report on Government Manufacture of Munitions.* Washington, D.C.: Government Printing Office, 1936.

——. Special Committee on Investigation of the Munitions Industry. *Report on War Department Bills.* Washington, D.C.: Government Printing Office, 1936.

——. Special Committee on Investigation of the Munitions Industry. *Supplemental Report on the Adequacy of Existing Legislation.* Washington, D.C.: Government Printing Office, 1936.

U.S. Department of Justice. File 235644. Record Group 60. National Archives, Washington, D.C. Includes a small number of important items.

U.S. Department of State. Decimal File, 1930–1939. Record Group 59. National Archives, Washington, D.C. Contains many important items that are well arranged and easy to use.

——. *Foreign Relations of the United States, 1934–1936.* Washington, D.C.: Government Printing Office, 1951–1953.

MANUSCRIPT SOURCES

Cummings, Homer. Diaries. Microfilm. Franklin D. Roosevelt Library, Hyde Park, New York. Includes several useful notations on cabinet meetings.

Detzer, Dorothy. Papers. Swarthmore College Peace Collection, Swarthmore, Pennsylvania. Includes numerous memoranda and letters.

Hull, Cordell. Papers. Microfilm. Library of Congress, Washington, D.C. Includes a small number of significant items related to the munitions investigation.

Hull, Hannah Clothier. Papers. Swarthmore College Peace Collection, Swarthmore, Pennsylvania.

Johnson, Hugh S. Papers. Franklin D. Roosevelt Library, Hyde Park, New York.

Moore, R. Walton. Papers. Franklin D. Roosevelt Library, Hyde Park, New York. Includes several important letters and memoranda.

National Council for the Prevention of War. Records. Swarthmore College Peace Collection, Swarthmore, Pennsylvania. Contains a small number of significant letters and memoranda.

Nye, Gerald P. Papers. Herbert Hoover Library, West Branch, Iowa. Includes some useful materials, but few items related directly to the munitions investigation. Documents related to Nye's chairing of the investigation are held in the National Archives, Record Group 46.

Roosevelt, Franklin D. Papers. Franklin D. Roosevelt Library, Hyde Park, New York. FDR left few items directly related to the munitions investigation, but the collection includes letters and memoranda concerned with FDR's thoughts about the Du Ponts.

Stimson, Henry Lewis. Diaries. Manuscripts and Archives, Yale University Library, New Haven, Connecticut. Includes a few entries on meetings with FDR that indicate the president's thoughts on general foreign policy concerns.

——. Papers. Manuscripts and Archives, Yale University Library, New Haven, Connecticut. Includes a few letters relevant to the munitions investigation.

Women's International League for Peace and Freedom, U.S. Section. Records. Swarthmore College Peace Collection, Swarthmore, Pennsylvania. Contains many items of interest, including numerous letters, telegrams, and memoranda, some written by Dorothy Detzer.

PUBLISHED PRIMARY SOURCES

Allison, Brent Dow. "Senator Nye Sums Up." *Christian Century* (16 January 1935): 80–81.

"Arms and the Men." *Fortune* 9 (March 1934): 53–57, 113–26.

"Arms Manufacturers and the Public." *Foreign Affairs* 12 (July 1934): 639–53.

Barnes, Harry Elmer. "Woodrow Wilson." *American Mercury* 1 (April 1924): 484.

Beard, Charles A. *The Open Door at Home.* New York: Macmillan, 1934.

Becker, Carl L. "Everyman His Own Historian." *American Historical Review* 37 (1932): 228–31.

Brown, Francis E. "The Crusading Mr. Nye." *Current History and Forum* (February 1935): 521–27.

"Chemistry's Tremendous Tomorrow." *Literary Digest* (3 November 1923): 23.

Complete Presidential Press Conferences of Franklin D. Roosevelt. New York: DaCapo Press, 1972.

Day, Donald, ed. *Franklin D. Roosevelt's Own Story: Told in His Own Words from His Private and Public Papers.* Boston: Little, Brown and Company, 1951.

Detzer, Dorothy. *Appointment on the Hill.* New York: Henry Holt and Company, 1948.

Engelbrecht, Helmuth Carol and Hanighen, Frank Cleary. *Merchants of Death: A Study of the International Armament Industry.* 1934. Reprint. New York: Garland Publishing, 1972.

Freedman, Max, ed. *Roosevelt and Frankfurter: Their Correspondence, 1928–1945.* Boston: Little, Brown and Company, 1967.

Hull, Cordell. *The Memoirs of Cordell Hull.* 2 vols. New York: Macmillan, 1948.

Ickes, Harold L. *The Secret Diary of Harold L. Ickes.* New York: Simon and Schuster, 1953.

Johnson, Hiram. *Diary Letters of Hiram Johnson, 1917–1945.* New York: Garland Publishing, 1983.

Kilpatrick, Carroll, ed. *Roosevelt and Daniels: A Friendship in Politics.* Chapel Hill: University of North Carolina Press, 1952.

MacArthur, Douglas. *Reminiscences.* New York: McGraw-Hill, 1964.

Moffat, J. Pierrepont. *The Moffat Papers: Selections from the Diplomatic Journals of Jay Pierrepont Moffat, 1919–1943.* Cambridge, Massachusetts: Harvard University Press, 1956.

Niebuhr, Reinhold. *An Interpretation of Christian Ethics.* New York: Harper and Brothers, 1935.

——. *Moral Man and Immoral Society: A Study in Ethics and Politics.* 1932. Reprint. New York: Charles Scribner's Sons, 1949.

Nixon, Edgar B., ed. *Franklin D. Roosevelt and Foreign Affairs.* 3 vols. Cambridge, Massachusetts: Harvard University Press, Belknap Press, 1969.

Rauschenbusch, Walter. *Christianity and the Social Crisis.* New York: Macmillan, 1907.

——. *Christianizing the Social Order.* New York: Macmillan, 1912.

Roosevelt, Elliott, ed. *FDR: His Personal Letters, 1928–1945.* 4 vols. New York: Duell, Sloan, and Pearce, 1950.

Rosenman, Samuel I. *Working With Roosevelt.* New York: Harper and Brothers, 1952.

Schlesinger, Arthur M., Jr. and Bruns, Roger, eds. *Congress Investigates: A Documented History, 1792–1974.* 5 vols. New York: Chelsea House, 1975.

Slater, Ellis D. *The Ike I Knew.* Ellis Slater Trust, 1980.

Truman, Harry S. *Memoirs by Harry S. Truman.* 2 vols. Garden City, New York: Doubleday and Company, 1955.

Tugwell, Rexford G. *The Democratic Roosevelt.* Garden City, New York: Doubleday and Company, 1957.

"War Profits." *Business Week* (22 December 1934): 22.

Wohlforth, Robert. "Armaments Profiteers: 1934." *Nation* (March 1934): 299–301.

SECONDARY SOURCES

Allen, Frederick Lewis. *Since Yesterday: The 1930s in America*. New York: Harper and Row, 1939.

Barr, Eleanor M., ed. "Records of the Women's International League for Peace and Freedom, United States Section, 1919–1959: Guide to the Scholarly Resources." Wilmington, Delaware: Scholarly Resources, undated.

Biographical Dictionary of the United States Congress, 1774–1989. Washington, D.C.: Government Printing Office, 1989.

Burke, Robert E. Review of *In Search of Peace*, by John E. Wiltz. *Journal of American History* 51 (June 1964): 131.

Burner, David. *The Politics of Provincialism: The Democratic Party in Transition, 1918–1932*. 1967. Reprint. New York: Alfred A. Knopf, 1968.

Burns, James MacGregor. *The Crosswinds of Freedom*. New York: Alfred A. Knopf, 1989.

———. *Roosevelt: The Lion and the Fox*. New York: Harcourt Brace and Company, 1956.

Burns, Richard D. Introduction to *Merchants of Death: A Study of the International Armament Industry*, by Helmuth Carol Engelbrecht and Frank Cleary Hanighen. 1934. Reprint. New York: Garland Publishing, 1972.

Cohen, Warren I. *The American Revisionists: The Lessons of Intervention in World War I*. Chicago: University of Chicago Press, 1967.

Colby, Gerard. *DuPont Dynasty*. Secaucus, New Jersey: Lyle Stuart, 1984.

Cole, Wayne S. *Roosevelt and the Isolationists, 1932–1945*. Lincoln: University of Nebraska Press, 1983.

———. *Senator Gerald P. Nye and American Foreign Relations*. Minneapolis: University of Minnesota Press, 1963.

Curti, Merle Eugene. *Peace or War: The American Struggle, 1636–1936*. Boston: J. S. Canner and Company, 1959.

Dallek, Robert. *Franklin D. Roosevelt and American Foreign Policy, 1932–1945*. New York: Oxford University Press, 1979.

Daniels, Roger. *The Bonus March: An Episode of the Great Depression*. Westport, Connecticut: Greenwood Press, 1971.

Divine, Robert A. *The Illusion of Neutrality*. Chicago: University of Chicago Press, 1962.

———. *The Reluctant Belligerent: American Entry Into World War II*. New York: John Wiley and Sons, 1965.

———. *Second Chance: The Triumph of Internationalism in America During World War II*. New York: Atheneum, 1967.

Fox, Richard Wightman. *Reinhold Niebuhr: A Biography*. New York: Pantheon Books, 1985.

Freidel, Frank. *Franklin D. Roosevelt: The Apprenticeship*. Boston: Little, Brown and Company, 1952.

———. *Franklin D. Roosevelt: Launching the New Deal*. Boston: Little, Brown and Company, 1973.

———. *Franklin D. Roosevelt: A Rendezvous with Destiny*. Boston: Little, Brown and Company, 1990.

Johnson, Robert David. *The Peace Progressives and American Foreign Relations*. Cambridge, Massachusetts: Harvard University Press, 1995.

Jonas, Manfred. *Isolationism in America, 1935–1941*. Ithaca, New York: Cornell University Press, 1966.

Koistinen, Paul A. C. "The 'Industrial-Military Complex' in Historical Perspective: The Interwar Years." *Journal of American History* 56 (March 1970): 819–39.

Kuehl, Warren F. "Midwestern Newspapers and Isolationist Sentiment." *Diplomatic History* 3 (Summer 1979): 283–306.

——. "Webs of Common Interests Revisited: Nationalism, Internationalism, and Historians of American Foreign Relations." *Diplomatic History* 10 (Spring 1986): 107–20.

LaFeber, Walter. *The American Age: United States Foreign Policy at Home and Abroad Since 1750*. New York: W. W. Norton and Company, 1989.

Leuchtenburg, William E. *Franklin D. Roosevelt and the New Deal, 1932–1940*. New York: Harper and Row, 1963.

——. *The Perils of Prosperity, 1914–1932*. Chicago: University of Chicago Press, 1958.

Livingston, Ellis N. "Senate Investigating Committees, 1900–1938." Ph.D. diss., University of Minnesota, 1953.

Maney, Patrick J. *The Roosevelt Presence: A Biography of Franklin Delano Roosevelt*. New York: Twayne, 1992.

Minus, Paul M. *Walter Rauschenbusch: American Reformer*. New York: Macmillan, 1988.

Novick, Peter. *That Noble Dream: The "Objectivity Question" and the American Historical Profession*. Cambridge: Cambridge University Press, 1988.

Parrish, Michael E. *Anxious Decades: America in Prosperity and Depression, 1920–1941*. New York: W. W. Norton and Company, 1992.

Patenaude, Lionel V. *Texans, Politics, and the New Deal*. New York: Garland Publishing, 1983.

Patterson, James T. *Congressional Conservativism and the New Deal*. 1967. Reprint. Westport, Connecticut: Greenwood Press, 1981.

Pessen, Edward. *Losing Our Souls: The American Experience in the Cold War*. 1993. Reprint. Chicago: Ivan R. Dee, 1995.

Pickens, Donald K. "Domestic Feminism and the Structure of American History." *Contemporary Philosophy* 12 (November/December 1989): 14–22.

Ritchie, Donald A. "The Pecora Wall Street Exposé, 1934." In *Congress Investigates: A Documented History, 1792–1974*, edited by Arthur M. Schlesinger, Jr. and Roger Bruns, 2555–78. New York: Chelsea House, 1975.

Schapsmeier, Edward L. and Schapsmeier, Frederick H. *Henry A. Wallace of Iowa: The Agrarian Years, 1910–1940*. Ames: Iowa State University Press, 1968.

Schlesinger, Arthur M., Jr. *The Coming of the New Deal*. Vol. 2, *The Age of Roosevelt*. Boston: Houghton Mifflin, 1958.

——. *The Politics of Upheaval*. Vol. 3, *The Age of Roosevelt*. Boston: Houghton Mifflin, 1960.

Tompkins, C. David. *Senator Arthur H. Vandenberg: The Evolution of a Modern Republican, 1884–1945*. East Lansing: Michigan State University Press, 1970.

Weinstein, Allen. *Perjury: The Hiss-Chambers Case*. New York: Alfred A. Knopf, 1978.

Wiltz, John E. *From Isolation to War, 1931–1941*. Arlington Heights, Illinois: Harlan Davidson, 1968.

——. "The Nye Munitions Committee, 1934." In *Congress Investigates: A Documented History, 1792–1974*, edited by Arthur M. Schlesinger, Jr. and Roger Bruns, 2735–67. New York: Chelsea House, 1975.

——. *In Search of Peace: The Senate Munitions Inquiry, 1934–1936.* Baton Rouge: Louisiana State University Press, 1963.

Wolfskill, George. *The Revolt of the Conservatives: A History of the American Liberty League, 1934–1949.* Boston: Houghton Mifflin, 1962.

Index

Router bits - woodenott

monarch collett —
f.t old machine?

STEEL plate — — —
plate

N: nod

Sawdust.

12" makita ?

Bandsaw blad(e)

Pima International

Units 28/29
Atcham Business Park
Upton Magna
Shrewsbury
SY4 4UG

E-mail:
salesusa@pimainternational.co.uk

With Complements

Please find enclosed your recent Abebooks order.

We hope you are happy with your purchase.

Should you require any further information please feel free to contact us at the above

Email address.

About the Author

MATTHEW WARE COULTER is Professor of History at Collin County Community College.

ISBN 0-313-30394-0

90000>

EAN

9 780313 303944

HARDCOVER BAR CODE